Form and Style

Form and Style

Research Papers, Reports, Theses

NINTH EDITION

Carole Slade, *Columbia University*

William Giles Campbell

Stephen Vaughan Ballou

Houghton Mifflin Company   Boston   Toronto
Geneva, Illinois   Palo Alto   Princeton, New Jersey

Senior Sponsoring Editor: Dean Johnson
Senior Development Editor: Barbara Roth
Associate Project Editor: Danielle Carbonneau
Production/Design Coordinator: Sarah Ambrose
Senior Manufacturing Coordinator: Marie Barnes
Marketing Manager: George Kane

ISBN: 0–395–676584

3456789–B–98 97 96 95

Contents

Preface

The ninth edition of *Form and Style: Research Papers, Theses, Reports* provides guidance to writers of research papers, theses, and reports in college, graduate school, business, government, and professions. The review of the fundamental processes of research makes *Form and Style* suitable as a text in courses of many kinds: composition courses, writing courses in the disciplines, and courses in research and methods at both the undergraduate and graduate levels. The book also continues to serve experienced writers with its discussion of procedures for writing various types of theses, its thorough presentation of principles of documentation and bibliographic forms, and its comprehensive treatment of the conventions for presenting the results of research.

This book will serve as either a reference work or an instructional text. The index allows the reader to locate particular subjects quickly and easily; the glossary provides explanations of abbreviations. At the same time, because the book provides an approximately sequential guide to the processes of research and writing, some writers may wish to begin by reading straight through it.

Chicago Manual, MLA, and APA Documentation Systems

This new edition of *Form and Style* treats three frequently used documentation systems in three separate chapters. Coverage of these systems is drawn from *The Chicago Manual of Style,* 14th ed. (1993), *Publication Manual of the American Psychological Association,* 3rd ed. (1983), and the *Modern Language Association Handbook for Writers of Research Papers,* 3rd ed. (1988), by Joseph Gibaldi and Walter S. Achtert. These systems are abbreviated in *Form and Style* as *Chicago Manual* (or simply *Chicago*), MLA, and APA. An appendix provides information on legal citation and the author-number system of references.

I am grateful to The University of Chicago Press for the privilege of receiving page proof for *The Chicago Manual of Style,* 14th ed. (1993). This edition of *Form and Style,* then, reflects changes in the new *Chicago Manual.* The changes appear throughout *Form and Style* but are concentrated in the revised note and bibliography formats in Chapter 7 and in the bibliography entries on the sample pages.

A writer's choice of documentation system usually depends on the suggestions of an adviser, the requirements of a department or university, or the conventions of a field of study. If not guided by any of these stipulations, writers of papers with general interest probably will want to use the widely accepted *Chicago Manual* system, while writers within particular disciplines will select either the MLA or the APA system, as appropriate.

As my authority for usage and spelling, I have continued to rely on *The American Heritage Dictionary*, 3rd ed. (1993).

Organization and Coverage

Reorganized for this edition, *Form and Style* divides into two sections: Part I, The Processes of Research and Writing, covers the essential procedures that most writers employ as they create a paper; Part II, Systems of Documentation, after a general introduction to citation, provides separate chapters on using *Chicago Manual*, Modern Language Association, and American Psychological Association documentation.

▪ Part I: The Processes of Research and Writing

Chapters 1 through 6 focus on the processes required for producing the texts of a research paper, thesis, or report. In the interest of clarity, instruction and examples in these chapters draw on *Chicago Manual* style. Most of the principles also apply to MLA and APA styles, but where differences exist, the alternatives are provided. Throughout, this edition includes current information on doing research and writing with computers.

Chapter 1 explains the process of writing a research paper from the initial steps of choosing a topic, preparing a working bibliography, and collecting information through outlining, drafting, and revising the paper. These explanations of fundamental principles make the book accessible and useful to undergraduates at all levels. Some graduate students may want to use this chapter to review the essential stages in writing a research paper. This edition includes a new section on using electronic sources.

Chapter 2 presents the elements of a thesis or dissertation, along with requirements for research and writing of such projects. The chapter offers guidelines for preparing three types of graduate papers: theses based on the collection of empirical data, theses based on critical analysis or philosophical speculation, and theses based on historical research.

Chapter 3 provides a full explanation of principles for attributing ideas and quotations to their sources. Because most plagiarism results from careless application of the rules for documentation, the chapter thoroughly discusses the documentation of direct and indirect quotations.

Chapter 4 presents the principles of grammar and mechanics most often needed in writing and revising research papers. Chapter 5 offers full instructions for preparing tables and figures, as well as for including figures, graphs, and computer-generated materials. Chapter 6 discusses the process of preparing the finished copy, and it collects the instructions for typing and printing that were previously dispersed through the book.

▪ Part II: Systems of Documentation

Part II gives detailed coverage of the *Chicago Manual,* MLA, and APA documentation systems. The introduction to this section reviews the principles of documentation applicable to all three systems, such as the purposes of citation and the organization of entries in bibliographies and lists of works cited. Chapter 7 explains the *Chicago Manual* system for notes accompanied by a bibliography. A section of facing note and bibliography entries helps the writer to translate information about a work from bibliography form into note form, and vice versa. Chapter 8 provides instructions for MLA documentation, and Chapter 9 provides instructions for APA documentation. All of these chapters offer expanded coverage of citations for computer materials. For ease of reference, a tab marks each chapter.

▪ Sample Pages

Sample pages in chapters 1, 2, and 5 illustrate the formats for research papers and systems of documentation described in *Form and Style.* These pages have been designed to resemble pages typed on a typewriter or printed by a computer so that they can serve as models for research papers, theses, and dissertations. The appearance of any printed book necessarily differs from that of a typescript, particularly in its spacing, margins, and typefaces; therefore, the printed text of *Form and Style* may vary slightly from the format recommended here for typescripts.

Acknowledgments

I wish to thank Anita Lowry, reference librarian at Columbia University, for information and instruction on using electronic sources; George E. Harlow for new figures and illustrations; Jeffrey C. Slade for advice on legal citation; and Marsha Z. Cummins, Bronx Community College of the City University of New York, for a continuing conversation on teaching writing. For their valuable suggestions on the preparation of the ninth edition of *Form and Style,* I am also indebted to the following:

Gordon Bachus, Central Missouri State University
Kenneth Collins, Northeastern State University, Oklahoma
H. E. Dantzler, Pennsylvania State University, Fayette Campus
Geneva England, Holmes Community College-Grenada, Mississippi
Robert J. Fallows, Northern Arizona University
Judith Z. Flynn, Framingham State College, Massachusetts
Omer V. Frank, Central Missouri State University
Margaretta S. Handke, Mankato State University, Minnesota
John W. Hansen, California State University, Fresno

Jerry Harmon, Northern State University, South Dakota
Walter Howard, Bloomsburg University, Pennsylvania
Raymond H. Merritt, St. Cloud State University, Minnesota
George Rawlins, Austin Peay State University, Tennessee
Russ Romans, City University, Bellevue, Washington
Ujjwala Salve Titus, Cheyney University, Pennsylvania
Robert Wall, Towson State University, Maryland.

Carole Slade

Introduction

Although this book has long been entitled *Form and Style,* it considers not only details of format and matters of style but also the essential processes of research and writing for research papers of all types, including reports, review articles, theses, and dissertations. These kinds of papers draw on information gathered systematically in the library or in the laboratory—research conducted either in collections of printed materials or through direct observation and experimentation. Although writers of such papers often work with materials compiled by others, they make an original contribution by organizing the information in a new way or by drawing a new conclusion on the basis of existing knowledge. The writer's creativity reveals itself in the choices made at every stage: selecting the topic, locating appropriate sources, organizing information, and presenting a clearly written and accurately documented paper.

The academic community designates research papers by a number of different names—research paper, term paper, report, thesis, dissertation—depending in part on the level, scope, and nature of the paper, as well as on individual and institutional preferences. Widely accepted definitions of these types of papers follow. For convenience and brevity, *Form and Style* refers to any paper based on research as a research paper.

■ Report

The word *report* generally refers to a thorough record or description of the results of firsthand experiences, empirical studies, or reading in primary sources. A report might present the results of mixing particular chemicals under specified conditions, a compilation of observations of classes in a school for gifted children, or a summary of attitudes toward new business in a particular region. Although the writer of a report may evaluate or interpret the results of research, most often a report presents information as objectively as possible so that readers may make judgments or decisions for themselves.

▪ Review Article

A *review article* refers to a presentation of secondary sources on a topic, which are evaluated, organized, and analyzed. The review article might further serve to represent the current thinking on a topic, to identify problems with the research, or to suggest possibilities for future research.

▪ Thesis

The word *thesis* commonly refers to a substantial research project. As the word (which also means a proposition or point of view defended through argument) implies, a thesis should draw an original conclusion based on information derived from research. Although the term can refer to the paper written for a doctoral degree, American usage generally reserves the name *thesis* for the master's paper or the undergraduate honors paper.

▪ Dissertation

A *dissertation* is a research paper submitted by a candidate for the doctoral degree. This paper requires more research and more extensive development of ideas than a master's thesis. The word *thesis* can generally be used interchangeably with *dissertation,* depending on the field and on the preference of the institution.

Theses and dissertations are usually written under the supervision of a professor but outside of any particular course and after the completion of all course work and qualifying examinations. Most institutions require a thesis or dissertation to draw upon substantial research, to demonstrate mastery of research techniques, and to reveal an ability to communicate knowledge to the academic community. A doctoral dissertation should make an original contribution to knowledge in the field through presentation of new conclusions, previously undiscovered materials, or new methods of analysis. Theses and dissertations usually require the approval of a group of readers and an oral defense, or justification, of the procedures and conclusions before readers and other members of the department.

Most doctoral dissertations accepted by American universities are indexed in one of several bibliographies, such as *Dissertation Abstracts International (DAI)* and the *Comprehensive Dissertation Index.* Microfilm copies of dissertations can be purchased from University Microfilms, Ann Arbor, Michigan 48106.

▪ Research Paper

The library paper assigned in undergraduate courses is most often labeled a *research paper.* This name distinguishes a paper based on work in the library from an essay, which usually draws on common knowledge and the writer's personal experience. An essay on the situation facing the elderly today, for example, could derive from conversations with the writer's grandparents. A research paper on the same topic might be based on a thorough review of sources such as government statistics on Social Security benefits or on a critical reading of books such as Simone de Beauvoir's *The Coming of Age,* a study of society's attitudes toward the elderly. The writer of a research paper carefully documents the sources of information and conclusions presented in the paper. In general, the more advanced the course, the more extensive is the research required for the assigned paper.

▪ Term Paper

The name *term paper* refers to a project that summarizes or demonstrates mastery of the work of a term or semester. Many instructors use this label interchangeably with *research paper.* Depending on the course, a term paper may or may not include formal research. A course that includes field work in teaching, for example, could require a term paper summarizing the development of teaching skills during the semester. A literature course could require a critical paper as evidence of the development of analytical techniques during the term. Similarly, a paper for either of these courses might require library research in secondary sources to substantiate the student's observations and conclusions.

I The Processes of Research and Writing

1 Writing Research Papers

The principles discussed in this chapter apply to all types of research projects, reports, theses, and dissertations. Whatever the subject and scope of the project, the processes involved are quite similar. The usual steps in preparing a research paper are (1) choosing a topic, (2) preparing a working bibliography, (3) collecting information, (4) outlining the paper, (5) drafting the paper, and (6) preparing the final copy. The process of writing a research paper does not necessarily proceed sequentially; you may find yourself going back and forth or working on two or three steps at once.

Choosing a Topic

The choice of a topic involves identifying a general subject area, limiting and defining the topic, and stating the topic as a question or hypothesis.

■ General Subject Area

Choice of topic

The instructor or adviser sometimes specifies a broad area of study. The instructor may assign a particular topic, provide a list of possible topics, or give the writer a free choice of topics within a broad range. You should begin to consider possible topics for a research paper as soon as the assignment is announced. Graduate students can begin to compile a list of possible thesis or dissertation topics early in their academic careers, perhaps trying out some of their ideas in papers for seminars.

Possibilities for research

Even in fields that seem to have been well covered by other scholars, possibilities for further research can often be found. Scholars frequently suggest new or undiscussed areas of inquiry in their studies. Also, commonly held but unsubstantiated conclusions or new ways of testing some basic assumptions in a field can provide subjects for research papers. Recently published books or new developments in current events can afford new insight into existing ideas and thus lead to opportunities for research. As you make decisions leading to a topic, you should also consider such factors as your interest in the subject, your ability to be objective (especially if the topic is controversial), and the time available for completing the assignment.

▪ Definition of the Topic

As you begin to focus on a specific topic within the general subject area, you should evaluate the possibilities according to the following criteria: importance and interest, manageability, and availability of resources. You do not want to begin working on a topic that will not hold your interest, that is not significant, that is not practical under the circumstances, or that cannot be completed within the time allowed for the assignment.

IMPORTANCE AND INTEREST   Naturally, you will want to devote your time to a topic of considerable importance and interest to your readers. To a certain extent, importance and interest are subjective judgments that depend on the nature of the assignment and the requirements of the instructor. A topic that seems trivial to persons in one field of study might hold great significance for specialists in another. Your instructor or adviser should confirm the importance of your topic, and your paper should convince readers of its significance.

In some cases, a clearly important subject, such as gun control, may not make a good topic if the extensive public debate hampers your ability to make an original contribution or if your strong feelings prevent you from at least examining opposing viewpoints.

MANAGEABILITY   Careful limiting of a topic will help you conduct research successfully. Topics that are too vague or broad, too narrow, or too specialized prevent you from finding suitable material. A topic that is too broad will not give sufficient direction to research and probably will necessitate superficial treatment of the subject. A topic that is too narrow will yield inadequate information, limiting your ability to reach a valid conclusion. If a topic is too specialized or too technical, it may demand knowledge you cannot acquire in the time allotted for your project. For example, you probably would not want to choose a topic that requires statistics unless you have some background in mathematics or can consult with a statistician. Ultimately, of course, readers will judge the manageability of your topic by the treatment you give it because a good paper defends not only its content but also its scope.

AVAILABILITY OF RESOURCES   Even if a topic is worthwhile and manageable, it may not be suitable if the necessary research materials are not available. The holdings of the library or libraries in which you are working should influence your choice of topic. While trying to avoid areas in which your library's holdings are weak, you may discover a subject in which it is particularly strong. If your research paper entails a survey or an experiment, you need to determine whether you can collect the required data within the time limits of the assignment.

▪ Statement of the Topic

Initially, you might wish to state your topic as a question or as a hypothesis, depending on the nature of the assignment.

For most undergraduate research papers in the humanities and social sciences, it is useful to formulate your topic as a question:

Topics stated as questions

- What are the psychological effects of computer-assisted instruction?
- How have E. D. Hirsch's ideas of "cultural literacy" been received?
- How has the Vietnam War affected Americans' view of themselves?

You will then conduct your research by exploring a full range of possible answers to your question.

As you gather information, you may discover that you have asked the wrong question or that you are more interested in answering a related question. If so, you can revise your question. Probably, you will also narrow your question as you work. A question about the psychological effects of computer-assisted instruction might be narrowed to focus on instruction in foreign languages, perhaps even on one specific language, possibly even one particular program for learning that language. You might narrow your questions about the reception of the concept of "cultural literacy" to the reactions of college professors, elementary school teachers, or the general public.

As you become more experienced in doing research, you may want to state your topic as a hypothesis—a tentative explanation or argument that you will test with your research.

Topics phrased as hypotheses

- Students composing on computers write differently than they do when composing in longhand or on the typewriter.
- For the unexpected increase in December 1992 retail spending, consumers drew principally from savings, not from current income.
- Most scientists believe that the earth is experiencing the phenomenon known as global warming.

As you conduct research you will test your hypothesis against the facts and ideas you find, and you will revise it as many times as your information warrants. For example, the writer of the sample paper "Are Books Obsolete?" began with the hypothesis that, given rapid developments in computer technology, electronic materials will quickly replace printed books. After doing some research, she concluded that her initial hypothesis was wrong. (See page 43 for a more scientific use of the word *hypothesis*.)

Your answer to the question or your revised hypothesis will become the *thesis statement*, or what some instructors call the *controlling idea*, of your paper.

Preparing a Working Bibliography

After selecting the broad subject of your paper, you should begin to work in the library to determine how to shape and limit the topic with the materials available. This effort should result in a *working bibliography*, a list of sources that appear to be relevant at the initial stage of your research. Developing the working bibliography requires knowledge of library resources, the use of reference systems to locate sources, and a consistent method of preparing bibliography cards (see page 14).

During the first phase of your research, you will want to write down information about every source you encounter that might be relevant to your study, even if you are not certain you will be able to use it. You are likely to regret ignoring potential sources at this early stage. As your thinking develops, you will wish that you had made bibliography cards for works that seemed irrelevant at the time but later proved essential. Instructions and suggestions from your instructor, as well as the nature and scope of your topic, should indicate the appropriate number of sources for your working bibliography.

Library resources   Even before you begin to work on a particular assignment, you should become familiar with the resources offered by your library: the information desk, the reference area, the card catalog (in card form or on-line), indexes to periodicals, reading rooms, the reserve reference area, government documents, and special collections. Your library may also provide services such as interlibrary loan, computerized searches, and database services, as well as equipment such as computer terminals, typewriters, copy machines, and microform readers. Some libraries distribute printed guides and conduct tours of their facilities. If your library does not, you should spend some time locating library resources on your own. You should also investigate all the different libraries that you may be able to use, such as the libraries of other public and private universities and colleges, museums, art galleries, and businesses in your area.

Reference room   Your work in the library will probably begin in the reference room, where general and specialized indexes, bibliographies, and the card catalog can help you develop a list of relevant works. In many libraries, you can use these materials in computerized form. Whether you use them in book, card, or computerized form, however, the principles remain the same. If you have trouble locating information, you should consult a librarian, who will have not only knowledge about the library but experience and expertise in the use of reference materials.

▪ General and Specialized Indexes

The word *index* means an alphabetized list of names or topics. An index of topics covered appears at the end of most nonfiction books. *Index* also designates a kind of reference work that can be valuable in formulating a working bibliography. Many indexes now appear in computerized as well as the traditional print form. Indexes are useful for locating journal and newspaper articles, which are not entered in the card catalog. Some indexes contain abstracts, or brief summaries, of articles and book reviews, whereas certain indexes list books and other materials.

General indexes cover a wide range of subjects because they list every article, editorial, or review in each issue of the periodicals they survey. Specialized indexes focus on specific fields and subject areas, often collecting material from a wide range of periodicals and books. As you work in a particular field, you will accumulate a list of relevant indexes. To find out whether your library owns an index on a particular subject, consult the card catalog under the heading *Indexes,* or look up *Indexes* as a subdivision of a specific subject (as in *Spanish-American History—Indexes*).

A printed index will include a key to its organizational format and the abbreviations it uses. Indexes in computerized form may provide such information in a tutorial program or in instructions given on the screen. Brief study of this material before turning to the index will help you find the entries you want and to decipher the numbers and abbreviations used in a particular index.

A list of widely used general and specialized indexes appears below. The first date indicates the beginning of the series; the second date indicates the end of coverage.

INDEXES IN THE HUMANITIES

America: History and Life, 1974–
Art Index, 1929–
British Humanities Index, 1962–
Guide to the Performing Arts, 1957–
Humanities Index, 1974–; With *Social Sciences Index,* 1974–;
    Preceded by *Social Sciences and Humanities Index,* 1967–73;
    and by *International Index,* 1907–66
Index to Religious Periodical Literature, 1949–
International Bibliography of Historical Sciences, 1926–
Library Literature, 1933–
Music Index, 1949–
Philosopher's Index, 1967–
MLA International Bibliography of Books and Articles on the Modern
    Languages and Literatures, 1921–
World Literature Today, 1960–
Guide to the Performing Arts, 1957–
Year's Work in Modern Language Studies, 1929–

INDEXES IN THE SCIENCES

Applied Science and Technology Index, 1958–
Biological and Agricultural Index, 1964–
Energy Index, 1973–
General Science Index, 1978–
Science Citation Index, 1964–

INDEXES IN THE SOCIAL SCIENCES

America: History and Life, 1964–
Education Index, 1929–61; 1969–
Educational Studies, 1973–
International Bibliography of Economics, 1952–
Index of Economic Articles, 1961–
International Bibliography of Political Science, 1952–
International Bibliography of Social and Cultural Anthropology, 1955–
International Bibliography of Sociology, 1952–
LLBA: Language and Language Behavior Abstracts, 1967–
Resources in Education, 1966–
Social Sciences Index, 1974–; See the listing above for accompanying
    Humanities Index
Writings in American History, 1902–

JOURNAL INDEXES

Business Periodicals Index, 1958–
Current Index to Journals in Education (CIJE), 1969–
Readers' Guide to Periodical Literature, 1901–
New Periodicals Index, 1977–
Nineteenth-Century Readers' Guide, 1890–1922
Poole's Index to Periodicals, 1802–1907
Popular Periodicals Index, 1973–
Public Affairs Information Service (PAIS), 1915–
State Education Journal Index, 1963–

NEWSPAPER INDEXES

Christian Science Monitor Index, 1960–
New York Times Index, 1851–
The Times Index (London), 1906–
Wall Street Journal Index, 1958–
Chicago Tribune Index, 1972–
Los Angeles Times Index, 1972–
Washington Post Index, 1972–

INDEXES TO GOVERNMENT PUBLICATIONS

American Statistics Index, 1973–
The Monthly Catalog of the United States Government, 1898–
Congressional Information Service Index to Publications of the United States Congress, 1970–

INDEXES TO PARTS OF BOOKS

Biography Index, 1946–
Essay and General Literature Index, 1900–

INDEXES TO BOOK REVIEWS

Book Review Digest, 1906–
Book Review Index, 1965–
International Bibliography of Book Reviews, 1971–
New York Times Book Review, 1896–

For an exhaustive listing of reference works in the above categories, as well as in numerous others, see *Guide to Reference Books,* 10th ed., edited by Eugene P. Sheehy et al. (Chicago: American Library Association, 1986), and the supplement to the tenth edition, *Guide to Reference Books Covering Materials from 1985–1990,* edited by Robert Balay and Eugene P. Sheehy (Chicago: American Library Association, 1992).

▪ Bibliographies

The word *bibliography,* which means a systematic and comprehensive listing of works, refers not only to the section within a book that lists works cited or consulted for the study, but also to book-length compilations of bibliographical entries on a given subject. These reference works can be very helpful for the development of a working bibliography. To determine whether a bibliography on your subject exists, refer to the *Bibliographic Index: A Cumulative Bibliography of Bibliographies* (1937–) or to *A World Bibliography of Bibliographies* by Theodore Besterman. These works provide subject indexes to bibliographies of both types, those published separately as books and those included within other works.

After looking at these bibliographies, consult the card catalog under the heading *Bibliographies* alone, or look up *Bibliographies* as a subdivision of a specific subject. In addition, *union catalogs,* which list the holdings of books and/or periodicals in one or more libraries, can help you locate books relevant to your subject. So can *trade bibliographies,* which are guides to books currently in print.

▪ The Card Catalog

A catalog is an index of materials owned by a library. This catalog may take two forms: (1) a set of cards arranged in drawers, that is, a *card catalog*; or (2) entries in an electronic database that may be retrieved at computer terminals, that is, an *on-line catalog* (see page 10). Even if your library has a computerized catalog, you need to understand some of the principles governing the creation of a card catalog.

Library materials are classified by means of letters and numbers and are listed alphabetically in three ways—by author, by title, and by subject. Each work, then, has at least three cards, or entries, in the catalog. More than three cards may exist for some works: a book with two authors will have author cards for both authors; a book cataloged in more than one subject area will have more than one subject card.

Author listing   The *main entry card* is the author listing. Included in the category of authors are writers, editors, compilers, and translators. When you want to know which works by an author can be found in a library, you should consult the *author cards.*

Title listing   The *title card* can lead you to a work when you know the title but not the name of the author. Libraries usually interfile title cards alphabetically with author cards according to the first word of the title, excluding *A, An,* and *The.*

Subject listing   *Subject cards* are important tools for locating sources relevant to your topic; they indicate all the works in the library dealing with one subject. It is useful to note the subject areas under which the books for your topic are cataloged; those subject headings can lead you to related headings and additional sources of information. You can also find subject headings by looking up a general subject area, such as art, history, literature, linguistics, or physics, and noting the subdivisions and cross-references for the subject.

Related subjects   When you search through subject headings, you should be open-minded about subjects that seem peripheral to your topic: thoughtful and inventive use of subject listings can yield original approaches and materials.

Lists of subject headings   To use subject cards efficiently, you should first study the category headings, subheadings, and cross-references in the cataloging system used by your library. The two cataloging systems you may encounter are the Library of Congress and the Dewey Decimal systems. The Dewey Decimal system is older, and many libraries no longer use it to catalog new books. However, many libraries have books shelved under both systems, so you may have to look in two places for books in the same category. Knowing

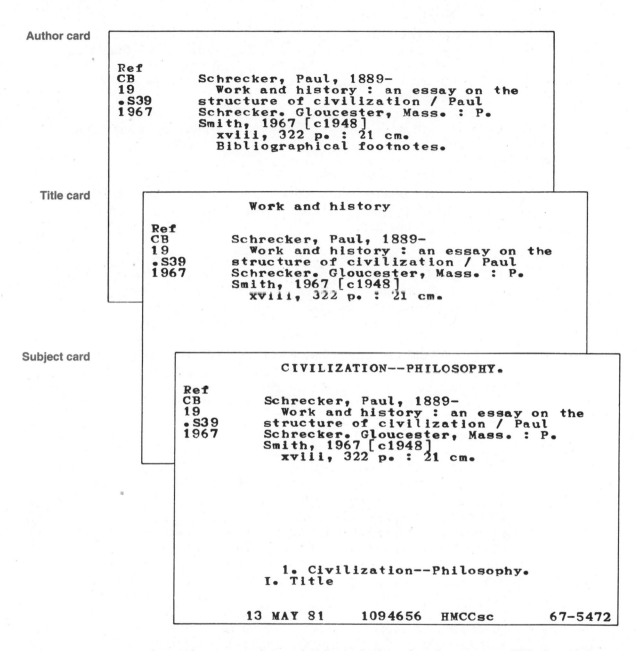

Author card

```
Ref
CB          Schrecker, Paul, 1889-
19             Work and history : an essay on the
.S39        structure of civilization / Paul
1967        Schrecker. Gloucester, Mass. : P.
            Smith, 1967 [c1948]
               xviii, 322 p. : 21 cm.
               Bibliographical footnotes.
```

Title card

```
                    Work and history

Ref
CB          Schrecker, Paul, 1889-
19             Work and history : an essay on the
.S39        structure of civilization / Paul
1967        Schrecker. Gloucester, Mass. : P.
            Smith, 1967 [c1948]
               xviii, 322 p. : 21 cm.
```

Subject card

```
                CIVILIZATION--PHILOSOPHY.
Ref
CB          Schrecker, Paul, 1889-
19             Work and history : an essay on the
.S39        structure of civilization / Paul
1967        Schrecker. Gloucester, Mass. : P.
            Smith, 1967 [c1948]
               xviii, 322 p. : 21 cm.




            1. Civilization--Philosophy.
            I. Title

    13 MAY 81      1094656    HMCCsc        67-5472
```

the major categories and subcategories of each system will help you locate sources, especially in a library with open stacks (shelves of books accessible to library users).

For a card catalog with headings based on the Library of Congress system, see either *Subject Headings Used in the Dictionary Catalogs of the Library of Congress* (with supplements), edited by Marguerite V. Quattlebaum, or *Outline of the Library of Congress Classification* (see box on page 13). The latter is organized under the following major categories, which serve as the basis for Library of Congress call numbers (found in the upper left-hand corner of the cards):

Library of Congress system

A	General Works—Polygraphy	N	Fine Arts
B	Philosophy—Religion	P	Language and Literature
C	History—Auxiliary Sciences	Q	Science

D	History and Topography (except America)	R	Medicine
E-F	America	S	Agriculture—Plant and Animal Husbandry
G	Geography—Anthropology	T	Technology
H	Social Sciences	U	Military Science
J	Political Science	V	Naval Science
K	Law	Z	Bibliography and Library Science
L	Education		
M	Music		

For a card catalog with headings based on the Dewey Decimal system, see *Sears List of Subject Headings* by Minnie Earl Sears. The major categories are as follows:

Dewey Decimal system

000–099	General Works	500–599	Pure Science
100–199	Philosophy	600–699	Technology
200–299	Religion	700–799	The Arts
300–399	Social Sciences	800–899	Literature
400–499	Language	900–999	History

You should use these lists of subject headings when you cannot find your topic in the card catalog. For example, *Equal Rights Amendment* does not appear in the card catalog. By consulting a work on subject headings, you would discover that material on the ERA is filed under *Women's Rights—United States*.

Alphabetization

Some familiarity with the rules of alphabetization can prevent confusion in locating materials. Most abbreviations are alphabetized as if they were fully spelled out (*Mr.* is filed as *Mister*). Names beginning with *Mc* or *M'* are listed as if they were spelled *Mac* (*McHenry* is alphabetized as *MacHenry*, for example). The articles *A, An,* and *The* are disregarded in the alphabetization of titles.

Word-by-word order

A library may use one of two systems of alphabetization: word by word or letter by letter. The word-by-word system is the most common. With this system, complete words precede longer words containing them. *Hard Times* would come before *The Harder They Come,* because *Hard* precedes *Harder* under this rule. Entries with the same spelling are ordered as person, place, thing: *Reading, Thomas* comes before *Reading, Pennsylvania,* which comes before *Reading Is Fun.* In the letter-by-letter system, every letter is considered. *The Harder They Come* precedes *Hard Times* because the *e* in *Harder* comes before the *t* in *Times.* Librarians will have information concerning the alphabetizing and cataloging rules followed in their library.

Letter-by-letter order

▪ Library Information On-Line

Many libraries have begun to catalog new books on electronic databases and to replace card catalogs with computerized listings that can be retrieved at computer terminals in the library. Such a computerized listing is known as a *card catalog on-line.* Libraries with computerized catalogs provide printed instructions and the assistance of librarians. You may be able to make arrangements to retrieve library information with your personal computer by using a modem, a device that enables computers to communicate with each other over the telephone lines.

Most libraries have individualized on-line systems, but all systems operate on the same principle as a card catalog. Entries for works available in the library are organized by author, title, and subject. Some on-line systems allow you to browse through a series of call numbers; some include materials that have been ordered or are being bound. Most libraries now have acquisitions from only a few years on-line. The statement that a library has works from 1980 on-line means that all books cataloged from 1980 on are included even though they may have been published in previous years. A book published in 1970 but not purchased until 1978 and not cataloged until 1980 would thus appear in the on-line catalog; alternatively, a book published in 1978 and cataloged in 1979 would appear only in the card catalog. Eventually, the entire catalogs of most libraries will be on-line, but in the meantime you will have to use both card and computer systems.

To use an on-line catalog, you will have to follow directions for entering the system. Once you have entered the system, you will be asked to request a work by author, title, or subject. If you want either a specific work by a particular author or a list of an author's works, you will type in the name of the author (last name first) at the appropriate place with whatever punctuation and commands the instructions request. If you know only the title of a work, you will type in the title, also at the appropriate place, again following instructions about punctuation and commands. If you have a general subject in mind, you will type in that subject. Most on-line catalogs use the standard headings and subheadings found in the card catalog and fully listed in *Subject Headings Used in the Dictionary Catalogs of the Library of Congress* (with supplements), edited by Marguerite V. Quattlebaum, and *Outline of the Library of Congress Classification*.

Many systems have printers that produce a paper copy of the entry as it appears on the screen. This service allows you to have complete bibliographical information without copying it by hand, a time-consuming and sometimes inaccurate process. You should remember, however, to verify the information in the entry when you consult the book itself. A sample print-out of an entry from an on-line catalog appears on page 12.

▪ Electronic Sources

Developments in computers and telecommunications have prompted rapid growth in the computerization of databases. These electronic databases take two forms: (1) CD-ROM (Compact Disk-Read Only Memory), the type of disk that is used in compact-disk stereo systems, and (2) on-line databases, which are retrieved by modem from a central databank or vendor, such as DIALOG or H. W. Wilson.

Many indexes and bibliographies are now available in both print and electronic form. These include, to name only a few, *Arts and Humanities Citation Index*, *Biological Abstracts*, *Chemical Abstracts*, *Dissertation Abstracts*, *Educational Resources Information Center (ERIC)*, *G.P.O. Monthly Catalog*, *Historical Abstracts*, *Humanities Index*, *Legal Resource Index*, *Linguistic and Language Behavior Abstracts*, *Modern Language Association Bibliography*, *Physics Abstracts*, *Public Affairs Information Service (PAIS)*, *Philosopher's Index*, *Psychology Abstracts*, and *Sociological Abstracts*. Other electronic databases have no equivalent in print form. These databases are updated weekly, quarterly, or yearly; often the electronic version is more current than the print one.

Print-out of an on-line catalog entry

```
                                    ①                 ②
         Personal author:  Jones, Emrys.
  ③      Names:    1. Eyles, John, Joint author.
  ⑥      Title:  An introduction to social geography / Emrys Jones and John Eyles.
         Publication facts:  Oxford (Eng.) ; New York : Oxford University Press,
            1977.         ④        ⑦      ⑧        ⑨       ⑩              ⑤
  ⑪      Physical description:  xi, 273 p.  :  ill.  ; 23 cm.
         Subjects:    1.  Anthropo-geography.    2.  Sociology, Urban.

         Library,  Item Location Code  (call number)  and Holdings:
            1. BURGESS  GF41.J66
                           ⑫
```

① Author of book		⑦ Number of pages in introduction	
② Co-author of book		⑧ Number of pages in book	
③ Title		⑨ Indication of illustrations	
④ Places for publication		⑩ Height of book	
⑤ Publisher		⑪ Subject entries for book	
⑥ Date of publicaton		⑫ Call number	

The card catalogs of some of the nation's major research libraries, such as the New York Public Library and the University of California, are available electronically nationwide. RLIN (Research Libraries Information Network) and OCLC (Online Computer Library Center) are national bibliographic databases, providing information about the location of books throughout libraries in the United States and in other countries as well.

Searching electronic databases

When you approach a new database, you will have to spend some time learning how it is organized, just as you would peruse the table of contents and the index in a book. Most electronic databases have a "Help" program—an on-line instructional program—as well as brochures in print form.

Because electronic sources have not been systematized by any one organization, they use a variety of different commands, symbols, and descriptors, which are the equivalent of subject headings in print sources. To find potentially useful descripters, you could refer to the Library of Congress listings, a section of which is shown on the next page.

Often it is useful to call up one or more titles on your subject that you already know to see how they are defined by a particular database. Some databases allow you to browse alphabetically through their list of subject descriptors. Other systems allow you to search for any word that appears in a title, abstract, or article, including place, date of publication, and language. All databases operate on the principles of a combinatory system known as Boolean logic, which functions with the operators *and*, *or*, and *not*. *And* and *not* function to narrow a search in different ways, whereas *or* expands a search. These examples of logical operators use RLIN commands (fin = find, pn = personal name, tw = title of work):

**Annotated List
of Library of
Congress Subject
Headings**

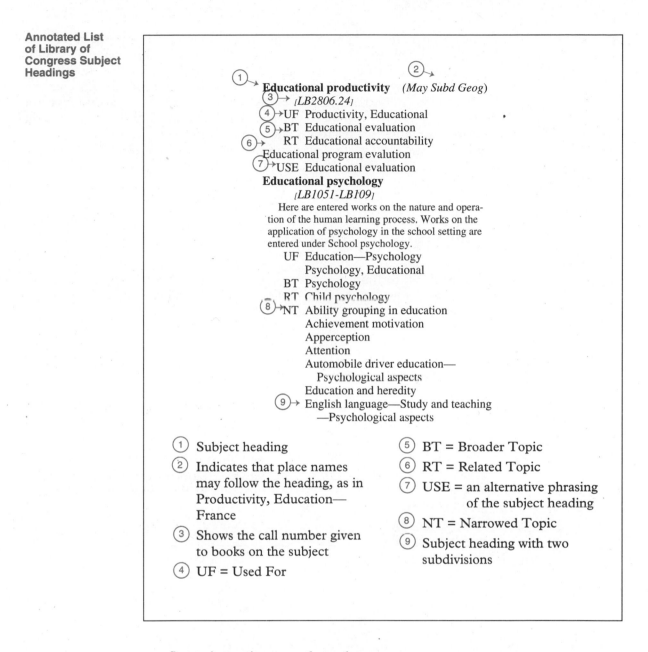

① **Educational productivity** *(May Subd Geog)*
③ [LB2806.24]
④ UF Productivity, Educational
⑤ BT Educational evaluation
⑥ RT Educational accountability
Educational program evalution
⑦ USE Educational evaluation
Educational psychology
[LB1051-LB109]
Here are entered works on the nature and opera-
tion of the human learning process. Works on the
application of psychology in the school setting are
entered under School psychology.
UF Education—Psychology
Psychology, Educational
BT Psychology
RT Child psychology
⑧ NT Ability grouping in education
Achievement motivation
Apperception
Attention
Automobile driver education—
Psychological aspects
Education and heredity
⑨ English language—Study and teaching
—Psychological aspects

① Subject heading
② Indicates that place names may follow the heading, as in Productivity, Education—France
③ Shows the call number given to books on the subject
④ UF = Used For

⑤ BT = Broader Topic
⑥ RT = Related Topic
⑦ USE = an alternative phrasing of the subject heading
⑧ NT = Narrowed Topic
⑨ Subject heading with two subdivisions

fin pn joyce, james and tw ulysses
(narrows the search to one work by James Joyce, *Ulysses*)
fin pn joyce, james and tw ulysses not gabler, hans walter
(indicates that the edition of *Ulysses* edited by Hans Walter Gabler
should not be included)
fin pn joyce, james and tw ulysses or tw finnegans
(expands the search to include Joyce's *Finnegans Wake* and *Ulysses*)

**Charges for
database
searches**   Libraries that own database services sometimes do not charge for their
use. Many libraries make some databases on CD-ROM available free of
charge. However, when a library must contact a database off campus, you
may have to pay for each computer search and for each title located.
Because the cost of such searches can be considerable, you should not
undertake them until you have precisely defined your descriptors.

Home use of electronic databases

For information on the electronic databases you can arrange to receive through a modem in your home, see the *Directory of Online Databases*, published quarterly, with two additional updates a year, by Cuadra/Elsevier.

Some encyclopedias, dictionaries, and other reference works may be purchased by individuals in CD-ROM form. To read these disks with a personal computer, you need a special drive unit. For information on materials available in CD-ROM form, see Norman Desmaraise, ed., *CD-ROMs in Print, 1992: An International Guide to CD-ROM, CD-I, CDTV, and Electronic Book Products* (Westport: Meckler, 1992).

Collecting Information

To gather information for your paper, you need to develop a bibliography, evaluate sources for their validity and accuracy, and take accurate, useful notes.

▪ Bibliography Cards

Books and articles that appear to be relevant to your topic should be listed systematically, one to a card and in the bibliographic format that you will use in your final draft.

For ease of revision and alphabetization, you should list each source on a separate card. Most researchers prefer three-by-five-inch cards, but other sizes may be used. It is important, however, to use consistently whatever size you choose.

Bibliography card for a book

McPherson, James M. *Battle Cry of Freedom: The Civil War Era.* New York: Ballantine, 1988.

You will save time if your entries on bibliography cards correspond to the documentation system that you will use for your paper. This book provides instructions for using note-bibliography system based on *The Chicago Manual of Style* (*Chicago*) and the parenthetical reference systems based on Modern Language Association style (MLA) and American Psychological Association style (APA). The introduction to Part II (pages 135–41) provides information on preparing bibliographies according to the *Chicago* system. For the MLA and APA systems, see the instructions for preparing a list of works cited on pages 198–212 for MLA, pages 213–28 for APA. Even though you may not find all the information you need for a particular bibliographical form in the index you consult, you can record the entry as the system indicates, leaving spaces for the missing elements as a reminder to locate them when you consult the source itself. If the entries on your cards follow the specified format, you will be able to prepare your final bibliography by simply copying the information from the cards.

▪ Critical Evaluation of Sources

As you select works to read and sources to use in your paper, you should continually evaluate the materials with regard to the primary or secondary nature of the source, the objectivity of the source, the qualifications of the author, and the level of the source.

PRIMARY AND SECONDARY SOURCES   You should consider whether a particular work is a primary or a secondary source for your purposes. *Primary sources* are basic materials with little or no annotation or editorial alteration, such as manuscripts, diaries, letters, interviews, and laboratory reports. *Secondary sources* derive from primary materials and include analysis, interpretation, and commentary on primary materials.

Depending on the point of view of your research paper, a set of materials may be considered either primary or secondary. A research paper on the contribution of E. B. White, a writer and editor, to the *New Yorker* magazine would treat White's articles in the magazine as primary materials. It would treat as a secondary source Brendan Gill's book *Here at the* New Yorker, an account of the editorial leadership of the magazine during the years White worked there. The writer of a paper on Brendan Gill, however, would consider *Here at the* New Yorker a primary source. Your topic may require you to emphasize either primary or secondary sources or to use a combination of the two.

OBJECTIVITY   The objectivity of a source is its lack of bias or prejudice. Total objectivity is not humanly possible, but the most valuable sources identify any biases that might be caused by the author's affiliations or allegiances—whether economic, political, philosophical, or religious—and any limitations inherent in the author's approach or the materials used. A writer with investments in farms that produce soybeans, for example, should indicate the possibility of bias for economic reasons in a study on the relative advantage of soybeans and seaweed as bases for new foods. Similarly, the writer of a study of the automotive industry based on information obtained from executives at Chrysler or Ford should make readers aware that the nature of the sources may have influenced his or her conclusions.

Bias and prejudice in sources

Even if a writer does not reveal possible reasons for bias, you should try to discern the writer's point of view and evaluate the work accordingly.

QUALIFICATIONS OF THE AUTHOR   An author's qualifications for writing a work, such as academic degrees, professional credentials, and experience and status in the field, may influence your choice of a source. Information about an author's qualifications may be found in preliminary or appendix materials in the source itself, in a biographical dictionary or directory such as *Who's Who,* or in an encyclopedia. The information may provide clues to the quality, nature, and objectivity of a source.

LEVEL   The intended audience determines the level of a work as regards diction, sentence structure, complexity, and assumed background knowledge. You may find sources that are too technical and advanced. When you do, you should seek guidance in understanding them or not use them. On the other hand, you may encounter works written for a wide audience that are too general or simplistic for your paper. You should not use these works either.

▪ Note Taking

To be able to organize and use the information you find requires you to devise a system for recording it before you begin. You will want to select note cards of a convenient size, a system of notation for relating the note cards to the bibliography cards and the outline, and a form for recording information. Some computer programs allow you to make and label note cards on a computer. If you use a computer for note taking, you will still follow the principles explained below, and you will need to be certain that you have carefully backed up your files.

Even though you will probably want to photocopy some materials in the library, you will still need to take notes on the works that you find useful for your paper. Having a photocopy of a work does not substitute for having a set of note cards on which you organize selected information from the work.

NOTE CARDS   The size of card you choose (three-by-five, four-by-six, or five-by-eight inches) should depend on the anticipated length of your notes. Some researchers prefer the discipline of using the small, three-by-five cards, which preclude placing too much material on one card. The four-by-six size provides more space for notes without being too large to use for bibliography cards. The five-by-eight size is convenient if you wish to make substantial comments or attach photocopied materials. Half-sheets of paper can substitute for five-by-eight cards, but papers tend to stick together and become rumpled. The temptation to take notes on large sheets of notebook paper or on both sides of a page should be avoided because this kind of note taking makes rearranging the material difficult. You will find that you are likely to follow the logic and development of each source rather than to impose your own organization on the material. Whatever size of card you choose, use it consistently.

SYSTEM FOR NOTE TAKING   Before you begin to take notes, enter on the card the information you will need to link the note card to the appropriate bibliography card. The last name of the author (and, if you have more than one entry for an author, the title) usually suffices. Some researchers number each bibliography card and put the corresponding number on each note card. Using the author's name, however, is more likely to be accurate than using numbers. You should check to be certain that you have recorded accurately the page number from which you are transcribing information. If you turn a page in the middle of a note, indicate precisely the point of division between the pages so that if you use only part of the note in the paper, you will know to which page in the source the note should refer. Also, before you put the note card aside, enter either the section of your outline or the area of your subject to which the information is relevant. Some researchers pencil in this comment so that they can make changes as their thinking develops.

Identification of sources on note cards

Subject headings on note cards

FORM   You may choose to record information in one of two basic forms: direct quotation or summary. A *direct quotation* is an exact copy of a portion of the original text (see note card 1 below). The quotation may encompass one or more words, phrases, clauses, complete sentences, or paragraphs. It is a good idea to take down a direct quotation when you feel there is a chance you will want to quote the passage or when the material meets one of the criteria for direct quotation discussed in Chapter 3 (see page 57). You should also write down a quotation when you wish to have the material on your note cards precisely as the author wrote it so that you can reread or verify it later. Before leaving the source, check direct quotations carefully so that you can be confident of their accuracy.

Direct quotation

Note card 1: direct quotation

Musical Settings – Novels
III. A.

Smith, Grover, ed.
p. 821
    Aldous Huxley to Leonard Bernstein, 4 Apr. 1957

"... I am writing to ask if you would be at all interested in reading a dramatic version of my novel <u>Brave New World</u>, which I have recently made, with a view to a musical setting."

The use of direct quotation in note taking helps ensure accuracy, but direct quotation can be a waste of time if you do not plan to use the quotations in the paper or if you merely copy information without understanding or digesting it. The use of summary or paraphrase rather than direct quotation forces you to comprehend as you read and leads naturally into the process of writing the paper. A *summary* is a brief restatement of the original material in your own words. A restatement of the author's ideas in about the same number of words as in the original is a *paraphrase*. The terms are commonly used interchangeably.

Summary or paraphrase

When you write a summary during note taking, you must be careful to avoid using the author's wording. Changing an occasional word or reversing the order of phrases or sentences does not result in an adequate summary. A good method is to try to write a summary without looking at the source. After writing a summary, look at the original and make a critical comparison, checking for duplication of wording and accuracy in the statement of ideas (see note card 2). If you find that you have used more than two consecutive words from the original (with the exception of articles and prepositions), place them in quotation marks. Carelessness in writing a summary can result in unintentional plagiarism. (See pages 55–57 in Chapter 3 for advice on avoiding plagiarism.) Even though the summary contains your own words, you will want to give credit for the ideas if you use them in your paper. Be as careful about recording the author's name and page numbers for a summary or a paraphrase as you would be for a direct quotation.

Precision in note taking

Unintentional plagiarism

Note card 2 is a summary of the contents of a letter. If you have large amounts of material to summarize, you might want to write your summary notes in outline form (see note card 3), either in an informal way or in a detailed, formal manner following the specific rules for outlining presented later in this chapter. Even when you outline, you should distinguish carefully between your own words and the words of the author.

Outlines in notes

Whatever form you choose for taking notes, you will want to strike a balance between taking enough notes to avoid having to return to your sources and taking repetitious or irrelevant notes. Judgment in this

Note card 2: summary

> Musical Settings – Novels
> III. A.
>
> Smith, Grover, ed.
> p. 821 Aldous Huxley wrote to Leonard
> Bernstein on April 4, 1957, to ask him to
> consider setting a "dramatic version" of
> <u>Brave</u> <u>New</u> <u>World</u> to music.

matter develops naturally as you learn more about your topic and as you master the process of writing a research paper.

Note card 3: outline form

Smith, Grover, ed.
 Aldous Huxley's letters on liberty
Threats to liberty
 1. Applied psychology (p.539) letter of 18 March 1946
        to Julian Huxley
 2. bureaucracy (p.451) letter of 19 March 1940
        to E.S.P. Haynes
 3. conditioning and mind control (p.837)
        letter of 12 December 1957 to
        Julian Huxley
 4. "urge for tidiness" (p.847) letter of
                                        cont.

Outlining the Paper

Some researchers begin with a tentative, or working, outline that guides the choice of research materials; others let the outline grow from their research and writing. If you develop an outline in advance, it should remain open to change as you read and take notes. Formulating and revising an outline throughout the processes of researching and writing can help you give your paper a logical and meaningful structure. After you have written a draft of your paper, you should either check it against an existing outline or attempt to make an outline from the draft.

Creating a final outline involves making decisions about the thesis statement, the principle of organization, the type of outline, and the format of the outline.

▪ The Thesis Statement

The answer to the question with which you began your research, or the substantiated hypothetical statement, will eventually become the thesis statement, or controlling idea, for the paper. As your outline evolves and your research leads you in new directions, your thesis statement may change, and you should frequently consider revising it as your work progresses. You might even find that you have completely reversed your conclusions in the process of doing research.

The scope and precision of your thesis statement will vary depending on your field of study, the level at which you are writing, and the nature of the assignment. For an undergraduate research paper on a subject new to the writer, the thesis statement might well be much more general than an appropriate thesis statement for a graduate paper. For the latter, a more knowledgeable and sophisticated approach to the subject would be required. The same would be true of a professional paper, which might delve into extremely specialized areas of the subject. Even when writing a very general paper, however, you might find a particular area of the subject on which you wish to concentrate. You will want to get some idea from your instructor or adviser about the scope of conclusions you are expected to draw for any given assignment.

Your final thesis statement should cover all the points made in the paper. It need not enumerate each point, but you should not disconcert your reader by straying into an area of inquiry not suggested by the thesis statement. The thesis statement for the sample paper on pages 32–33, "Although electronic means of publication have some advantages, electronic texts are not likely to replace books," refers briefly to two major sections of the paper, the advantages of electronic texts and the disadvantages to electronic publishing, and it suggests the writer's answer to the question of the title, "Are Books Obsolete?" A paper beginning with this thesis statement should not conclude that books are in fact obsolete; the writer who had come to that conclusion in the process of writing would have to revise the thesis and the rest of the paper accordingly.

▪ Principles of Organization

The organization of a paper often develops naturally in the course of research and during the writing of early drafts. Nevertheless, is is often instructive to try out various principles or patterns of organization with your material. Experimentation can help you to find the pattern most appropriate to your material or can lead you to new insights. Among the most useful principles for structuring a research paper are chronology, comparison and contrast, spatial pattern, cause and effect, and analysis. These patterns of development are often used in combination, and they can be applied to individual paragraphs as well as to an entire paper.

CHRONOLOGY   The chronological pattern explains each of the steps in a sequentially ordered process. The basic plan of this chapter, for instance, is chronological: the suggestions for writing a research paper begin with selecting a topic and progress step by step to proofreading the final copy. The chronological pattern is often appropriate for a paper describing a series of historical, political, or sociological processes or events.

COMPARISON AND CONTRAST   The pattern of comparison and contrast presents the similarities and/or differences between two or more persons, places, or things. A logical development by comparison and contrast entails discussion of the same qualities of both subjects. For example, the statement that one politician was a poor public speaker and another had a good understanding of the legislative system does not provide a basis for comparison and contrast. The speaking ability of both politicians, as well as their understanding of political institutions, should be discussed. Comparison and contrast are appropriate when a subject can best be understood by distinguishing it from others in its class.

SPATIAL PATTERN   The spatial pattern develops the physical layout or geographical dimensions of a topic. It can guide the reader through a topic that includes several locations, such as the seasonal habitats of various animals, the movement of troops in the Vietnam War, or the concentration of heavy industry in the United States.

CAUSE AND EFFECT   A cause-and-effect paper presents the events or forces that produced certain results, speculates about how things might have turned out if conditions had been different, or reports controlled experimentation to determine the factors important to a particular outcome. Cause and effect are difficult to determine, particularly in the social sciences, and valid work in this area should either control or take into account as many factors as possible. Topics such as possible explanations for the decline in students' reading scores in the United States in the past decade or reasons for population shifts away from inner cities lend themselves to development by cause and effect.

ANALYSIS   Some subjects can best be understood by an examination of their component parts. Analysis is the process of dividing a subject into its parts and classifying them. A research paper on the responsibilities of a hospital administrator might proceed by grouping the duties by types and discussing each type.

Major divisions of a paper

Your outline will develop naturally from the principle of organization you select. A paper involving comparison and contrast or cause and effect, for example, will usually have two major divisions. A paper organized chronologically, spatially, or analytically may have a number of major divisions. After you have identified the large segments of the paper, you can fill in the points to be made in each part.

▪ Types of Outlines

Your working outline may consist of casual jottings, but the outline you present to your instructor either in the middle of your research or with your final paper should be formal and consistently developed. You may choose either a topic outline or a sentence outline, depending on your preference and that of your instructor.

TOPIC OUTLINE   The entries in a topic outline are words, phrases, or clauses: they are not complete sentences. The entries should be parallel; they all should take the same grammatical form. If you use a noun phrase for one entry, you should continue using noun phrases consistently. You may have to rework some of your entries to make them parallel, but paying attention to grammatical form often leads to clear and logical thinking. (See the example topic outline on page 80 and the discussion of parallelism that begins on page 79 in Chapter 4.)

SENTENCE OUTLINE   The entries in a sentence outline are complete sentences. The process of writing a research paper involves writing sentences from the topics in the topic outline, in effect producing a sentence outline. A sentence outline therefore serves as a beginning for the paper and as a test of the logic of the outline. (See the example sentence outline in Chapter 4 on pages 80–81.)

■ Outline Formats

Number-letter sequence

The two basic formats for an outline are the number-letter sequence and the decimal pattern. The number-letter sequence is shown in the following example:

```
I.  The two reasons for . . .

    A.  The first reason . . .

        1.  The women . . .

            a.  They could . . .

                (1)  The time . . .

                    (a)  The technology . . .

                        i)  The latest development . . .

                        ii)  The plans for . . .

                    (b)  The receptive public . . .

                (2)  The place . . .

            b.  They could . . .

        2.  The men . . .

    B.  The second reason . . .

II.  The reasons against . . .
```

Decimal outline

The sequence for a decimal outline proceeds as follows:

```
1.  The two reasons for . . .

    1.1 The first reason . . .

        1.1.1 The women . . .

            1.1.1.1 They could . . .
```

```
                    1.1.1.1.1 the time . . .

                    1.1.1.1.2 the receptive public . . .

                1.1.1.2 They could . . .

            1.1.2 The men . . .

        1.2 The second reason . . .

    2.  The reasons against . . .
```

With either format, logic requires that there be at least two items at each level or subdivision; that is, an A must not appear without a B and a 1.1.1 must not appear without a 1.1.2 because nothing can be divided into fewer than two parts. When you find that you have only one subdivision for a section, you should either restate the major heading to include the subdivision or search for another logical division for the heading. (See the sample outline on page 31.)

Writing the Paper

Writing a research paper involves preparing a first draft, revising the draft as often as necessary, editing the draft, preparing the documentation and attending to other elements of the format, and proofreading.

Although to some extent you will approach these tasks in the order they are listed here, you should not expect to complete any of them until you have a finished copy. Each activity proceeds both linearly and recursively. Even as you proceed with writing your first draft, you will constantly be thinking back to the sentences and paragraphs you have already written and thinking ahead to the projected design of your entire paper. Similarly, throughout the writing process you may be preparing parts of the final format, such as the notes and bibliography.

▪ The First Draft

Exploratory writing

As you do research, you may want to write brief, exploratory pieces to develop your thinking. You may eventually incorporate them into your paper, or you may set them aside. Either way, because writing not only reflects thought but generates it, writing during all stages of research will help you refine your thesis statement and outline.

When you write short papers or portions of a long paper, you may not need an outline in advance. For a lengthy research paper, however, you probably will want to have a relatively complete outline, with your notes organized by topics and subtopics, before you begin to write. As you write, you may find that you will need to rework your outline or that you will need to do additional research.

Even if they plan to use a word processor to type their papers, many writers prefer to draft their papers by hand. Some find that they choose their words more carefully and that they write more varied and complex sentences that way. Others prefer to write the first and other drafts on a typewriter or a word processor. Whichever mode of drafting you choose, you should be aware that your choice may affect your writing.

Writing on a word processor

One of the advantages of a word processor is that it allows you to write as fast as your fingers can press the keys. This capacity to produce a great deal of prose quickly may allay your fear of the blank page and help you cut short the slow process of writing in longhand. Many people who use a word processor, however, tend to produce prose that is repetitive and loosely structured, that contains many superficial errors, some of which may be typographical, and that resembles spoken rather than written language. Such writers may overcome the initial impediments to writing, but they must develop the ability to correct for any deficiencies fostered by the machine. Other writers derive pleasure from writing with their favorite pen and on paper of a particular size or color and then typing their draft into a word processor or on a typewriter. Whatever your preference, you should constantly monitor your writing process and scrutinize your writing, making changes in your tools and techniques to best serve your work.

▪ Revision

Writers often resist revising because they do not want to mess up a clean handwritten or typed copy. Writing, however, is a craft; and writers, like other craftspeople, should be prepared to cut, discard, and reshape their materials. Most workshops contain a clutter of scraps. Some of the scraps can be collected and reused; others are eventually swept away. Most artisans cherish such evidence of the progress of their work. Experienced writers have generally learned to do likewise. Rather than seeing a draft with insertions and deletions marked in pencil as a mess, they see it as a work in progress. This is not to deny that revision is a sometimes painful, though natural, part of the creative process.

If you use a word processor, your printed copy will give you a view of your drafts that is different from the view that appears on the screen. Seeing your writing in different formats will help you to revise, which means to re-envision. You also give yourself the opportunity to have this double perspective on your work if you type a handwritten draft (or have someone else type it).

Revising on a word processor

Although word processors facilitate revision, most writers who use them tend to make the small changes, of words and individual sentences, more readily than they rearrange paragraphs and sections. Working on a screen that allows you to see only twenty-four lines at a time makes it difficult to keep the structure of the entire paper in mind. Often it is easier to print out several pages and make your revisions on paper. It is quite common for writers to rework a sentence or paragraph on the computer screen, only to find that it no longer fits logically into the paper.

The computer also allows you to shift entire paragraphs and sections by pressing only a few keys. Any change in the position of a paragraph nearly always requires other revisions, such as changes in transitions and the reordering of sentences elsewhere in the paper. As you revise, you would be wise to keep all versions of your draft because you may find that you want to restore something you had deleted. Some writers keep each draft in a separate, dated file; others keep a file of deleted paragraphs, sentences, or even single words for possible use in another part of the paper.

Questions for revision

The following questions can help you notice passages in your work that need revision:

- Does the thesis statement govern everything in the paper?
- Does the introduction prepare the reader for the paper?
- Are the paragraphs developed logically and arranged in a sequence that is coherent?
- Do any sections repeat or contradict other sections?
- Does the entire paper read smoothly, with transitions that carry the reader from one idea to the next?

After you have answered all these questions affirmatively, you can begin your editing.

▪ Editing

When you have a thoroughly revised draft ready for final typing, you should read through it at least once more, paying attention to every detail. Once again you should evaluate every sentence for clarity, check every paragraph for coherence, think about every choice of diction and sentence structure. In addition, you should look for mechanical errors in spelling and punctuation as well as for typographical errors. Chapter 4 discusses the problems that most often arise in editing a research paper.

Editing on a word processor

Many word-processing programs have features that you can use to help identify and correct errors. When you find an error, you can use the search command to retrieve other instances of it and to replace it automatically with the correct form. An adjunct to most word-processing programs is the spell checker, which identifies the misspelling of any word in its dictionary and allows you to add to the dictionary any words that you tend to misspell. Other programs can be used to check grammar and mechanics and to identify stylistic problems.

When you use any of those features or programs, you should remember that the computer does not think; it only simulates thinking. The only misspellings that a spell checker can identify are errors in words that are in its dictionary. If you type the wrong word but spell it correctly—if you type *there* when you meant to type *three*—the spell checker will not find the error. Other error identification programs may point out problems, but they cannot help you find the most effective way to revise.

▪ Format

Instructors in different disciplines have different requirements for the format of research papers. Most undergraduate papers, however, include the following parts in addition to the body, or text: a title page, an outline page, documentation (through parenthetical references in the text or through endnotes or footnotes), and a bibliography. Any given paper or instructor may require only some of these elements or additional ones. (See Chapter 2 for the elements of a thesis or dissertation and Chapter 6 for typing instructions for research papers, theses, and dissertations.)

TITLE PAGE   The title page of a research paper should include the title of the paper, the student's name, the course and section, the instructor's name, and the date. (See the sample title page on page 30.) If your instructor does not require a title page, you should include this information on the first page of the text. (See page 32 for a sample paper without a title page.)

OUTLINE PAGE   The outline page of a research paper presents a topic or sentence outline and sometimes includes the thesis statement. The numbers and headings on the outline page should not appear within the text of your paper. (See the sample outline on page 31.)

BIBLIOGRAPHY   When your instructor or publisher does not specify a system of documentation, you probably will want to follow the requirements of *The Chicago Manual of Style* (detailed in Chapter 7), the most widely used documentation system. The type of bibliography most often requested for an undergraduate research paper is a list of the works that are referred to in the paper. If you read a work but did not cite it, that work is not included in your list. The introduction to Part II (pages 136–41) and Chapter 7 present information on preparing bibliographies according to the *Chicago Manual* system. If you use the MLA or APA system, see the instructions for preparing a list of works cited on pages 202 through 204 for MLA, pages 216 through 217 for APA. (See the sample bibliography page for a short research paper on page 35.)

DOCUMENTATION   Each fact or opinion obtained from a source, whether quoted directly or summarized, must be documented with a note or with a parenthetical reference. Notes may be in one of two forms: footnotes or endnotes. Footnotes are placed at the bottom of the page that contains the material they refer to. Endnotes are grouped together in a separate section at the end of the paper. (See the sample endnotes page on page 34.) Chapter 7 discusses the documentation of first and subsequent references in the note-bibliography format required by the Chicago system. For the parenthetical-reference format required by the MLA, see pages 201 through 202, and for that of the APA, see pages 213 through 216.

▪ Proofreading

Rereading the finished copy, or proofreading, can make the difference between a mediocre paper and an excellent one. You should read your paper just one more time, even though you may be tired of it. Better yet, if possible, you should allow yourself enough time to set the paper aside for at least one day so that you can read it from a fresh perspective.

Speed-reading techniques are not appropriate for proofreading. You need to read almost letter for letter. Careful proofreading will help ensure that the paper you submit does justice to the time, energy, and thought you invested in its creation.

ELEMENTS OF RESEARCH PAPERS

Sample Pages

On the following pages are sample pages from research papers illustrating principles of layout and format described in Chapter 1. The pages presented here follow the Chicago note-bibliography system.

[5 inches]

Are Books Obsolete?:   The Prospects for Electronic Texts

[quadruple space]

Elizabeth Barnes

Professor Smith

English 1302.15

19 May 1993

[1 inch]

Title page for a research paper (optional)

[double space]

Outline

[double space]

Thesis Statement: Although electronic means of publication have many

advantages for both readers and publishers,

electronic texts are not likely to replace books.

  I. The New Electronic Medium

 II. Advantages of Electronic Texts

     A. For Publishers

          1. Publishing on Demand

          2. On-line Publishing

          3. Electronic Texts

     B. For Readers

          1. Instantaneous Access

          2. Capacity to Read the Text in Different Ways

          3. Elimination of Storage Problems

     C. For Authors

III. Drawbacks to Electronic Publishing

     A. For Publishers

     B. For Readers

     C. For Authors

 IV. The Enduring Appeal of Books for Readers

     A. Portability

     B. Price

     C. Nostalgia

Outline page for a research paper (optional)

[1 inch]

Elizabeth Barnes

[double space]

English 1302.15

Professor Smith

19 May 1993

[double space]

[5 spaces]   Are Books Obsolete?: The Prospects for Electronic Texts

[double space]

Word processors have replaced typewriters in most offices; the click of typewriter keys no longer resounds even in the newsroom. The computer has changed the way the printed word is produced, but so far it has had little effect on the way it is read. Recipients of business letters and subscribers to magazines read electronically processed words on the traditional printed page. The technology exists that could eliminate books as effectively as it has displaced typewriters. The book is not obsolete, however, nor is it likely to be. Although electronic means of publication have some advantages, electronic texts are not likely to replace books.

[5 spaces]   For publishers, electronic publishing has some alluring advantages. It holds out the promise of eliminating one of the most persistent problems of both publishers and booksellers, the overstock that is necessary to keep a large backlist in print and before the public.[1] The new technology for electronic publishing could allow for publishing on demand, the publication of books as they are ordered. This system would permit publishers to keep books in print indefinitely, even those that have a limited market, and it would reduce the storage and space problems that bookstores now face.[2]

First page of a research paper with endnotes and no title page

[double space]

some disadvantages. It might even restrict the accessibility of information. The cost of the necessary equipment, even though it has been falling, could reduce the number of people with ready access to reading materials. While libraries have long lent books, it is unclear that they would be able to provide electronic texts to as large an audience. Also, if the proliferation of electronic databases on different systems is any guide, electronic texts might be published in different formats and for various systems. Because it would require a larger range of skills, reading would require more training. And because on-line publishing would of necessity be more centralized, Paul Starr suggests that it could actually undermine individual freedom to write and to read:

[10 spaces]   [double space]

On-line publishing also has some sinister possibilities.

> In the hands of a totalitarian government, it could be used to monitor what citizens were reading. When it suited the regime, the texts of past newspapers, journals, and books could be permanently altered.[12]

[double space]

These scenarios seem far-fetched, but it is sobering to remember that the books might be destroyed more efficiently by pulling the plug on electronic texts than by throwing large numbers of copies on bonfires.

While the possibilities of electronic publishing seem to outweigh the risks, books probably will not become obsolete. Starr judges that "the printed page has such obvious advantages in ease of

Page of text using endnotes

[1 inch]

Barnes 11

Notes [double space]

[double space]

[1] Leonard Shatzkin, <u>In Cold Type: Overcoming the Book Crisis</u> (Boston: Houghton Mifflin, 1982).

[2] Paul Starr, "The Electronic Reader," in <u>Reading in the 1980s</u>, ed. Stephen Braubard (New York: Bowker, 1983), 149.

[3] Gregory Crane, "'Hypermedia' and Scholarly Publishing," <u>Scholarly Publishing</u>, Apr. 1990, 131.

[4] Shatzkin, 79.

[5] Starr, 149.

[6] Elizabeth I. Eisenstein, <u>The Printing Press as an Agent of Change</u> (Cambridge: Cambridge University Press, 1979), 107.

[7] Eisenstein, 72.

[8] Walter W. Powell, <u>Books: The Culture and Commerce of Book Publishing</u> (New York: Basic Books, 1982), 97.

[9] Eisenstein, 125.

[10] Nicholas E. Davies, "The Health-Sciences Information Struggle: The Private Information Industry versus The National Library of Medicine," <u>New England Journal of Medicine</u> 307 (15 July 1982): 201.

[11] Davies, 202.

[12] Starr, 155.

[13] Powell, 97.

[14] Irving Louis Horowitz and Mary E. Curtis, "The Impact of Technology on Scholarly Publishing," <u>Scholarly Publishing</u>, Apr. 1982, 210.

Endnotes page

[double space]
Bibliography
[double space]

Barzun, Jacques, and Henry F. Graff. The Modern Researcher. 5th ed.

  Fort Worth: Harcourt Brace, 1992.

Choldin, Harvey M. "Electronic Community Fact Books." Urban Affairs

  Quarterly 15 (Mar. 1980): 269-89.

Crane, Gregory. "'Hypermedia' and Scholarly Publishing." Scholarly

  Publishing, Apr. 1990, 131-55.

Cullen, Murphy. "Caught in the Web of Bytes: The Electronic Oxford

  English Dictionary." Atlantic, Feb. 1989, 68-70.

Davies, Nicholas E. "The Health-Sciences Information Struggle: The

  Private Information Industry versus The National Library of

  Medicine." New England Journal of Medicine 307 (15 July 1982):

  201-04.

Directory of Electronic Journals, Newsletters and Academic Discussion

  Lists. 2nd ed. Washington, D.C.: Association of Research

  Libraries, 1992.

Eisenstein, Elizabeth I. The Printing Press as an Agent of Change.

  Cambridge: Cambridge University Press, 1979.

Horowitz, Irving Louis, and Mary E. Curtis. "The Impact of Technology

  on Scholarly Publishing." Scholarly Publishing, Apr. 1982,

  210-28.

Shatzkin, Leonard. In Cold Type: Overcoming the Book Crisis. Boston:

  Houghton Mifflin, 1982.

Starr, Paul. "The Electronic Reader." In Reading in the 1980s, ed.

  Stephen Braubard, 143-56. New York: Bowker, 1983.

Bibliography page

[1 inch]

Smith 79

[double space]

Annotated Bibliography

[double space]

Daiute, Colette A. "The Computer as Stylus and Audience." College Composition and Communication 34 (May 1983): 134-45.

  Daiute argues that computers can help writers overcome what she calls "psychological difficulties" in writing, such as the limits of short-term memory and the necessity of considering the reader's point of view.

Dobrin, David N. "Some Ideas about Idea Processors." In Writing at Century's End: Essays on Computer-Assisted Instruction, ed. Lisa Gerrard, 17-23. New York: Random House, 1987.

  Dobrin argues that idea processors, programs such as ThinkTank that produce outlines, can help some writers to order their thoughts, but for most writers they limit creativity.

Gottesman, Polly. "Writing Papers on the Word Processor: A Winter Study Experiment, 1984." Department of English, University of Colorado, Boulder. Photocopy.

  In an independent study project in science writing, Gottesman experimented with teaching students to write and revise on computers. Although the computer ultimately promoted revision, students had to overcome the tendency to see a beautifully typed draft as correct, and they had to learn to shift and alter large sections of the text.

Schwartz, Helen J. "Teaching Writing with Computer Aids." College English 46 (Mar. 1984): 239-47.

  Schwartz analyzes programs useful for teaching invention, organization, and revision in the composition classroom.

Teichman, Milton. "What College Freshmen Say about Word Processing." Perspectives in Computing 5 (1985): 43-48.

  In response to a questionnaire prepared by Teichman, students listed the benefits and drawbacks of word processing. The most important advantages they cited were saved time, ease of revision, and a professional-looking copy. Among the disadvantages mentioned were the inconvenience of working in one place, preoccupation with the machine itself, and technical difficulties.

Annotated bibliography

[double space]
Bibliography
[double space]
Primary Sources
[double space]
Collected Documents

Commager, Henry Steele, ed. Documents of American History. 2 vols.
    in 1. 5th ed. New York: Appleton-Century-Crofts, 1949.

MacDonald, William H., ed. Select Charters and Other Documents
    Illustrative of American History, 1606-1775. New York:
    Macmillan, 1899.

Whitmore, William H., ed. The Andros Tracts: Being a Collection of
    Pamphlets and Official Papers. 3 vols. Boston: n.p., 1868-74.

Diaries, Letters, and Narratives

Andrews, Charles McL., ed. Narratives of the Insurrections, 1675-
    1690. Original Narratives of Early American History. New York:
    Scribner's, 1915.

Bradford, William. Of Plymouth Plantation, 1620-1647. Ed. Samuel E.
    Morison. New York: Knopf, 1952.

Dreuilletes, Father Gabriel. "Narrative of a Journey to New England,
    1650." In The Jesuit Relations and Allied Documents . . . 1610-
    1791, ed. Reuben G. Thwaites. Cleveland: n.p., 1898.

Dudley, Thomas. "Letter to the Countess of Lincoln." In Collections
    of the New Hampshire Historical Society. Concord: New Hampshire
    Historical Society, 1834.

Homes, William. "Diary of Rev. William Homes of Chilmark, Martha's
    Vineyard, 1689-1746." New England Historical and Genealogical
    Register 48 (1894): 446-53; 49 (1895): 413-16; 50 (1896):
    155-66.

Usher, John. "Report on Northern Colonies, 1698." William and Mary
    Quarterly, 3rd ser., 7 (1950): 95.

Bibliography divided by type of source

2 Elements of Theses and Dissertations

A thesis or a dissertation contains three categories of materials: the preliminaries (front matter), the text (body) of the paper, and the reference materials (back matter or end matter). When the thesis or dissertation is bound in book form for library use or reproduced on microfilm, these elements are included.

This chapter presents descriptions and models of the parts of a thesis or dissertation, along with procedures for preparing the entire typescript. A university graduate office usually provides information on required format. Consult university regulations before you begin to prepare final copy.

The Preliminaries (Front Matter)

The preliminaries, or front matter, of a thesis or dissertation consist of any or all of the following elements: abstract; approval sheet; title page; copyright page; table of contents; lists of tables, figures, and plates; clearance forms; acknowledgments; and preface. Not every thesis will include all these elements. They usually appear in this order, but a dissertation adviser or university regulations may require another arrangement. All the preliminaries, with the exception of the abstract and the approval sheet, are counted as pages of paper. The title page and the copyright page, though counted, remain unnumbered. All other pages of front matter are given lowercase roman numerals centered at the bottom of the page.

■ Abstract

Most universities require that a doctoral candidate submit an *abstract*, a brief descriptive summary, of the dissertation. The abstract should include a statement of the problem or issue, a brief description of the research method and design, major findings and their significance, and the conclusions. A reader should be able to decide from the abstract whether to read the entire dissertation. Because the abstract is not part of the dissertation, it is neither numbered nor counted as a page.

To fulfill the requirement that the doctoral dissertation be available to other scholars, the graduate office generally sends a copy of the abstract to University Microfilms, which prints an abstract in *Dissertation Abstracts International (DAI)* for each dissertation available on microfilm. Abstracts published in *DAI* are limited to a maximum of 350 words.

Universities or individual departments may require an abstract for these and other types of reports. An abstract for a short paper is usually limited to one page.

▪ Approval Sheet

The approval sheet provides space for the signatures of the adviser, readers, department chairperson, graduate deans, and others indicating their acceptance of the work. Most institutions have a model or form printed for this purpose, and local requirements should always determine the format of this page. Approvals are sometimes incorporated into the title page. Many institutions do not bind the separate approval sheet into the dissertation.

▪ Title Page

The first page of a thesis or dissertation is the title page. The graduate school office usually prescribes the form of the title page (see pages 49 and 50 for typical examples). The title page presents the title, the full name of the writer, and the submission statement, which includes the faculty or school, such as the Graduate School of Arts and Sciences or the School of Business Administration, and the institution, the degree sought (or granted), and the month and year in which the degree is to be (or was) granted. A particular institution may require different combinations of the elements shown in the samples, or it may require additional information, such as the writer's previous academic degrees.

The title should be concise as well as descriptive and comprehensive. Its wording should indicate the content of the paper so that scholars encountering mention of it in a bibliography will know whether it relates to their research. A title like "The Tourist Industry in the Bahamas" does not sufficiently describe a dissertation devoted to the economic aspects of the industry there; a title such as "The Economic Dynamics of the Tourist Industry in the Bahamas" would more accurately describe the content. Keep in mind that computerized databases cannot distinguish words used metaphorically from words used literally. An article on T. S. Eliot's poetic drama might colorfully, and accurately, be entitled "T. S. Eliot's Marriage of Poetry and Drama." However, the writer, aware that a computerized database would retrieve this title for a researcher interested in T. S. Eliot's marriage to Valerie Eliot, might consider a more literal title, such as "T. S. Eliot's Poetic Drama," particularly if the metaphor did not serve an important purpose.

Phrases like "A Critical Analysis and Evaluation of . . ." or "An Investigation of . . ." should be avoided when they are unnecessary. Subtitles, if any, should function to delimit the subject described in the title. The following excessively long titles have been shortened yet adequately identify the topic:

Wordy title   AN EVALUATION OF THE IMPLEMENTATION PROCESS AND IMPACT
OF A PROGRAM TO EDUCATE TEACHERS IN ECUADOR

Revision   THE IMPLEMENTATION AND IMPACT
OF A TEACHER-TRAINING PROGRAM IN ECUADOR

Wordy title   A STUDY OF THE EFFECTS OF FOREIGN INVESTMENT
ON THE ECONOMIC GROWTH IN SPAIN
DURING THE PERIOD BETWEEN 1976 AND 1990

Revision   THE EFFECTS OF FOREIGN INVESTMENT
ON ECONOMIC GROWTH IN SPAIN: 1976-1990

▪ Copyright Page

The microfilming of a dissertation is a form of publication. Thus you need to follow the law regarding copyright, both to protect your own work and to ensure that your use of other people's work meets legal requirements.

According to federal law, you own the copyright for your thesis or dissertation from the time you write the work until you formally transfer the copyright to a publisher or to some other organization or individual. Before such transfer takes place, you control all the rights to your work, including the right to make and distribute copies of it (that is, to publish it).

Whether or not you put a copyright notice on the second page of your unpublished thesis or dissertation (see the sample copyright page on page 51), you are legally protected against the unauthorized use of your work. Depositing a thesis or dissertation in a library and microfilming it, however, are equivalent to publication, and the law requires a copyright notice in any published work in which a copyright is claimed. You are not obliged to register your copyright with the Library of Congress, but you should consider doing so. Registering is a public record of copyright ownership and a prerequisite for legal action in the event of inappropriate use of your material.

If your thesis or dissertation is to be microfilmed, University Microfilms will register the copyright for a fee. If your paper is not to be microfilmed, you can register the copyright with the Library of Congress by writing directly to the Copyright Office, Library of Congress, Washington, DC 20559.

Just as federal law safeguards your copyright in your thesis or dissertation, it safeguards the rights of other writers in their work. In using material from other sources, you must follow the guidelines of *fair use*, a legal concept interpreted in various ways. According to one rule of thumb, you may quote up to 150 words from a source, or two lines of poetry, for critical or evaluative purposes without obtaining permission from the copyright holder. In most cases, the copyright holder is the publisher (because the author has transferred the copyright to the publisher). Some publishers allow the quotation of 250 words without written permission; others allow up to 500 words.

When a quotation, even of fewer than 150 words, constitutes a substantial proportion of the source, you need to write to the copyright holder and request permission to quote. If you are in any doubt about whether the direct quotations in your thesis or dissertation qualify as fair use, consult your graduate school office or contact the publisher of the work you are quoting. Any permissions you receive should be acknowledged on the copyright page or in the acknowledgments section.

▪ Table of Contents

In a thesis or dissertation, the table of contents precedes all the sections it lists. The table of contents should list all elements of the preliminaries—the chapter (part or section) titles, the main headings and subheadings in the text, and the reference materials. The beginning page number for each section is indicated along the right-hand margin. The numbering of chapters and the wording, capitalization, and punctuation of titles and headings should be exactly the same as they are in the text. (See the sample table of contents on page 52.)

▪ Lists of Tables and Figures

Lists of tables and figures should follow the table of contents. Each type of illustrative matter should be listed on a separate page. Charts, graphs, maps, and illustrations of other kinds are usually grouped as figures, but they may be designated by their more descriptive names, as in "Chart 3" or "Map 7." When there are only two or three tables or figures in a thesis or dissertation, local policy may permit omission of a listing in the front matter. All captions should appear in the listing exactly as they are in the text.

Capitalization of captions The traditional form for listing titles or captions of tables and figures calls for capitalization of the first letter of the first and last words and of all nouns, pronouns, adjectives, adverbs, and verbs. Figures are sometimes listed in capital letters.

Numbering of captions Tables and figures should be numbered consecutively in arabic numerals throughout the paper. If tables and figures are especially numerous, they should be double-numbered by chapter. Table 1.1 would be the first table in Chapter 1; Table 1.2, the second, and so on. Figure 2.1 would be the first figure in Chapter 2; Figure 2.2, the second. A period should separate the chapter from the item number. Chapter 5 contains a full discussion of the presentation of tables and figures, with explanations and examples.

▪ Clearance Forms

When human beings are the subjects of experimental study or when the facilities of an institution are used, clearance forms may be necessary. If the forms are short, they can be placed in the preliminaries. Any long or complex information on clearance should be placed in an appendix.

Design of the experiment and requirements of the institution dictate the nature of the clearance forms.

▪ Acknowledgments

The acknowledgments section contains expressions of appreciation for assistance and guidance. The help given by advisers and readers does not require written acknowledgment, but the recognition of generosity with time and knowledge is a courtesy that is widely appreciated. Acknowledgments should be expressed simply and tactfully.

Permissions that you have obtained for quotations may be presented in the Acknowledgments or on the copyright page. When permissions are granted as a special favor, they are best placed in the Acknowledgments.

▪ Preface

The preface, usually an optional section for a dissertation or thesis, might include brief comment on subjects such as the motivation for the study or methods of research. Substantial development of these issues and significant historical or background information belong in the text of the paper. The preface should be an adjunct to the paper rather than an essential part of it.

The Text (Body)

The text, or body, of a thesis or dissertation begins with the first page of Chapter 1, which follows the preliminaries discussed above. Numbering in arabic numerals starts on this page with number 1; all pages are numbered, including chapter and section title pages. Position all page numbers one inch from the top of the page, flush with the right margin.

▪ Organization of Chapters

Each topic calls for an organization appropriate to its own logic and to the discipline or field. Your research will determine the nature of the text, and your adviser will have suggestions concerning the design of your paper. Formats for the body of the paper differ for the three general types of theses: (1) theses based on the collection of empirical data, (2) theses derived from critical analysis or philosophical inquiry, and (3) theses based on historical research.

THESES BASED ON THE COLLECTION OF EMPIRICAL DATA

A standard format is often followed in theses based on the collection of empirical data, that is, information derived from direct observation or experience. The chapters are usually divided into five categories, corresponding to the stages of research. Although these parts may be variously labeled, essentially they consist of an introduction, a review of the literature, a presentation of the method, a report of the findings, and a summary and discussion.

Introductory chapter(s)

The introductory chapter(s) should contain the following:

1. An introduction to the subject area indicating the importance and validity of the problem chosen for study. The potential contribution of the study, the need for the research, and background information may also be included here.

2. A clear and concise statement of the problem, together with an analysis of its delimitation or scope. An experimental study should be stated as one or more hypotheses (tentative statements of the relationship between variables) and, particularly in the case of a statistical study of variables, an accompanying null hypothesis (a statement of the absence of the hypothesized correlation). Other kinds of research problems may be posed in the form of questions. The schedule and procedures for gathering data should be explained.

3. A section that establishes the theoretical framework within which the investigation was conducted. This section usually includes basic assumptions of the study and definitions of terms.

Review of the literature

The review of related research and literature, usually a separate chapter, should give readers the context for the present study. The review should not merely summarize a series of books and articles; rather, it should call attention to the most important previous work, identify the place of your study in relation to other research, and delineate areas of agreement and disagreement in the field. The review should evaluate and interpret existing research—not just repeat it. Organizing the review by topic rather than by author and avoiding unnecessary direct quotation can help you focus the review of research.

Design of the investigation

The chapter(s) devoted to the design of the investigation should discuss such matters as the method of research, the nature of the sample and any control groups, the data needed to test the hypotheses or to answer the questions, the sources of data, and the procedures followed in gathering and analyzing the data.

Analysis of the data

The analysis chapter(s) should present the results of the investigation, usually without interpretation or evaluation. This nonevaluative analysis of data constitutes the heart of a thesis based on the collection of empirical data. You will want to decide on the most effective method for presenting the data. The information should be explained in clear, coherent prose. You may wish to accompany your analyses with charts or tables, but these should supplement the text rather than substitute for it. The body of the paper should be comprehensible even if the reader chooses not to consult the tables. (See Chapter 5 for information on presenting tables, figures, charts, and computer data.)

Summary and interpretation

The chapter(s) of summary and discussion should be devoted to evaluation and interpretation of the data and formulation of conclusions. Also covered here, as appropriate, are implications of the findings for revising the existing body of knowledge, possible contributions of the thesis to research methodology, the relation of the results to previously published studies, limitations of the study, and unexpected conclusions. Practical applications of the findings or speculation about further studies might conclude this section.

THESES BASED ON CRITICAL ANALYSIS OR PHILOSOPHICAL SPECULATION

No specified format governs theses based on critical analysis or philosophical speculation. Rather, they contain a number of common elements either developed in separate chapters or interwoven in each chapter.

The introductory section usually places the study against the background of previous work in the field. The importance of the topic, its role in current controversy or developments, and the scholarly tradition in which the thesis belongs might be developed here. Although you want to acknowledge any studies that have influenced or guided your work, as well as those you may have reacted against, this section should not turn into a summary of the works in question. Instead, discussion of these works should always demonstrate their relationship to your topic. Although you will probably be critically evaluating theories advanced by other writers, your comments should remain fair and evenhanded. You need not demolish previous studies to give your own work validity.

The central chapters of such a thesis should present the results of your research and analysis. These results should be set forth clearly and systematically in order to convince readers that you have considered every facet of the topic and that the material uncovered by your research confirms your thesis statement. One of the challenges of writing these chapters is to present a good deal of information while continually keeping the central point of the thesis before the reader.

The interpretation or statement of the significance of the thesis may be integrated with the exposition of the findings or may be presented in the concluding chapter(s). The conclusion might include the implications of the work for the revision of previous interpretations, proof or disproof of assumptions or theories in the field, or new areas of inquiry opened by the study.

THESES BASED ON HISTORICAL RESEARCH

Because historical research serves to discover data rather to create it, the organization of the thesis developed from it depends largely on the kind and quantity of information the researcher gathers. The historical thesis thus follows no established format, but it usually contains several elements. (The elements of theses based on critical analysis, described above, may be useful for the historical paper as well.)

Commonly, the major portion of the historical thesis is devoted to reporting the researcher's findings, often in a style that strives for objectivity. Chronological organization is the most obvious, and very often the most useful way of arranging historical information. However, this information might also be ordered by another logical principle, such as cause and effect, or divided or subdivided into categories such as concepts, persons, or events.

The introductory chapter(s) might be used to present the motive for the study, to detail the problems or deficiencies of previous scholarship, or to chronicle difficulties and peculiarities of the process of retrieving the information in question. Whereas some historical theses may serve solely to present new information, others will attempt to explain a current situation in light of the past or to revise theories about the nature or significance of a sequence of events. This kind of interpretive material may be woven into the whole study, but often it takes the form of the concluding chapter(s).

■ Parenthetical Documentation

If you use parenthetical references, your documentation will appear in the body of the text within parentheses. See pages 198 through 202 for a full explanation of the principles of the parenthetical documentation system preferred by the Modern Language Association (MLA) and pages 213 through 217 for a discussion of the parenthetical-reference system favored by the American Psychological Association (APA). A brief account of the author-number system of parenthetical referencing appears in Appendix C.

■ Chapter Titles and Headings

The way in which a thesis or dissertation is divided is determined by its length and complexity. Papers under twenty-five pages usually do not require division of any kind; in fact, dividing a short paper can be distracting rather than helpful. Longer research papers may benefit from the insertion of headings, centered or flush with the left margin; organization into chapters; and grouping of chapters into parts.

Chapter titles and headings should be used to clarify the organization of the thesis or dissertation. They should never be used to cover up inadequate organization, incoherent development, or insufficient transitions. A chapter should be clear and complete without its subheadings.

Chapter titles   A title should indicate clearly and concisely the contents of a chapter and its relationship to the paper as a whole.

Headings   Headings may be used to divide a long or complicated chapter. The same principles of parallelism and logic of division that govern outlining apply here as well. Every division of a subject must yield at least two subdivisions. All headings at the same level should be parallel grammatically and logically.

Levels of headings   The five generally accepted levels of headings proceed in the following order:

CENTERED UPPERCASE

Centered Uppercase and Lowercase

<u>Centered, Underlined Uppercase and Lowercase</u>

<u>Flush left, Underlined Uppercase and Lowercase</u>

    <u>Indented five spaces, underlined lowercase ending with a period.</u> The paragraph begins at the end of the heading.

Divisions beyond the third level should be avoided. If fourth-level headings are necessary, they should take the form of enumerated paragraphs. At least one paragraph of text should be placed between a heading and its first subheading.

The first two levels of headings are appropriate for titles of dissertations, parts of long papers, and titles of short papers.

TITLE OR MAJOR DIVISION OF LONG PAPER

Title of Short Paper or Chapter of Long Paper

The next three levels divide the body or text of the paper.

First Level within the Text

Second Level within the Text

Third Level within the Text.

Most research papers and dissertations will not require all these levels of headings. In such cases, you need not begin with a head of the highest level and proceed consecutively; instead you may select headings appropriate for your purpose or institutional requirements. The number of levels of headings may vary from chapter to chapter, depending on the logic of organization in each.

APA suggests the following arrangement of headings when fewer than five are required: for one level of heading, level 2; for two levels of headings, levels 2 and 4; for three levels of headings, levels 2, 4, and 5; and for four levels of headings, levels 2, 3, 4, and 5.

Reference Materials (Back Matter, or End Matter)

The reference materials for a thesis or dissertation may include an appendix or appendixes, a glossary, endnotes, a bibliography, and an index.

▪ Appendix

Materials for appendixes

An appendix should be used for materials that supplement the text but are not appropriate for inclusion in it. Original data, summary tabulations, tables containing data of lesser importance (as distinguished from those presenting major data in the text), very lengthy quotations, supporting legal decisions or laws, computer printouts, and pertinent documents not readily available to the reader belong in an appendix. Questionnaires with their letters of transmittal and the verbatim comments of respondents belong in an appendix. Supplementary illustrative materials, such as forms and documents, may also be included. Placing lengthy tables and other matter in the appendix prevents the text from becoming unduly bulky.

The material in the appendix may be subdivided according to logical classifications. List each appendix by letter and title, if any, in the table of contents.

▪ Glossary

A *glossary* (a list of definitions of terms and concepts) is usually not necessary for a dissertation because it is directed toward a professional audience. For other types of papers, a glossary may be desirable when the typical reader might not be familiar with the terminology. See the glossary at the end of this book for a sample format.

▪ Notes

If you use the note-bibliography format, you will have footnotes appearing throughout the paper or you will have a section of endnotes. Even if you use parenthetical documentation, you are likely to want to include some informational or bibliographical notes in a section at the end of the paper.

A thesis or dissertation to be microfilmed should use footnotes rather than endnotes so that the reader of the film will not have to turn the film back and forth to follow the notes. Notes should be numbered consecutively throughout each chapter, beginning with 1 for the first note in each chapter. A research paper or report that is not to be microfilmed may use endnotes. (See page 34 in Chapter 1 for a sample endnotes page.)

▪ Bibliography, List of Works Cited, or References

Papers based on research should have a bibliography, works cited, or references section, listing the sources of information. See the introduction to Part II for a discussion of the various types of documentation, and see Chapters 7, 8, and 9 for specific formats.

▪ Index

A dissertation or unpublished report rarely includes an *index* (an alphabetical listing with page numbers of subjects treated in the work). If an index is required, it follows all the other reference material. (See the index at the end of this book.)

ELEMENTS OF THESES AND DISSERTATIONS

Sample Pages

This section contains sample pages showing various formats and layouts for the different elements of theses and dissertations.

[2 inches]

THE IMPLEMENTATION AND IMPACT

OF A TEACHER-TRAINING PROGRAM IN ECUADOR

[3 inches]

by
[double space]
John William Herbert

A dissertation
[double space]
submitted in partial fulfillment

of the requirements for the degree of

Doctor of Philosophy in the School of Education

University of New Mexico

May 1993

[1 inch]

Title page, Form A

50 · **B**

[2 inches]

THE POLITICS AND ECONOMICS

OF THE TOURIST INDUSTRY IN THE CARIBBEAN

[2 inches]

A Dissertation

presented to

the Faculty of the Graduate School

University of the Pacific

[3 inches]

In Partial Fulfillment

of the Requirements for the Degree

Doctor of Philosophy

by

Jennifer Christine Smart

December 1993

Title page, Form B

[1 inch]

[1 inch]

Copyright page

[1 inch]

Table of Contents [**or** TABLE OF CONTENTS]

[double space]

Page

Table of contents page (only chapter titles and first-level heads are included here; see pages 132–3 for contents format showing first-, second-, and third-level heads)

Tables [**or** TABLES]

[double space]

Table   Page

ix

[1 inch]

Smith 25

[double space]
CHAPTER 2
[double space]
The Relationship of Writing and Reading Abilities
[double space]
E. D. Hirsch's concept of cultural literacy developed in part

from his study of writing abilities. In The Philosophy of

Composition, Hirsch argued that writing is a skill and that successful

teaching of writing requires only isolating the principles that allow

students to master the skill. In that utopian book, he suggested that

the literacy problem might be solved within ten years if teachers and

researchers could agree on the right set of principles:

> The maxims should be sound ones, having a wide application.
> They should be explained persuasively, and in a form the
> student can apply directly to his own prose. They should be
> limited in number, and grouped according to their relative
> importance for their typical audience. The book should
> encourage the student to believe that he can master the
> elements of the craft and make future progress on his own.[1]

Hirsch abandoned this formalistic approach when his numerous studies

of high school students convinced him that their writing revealed a

lack of common knowledge rather than ignorance of such maxims.[2]

Convinced of the need for a shared reading background, Hirsch
[double space]
——————————————— [1½ inch rule]
[double space]
   [1] E. D. Hirsch, The Philosophy of Composition (Chicago:
University of Chicago Press, 1977), 168.
[double space]
   [2] E. D. Hirsch, "Cultural Literacy," American Scholar 52 (spring
1983): 159-69.

Chapter title page (dissertation text with footnotes)

3 Quotations

Quotations in a research paper may be either direct (verbatim) or indirect (paraphrased). You must document both types—that is, you must indicate the source of direct and indirect quotations with documentation, either with a superscript (raised number) in the text and a corresponding note containing bibliographical information or with a parenthetical reference in the text, as the MLA and APA documentation systems recommend. This chapter provides information about the general principles of direct and indirect quotation applicable to any of these documentation systems. Any differences in format are indicated with multiple examples. The first set of indirect and direct quotations is shown with footnotes in *The Chicago Manual of Style* format and with parenthetical documentation that accords with the MLA and the APA systems. Subsequent examples illustrate only the footnote format.

Documentation of direct and indirect quotations in no way diminishes the originality of your work. Documentation allows your reader to see the materials you used to reach your conclusions, to check your interpretations of sources, to place your work in a tradition of inquiry, and to locate further information on your topic. Your contribution consists of imposing your own order on the sources you use and drawing an original conclusion from them.

Plagiarism (the use of another person's ideas or wording without giving appropriate credit) results from inaccurate or incomplete attribution of material to its source. Ideas, as well as the expression of those ideas, are considered to belong to the person who first puts them forward. Therefore, when you incorporate in your paper either ideas or phrasing from another writer, whether you quote directly or indirectly, you need to indicate your source accurately and completely. Whether intentional or unintentional, plagiarism can bring serious consequences, not only academic, in the form of failure or expulsion, but also legal, in the form of lawsuits. Plagiarism is taken seriously because it violates the ethics of the academic community.

You should document any fact or opinion that you read in one of your sources, whether you first discovered the idea there or you have assimilated it so thoroughly that it seems to be your own. Some exceptions to this rule are facts that are common knowledge (for example, that John Hancock signed the Declaration of Independence), facts that can be verified easily and do not differ from one source to another (for example, that Madrid is the capital of Spain), and well-known sayings or proverbs (for example,

Plagiarism

Documentation to avoid plagiarism

that Theodore Roosevelt said, "Speak softly and carry a big stick"). Under most circumstances, these kinds of materials do not need to be documented. In contrast, material available in one source or in a limited number of sources (for example, a fact about changes in the birthrate in China) should usually be documented. Statistics other than those you have compiled yourself should be attributed to the source. Such attribution not only gives appropriate credit but also protects you in the event that the information in the source is erroneous.

Indirect Quotation

You should choose indirect quotation whenever you do not have a compelling reason for using direct quotation (see pages 57–58 for guidelines for choosing direct quotation). Indirect quotation calls less attention to itself than does direct quotation and thus concentrates the reader's attention on the development of your argument. It is likely that most of the quotations in any paper will be indirect.

When you choose to quote indirectly rather than directly, you should use your own words and sentence structure. Imitating syntax, rearranging words and phrases, and borrowing phrases even as brief as two or three words do not change the original sufficiently to avoid plagiarism. If you find that you cannot avoid using a phrase from the original, place those words in quotation marks. Any paraphrase used as indirect quotation should represent the original source accurately, avoiding distortion through imprecise or mistaken restatement, altered emphasis, or significant omissions (see page 18 for a discussion of paraphrase and summary).

Even when you have restated a passage completely in your own words, you must indicate that you encountered the information in your reading. In some cases, you may wish to attribute the statement within your text by citing the author (by first and last name for the first reference and thereafter by last name only) and, if necessary or desirable, the title of the work. Even if you choose not to name the author in your text, you must document the source of the idea in a note.

The versions of the passage below demonstrate adequate and inadequate paraphrasing.

Original   I have said that science is impossible without faith. By this I do not mean that the faith on which science depends is religious in nature or involves the acceptance of any of the dogmas of the ordinary religious creeds, yet without faith that nature is subject to law there can be no science. No amount of demonstration can ever prove that nature is subject to law.[1]

Plagiarism   Science is impossible without faith that nature is

subject to law.

(Borrowed wording without quotation marks.)

---

[1] Norbert Wiener, *The Human Use of Human Beings: Cybernetics and Society* (New York: Avon, 1967), 262–63.

Plagiarism   Faith makes science possible. This does not mean

that science rests on religious faith or the acceptance of

religious dogmas, but without the faith that nature

functions according to laws, science cannot exist.
(Imitated sentence structure.)

Correct indirect   The belief that nature functions in accordance with
quotation

laws makes science possible.[1]
(Documentation used to give credit for the idea even though the passage has been restated.)

MLA parenthetical   The belief that nature functions in accordance with
documentation
system
laws makes science possible (Wiener 262–63).

APA parenthetical   The belief that nature functions in accordance with
documentation
system   laws makes science possible (Wiener, 1967, pp. 262-63).

You may combine direct and indirect quotation, a technique that allows you to condense the original while preserving particularly forceful wording or the author's tone.

Science depends on faith--not religious faith, but the faith that "nature is subject to law."[1]

MLA parenthetical   Science depends on faith--not religious faith, but the
reference   faith that "nature is subject to law" (Wiener 262–63).

APA parenthetical   Science depends on faith--not religious faith, but the
reference   faith that "nature is subject to law" (Wiener, 1967, pp. 262-63).

Subsequent examples in the chapter show only the footnote type of documentation, in the form favored by *The Chicago Manual.*

Direct Quotation

Direct quotation presents material from a source verbatim, or word for word. While most of the quotations you use will be indirect, or paraphrased, direct quotation is appropriate when you wish to summon the voice of an authority, to preserve the source author's original wording, or to emphasize the accuracy of your borrowing from the source.

Authority   Direct quotation provides authority for controversial positions or statements requiring expertise in fields other than your own. For example, if in a thesis in higher education, you wish to substantiate a conclusion about the implications of a university's open-admissions policy for the region's economy, a quotation from a prominent economist or a local business-person could be effective. Or if you wish to buttress your assertion about the significance of a historical trend, you might show that a respected historian drew a similar conclusion from an analogous set of facts.

Original wording   When an author has stated an idea so inventively or forcefully that you cannot do it justice in a paraphrase, you should quote directly to lend color and power to your work. It would be difficult to improve on J. H. Plumb's way of stating the contrast between thriving, artistic Florence and declining, war-torn Milan: "If Florence belonged to Minerva, Milan belonged to Mars."[2] Direct quotation is also appropriate when you want to give your reader the flavor of the original. Malcolm X's sentence concerning the black nationalist Marcus Garvey communicates the importance of the leader to the community better than a paraphrase might: "I remember seeing the big, shiny photographs of Marcus Garvey that were passed from hand to hand."[3]

Accuracy   For statements in which accuracy is extremely important, direct quotation assures the reader that you have presented the information accurately. Materials you might consider quoting are laws, mathematical formulas, and complex theoretical formulations.

When you use a direct quotation in your text for whatever reason, you must reproduce the language of the source exactly, following the internal punctuation, spelling, emphasis, and even the errors found in the original.

Length of direct quotations   Direct quotations should be kept as short as possible; long quotations may be distracting to readers. It can be tempting to insert a quotation and thereby let someone else do some of your writing, but by yielding to this temptation, you evade some of your responsibility. Direct quotations should be pared down to the absolutely essential portions.

When very long quotations—more than one-half page of text—seem out of place in the body of your paper yet are essential to the paper as a whole, place them in an appendix and refer the reader to this appendix.

Fair use   When deciding how much direct quotation to use in a dissertation that will be microfilmed or a thesis that will be deposited in a library (both considered published materials), you need to take into account the concept of *fair use*. You may need to secure the permission of the publisher or the copyright holder for some quotations. (See page 40 in Chapter 2 for more information on fair use.)

▪ Quotations Run into Text

Brief quotations of prose   Direct quotations of prose that do not exceed four typewritten lines (about forty words) should be run into the text and enclosed in double quotation marks, as in the following example:

---

[2] J. H. Plumb, *The Italian Renaissance: A Concise Survey of Its History and Culture* (1961; reprint, New York: Harper Torchbooks, 1965), 63.

[3] Malcolm X with Alex Haley, *The Autobiography of Malcolm X* (New York: Grove, 1966), 6.

```
Ernst Robert Curtius's term "the Latin Middle Ages" covers a

range of Roman legacies, including "the share of Rome, of

the Roman idea of the state, of the Roman church, and of

Roman culture."4
```

Brief quotations of poetry

Direct quotations of poetry consisting of less than two full lines should be run into the text. Use a slanted line (called a virgule) with a space on each side between lines of the poem. Retain the capitalization of the original, even though the excerpt combines with the surrounding text to form a grammatical whole.

```
In his "Hymn to Intellectual Beauty," Shelley personifies

the immaterial, spiritual world: "The awful shadow of some

unseen Power / Floats though unseen amongst us."
```

You may, however, choose to set off brief passages of prose or poetry in order to emphasize them.

▪ Quotations Set off from Text

A direct quotation of more than four typewritten lines of prose (approximately forty words) or two lines or more of poetry should be set off from the text by indention (see specific formats for prose and poetry below). Nearly all publishers prefer that indented quotations be doubled-spaced, to make editing easier. APA requires double-spacing of all quotations. For dissertations and theses, however, single-spacing is often preferred because it more closely resembles a printed format. Set-off quotations are not enclosed in quotation marks. (See the sample pages at the end of Chapters 1 and 2.)

▪ Prose

Indention of set-off paragraphs

Set-off paragraphs should be indented ten spaces. If you quote from only one paragraph, you need not indicate whether it begins with a paragraph break.

```
William Barrett gives one explanation of the flattening of

space found in modern art.
```

---

[4]E. R. Curtius, *European Literature and the Latin Middle Ages,* trans. Willard R. Trask (New York: Harper and Row, 1953), 27.

```
When mankind no longer lives spontaneously turned
toward God or the supersensible world--when, to
echo the words of Yeats, the ladder is gone by
which we would climb to a higher reality--the
artist too must stand face to face with a flat and
inexplicable world.⁵
```

(In the original, the word "When" marks the beginning of a paragraph.)

When the quotation spans two or more paragraphs in the original, indicate second and subsequent paragraph breaks with additional indentions of three spaces.

APA style   APA indents set-off material five spaces. Second and subsequent paragraphs are indented five additional spaces.

```
Raymond Williams defends the use of jargon in appropriate

contexts.

    Every known general position, in matters of art and
    belief, has its defining terms, and the difference
    between these and the terms identified as jargon
    is often no more than one of relative date and
    familiarity.  To run together the senses of jargon
    as specialized, unfamiliar, belonging to a hostile
    position, and unintelligible chatter is then at times
    indeed a jargon.⁶
```

Letters   Quotations from letters should be treated like any other long prose quotation—that is, set off and double-spaced or single-spaced in keeping with the other quotations in your paper. If the salutation and date are quoted, they should be positioned as they appear in the original.

Oral sources   Quotations from oral sources, such as conversations and speeches, should also be treated like prose quotations. You will need to obtain approval from the speaker for statements you quote unless the material was recorded with the speaker's permission. See pages 224 and 227 for documentation of oral sources according to the APA system.

▪ Poetry

Quotations of poetry set off   Set off quotations of three or more lines from the text, introducing them as the syntax of your sentence requires. Indent poetry ten spaces from the left margin; indention may be five spaces when the line would

Run-over lines   otherwise have to be broken. Lines of poetry extending beyond one typescript line should be indented five spaces, broken, and indented ten spaces

---

⁵William Barrett, *Irrational Man: A Study in Existential Philosophy* .(Garden City: Doubleday, Anchor, 1962), 49.
⁶Raymond Williams, *Keywords: A Vocabulary of Culture and Society*, rev. ed. (New York: Oxford University Press, 1983), 176.

on the next line. Alignment, spacing, and punctuation within the set-off quotation should follow the original as closely as possible.

```
In "Song of Myself," Walt Whitman uses the diction and

rhythm of natural speech:

    A child said What is the grass? fetching it to me with
        full hands;
    How could I answer the child?  I do not know what it
        is any more than he.
    I guess it must be the flag of my disposition, out of
        hopeful green stuff woven.
```

Placement of partial lines   When a quotation from a poem begins in the middle of a line, place the first word approximately where it appears on the page in the original, as the placement of the following lines from Keats's "Endymion" illustrates:

```
                        When yet a child
    I oft have dried my tears when thou has smil'd.
    Thou seem'dst my sister: hand in hand we went
    From eve to morn across the firmament.
```

Alignment   Align quotation marks at the beginning of a line under the capital letter of the preceding line, as indicated in this quotation from Wordsworth's "Anecdote for Fathers":

```
    At this my boy hung down his head,
    He blushed with shame, nor made reply;
    And three times to the child I said,
    "Why, Edward, tell me why?"
```

Original spacing   Reproduce the spacing of a poem as accurately as possible, as in this typed version of the beginning of Robert Herrick's "The Pillar of Fame":

```
    Fame's pillar here, at last, we set,
    Out-during Marble, Brass, or Jet,
        Charmed and enchanted so,
        As to withstand the blow
            Of     overthrow:
```

MLA style   Follow the above guidelines for spacing, but include documentation within parentheses after the final punctuation mark, as in this quotation from Elizabeth Barrett Browning's "Sonnets from the Portuguese":

```
    How do I love thee?  Let me count the ways.
    I love thee to the depth and breadth and height
    My soul can reach, when feeling out of sight
    For the ends of Being and ideal Grace. (27.1-4)
```

(Parenthetical references should be abbreviated, as in this citation of sonnet 27, lines 1 through 4. If the divisions of a work are not well known, identify them in a note for the first of the quotations in your text.)

▪ Epigraphs

An *epigraph* is a quotation chosen for its pertinence to the topic that precedes the text of a chapter or book. Epigraphs should be indented twenty spaces from the left margin. Such indention eliminates the need for quotation marks. Indicate paragraphing in the source with an additional five-space indention. Cite the author and the title of the source below the quotation, placing all lines flush with the right margin. When the authors are widely known, further bibliographical information is optional. If you wish to supply such information, do so in a note.

> The last years of the eighteenth
> century are broken by a discontinuity
> similar to that which destroyed
> Renaissance thought at the beginning of
> the seventeenth.
> Michael Foucault, The Order of Things:
> An Archaeology of the Human Sciences

▪ Direct Quotations in Notes

Informational notes may contain direct quotations. All quotations should be run in with the text of the note and enclosed in quotation marks. If the quotation is longer than one paragraph, begin each paragraph at the left margin without indention. Place quotation marks at the beginning of each paragraph and at the beginning and end of the entire selection. Quoted material in notes should follow the spacing used throughout.

[1] On other issues the Supreme Court 'handed down these decisions in 1989: "Ruling unanimously in a copyright case (Community for Creative Non-Violence v. Redi, No. 88-293), the Court held that freelance artists and writers retain the right to copyright what they create as long as they were not in a conventional employment relationship with the organization that commissioned their work.
"The court unanimously refused to narrow the scope of the Federal racketeering law. The decision, H.J. Inc. v. Northwestern Bell, No. 87-1252, left the law, originally aimed at organized crime, as a powerful weapon in private civil lawsuits." (Linda Greenhouse, "The Year the Court Turned Right," New York Times, 7 July 1989, A10)

Ways of Introducing Direct Quotations

Introductions to quotations should be varied as appropriate, although you should not strain for novel effects for their own sake. Each introduction you select should indicate accurately the content and context of the source.

The introduction should also indicate your reason for using the quotation. It should specify the relationship between your argument or ideas and those of the source, indicating, for example, whether you disagree or agree with the source or whether the source differs from another source that you have cited. Notice how a change in the introduction can affect a reader's interpretation of a quotation:

George Orwell, the English political activist, complains

that "Dickens's criticism of society is almost exclusively

moral."[7]

(The introductory word *complains* and the characterization of Orwell's career as political suggest that Orwell condemns Dickens's neglect of political analyses and solutions.)

George Orwell, the English essayist and novelist, explains

that "Dickens's criticism of society is almost exclusively

moral."[7]

(The introductory word *explains* and the characterization of Orwell's career as literary suggest that Orwell analyzes Dickens's attitudes toward society with the empathy of a writer rather than as a critic of his politics.)

The introduction to a direct quotation should provide a smooth transition between your own words and those of the author you quote. The name of the author (the full name the first time; the last name only thereafter) and the author's profession or affiliation (the first time you quote; thereafter only if significant) should accompany the quotation.

▪ Introductions to Run-in Quotations

You may choose to introduce a run-in quotation in a variety of ways, depending on the style of surrounding sentences and the effect you wish to achieve. The following examples of run-in quotations indicate only a few of the many stylistic possibilities. Each sentence is punctuated as it would be if the quoted phrase or clause were part of the report or thesis writer's own work. The only necessary punctuation is that required by each particular grammatical structure.

Jean-Jacques Rousseau admits, "I felt before I thought."[8]

"I felt before I thought," Rousseau explains.[8]

---

[7] George Orwell, "Charles Dickens," in *A Collection of Essays* (New York: Harcourt Brace, 1946), 51.

[8] Jean-Jacques Rousseau, *The Confessions*, trans. J. M. Cohen (Harmondsworth: Penguin, 1953), 19.

"It is not alone by the rapidity, or extent of the conquest," Edward Gibbon observes, "that we should estimate the greatness of Rome."[9]

Gibbon concludes that "it is not by the rapidity, or extent of the conquest, that we should estimate the greatness of Rome."[9]

In his history of the Civil War, Bruce Catton describes Colonel Solomon J. Meredith as a "breezy giant of a man."[10]

According to Catton, Colonel Solomon J. Meredith was "a breezy giant of a man."[10]

Theodore Roosevelt counseled, "Speak softly and carry a big stick."

Theodore Roosevelt is the president who advised that leaders "speak softly and carry a big stick."

(When considered as a well-known saying, this quotation does not require a note.)

▪ Introductions to Set-off Quotations

Formal introduction with colon

Introductions to set-off, or block, quotations should be punctuated according to their grammatical form. An introduction that is a complete sentence containing a formal introductory word or phrase, such as *following*, *thus*, or *in this way*, usually ends with a colon.

Deborah Tannen characterizes women's use of speech as

follows:

> For most women, the language of conversation is primarily a language of rapport: a way of establishing connection and negotiating relationships. Emphasis is placed on displaying similarities and matching experiences.[11]

Informal introduction

An informal introduction that does not contain a formal introductory word and that is a complete sentence may close with either a period or a colon. The Tannen quotation thus might also be introduced as follows:

---

[9]Edward Gibbon, *The Decline and Fall of the Roman Empire*, vol. 1 (New York: Modern Library, 1961), 25.

[10]Bruce Catton, *Bruce Catton's Civil War*, 3 vols. in 1 (New York: Fairfax, 1984), 225.

[11]Deborah Tannen, *You Just Don't Understand: Men and Women in Conversation* (New York: Ballantine, 1990), 77.

Deborah Tannen distinguishes women's use of speech from

men's.

> For most women, the language of conversation is
> primarily a language of rapport: . . .

An introduction that is an incomplete sentence—a phrase or a clause—should end with the punctuation that would be necessary if the introduction and quotation were run together as one sentence:

James Moffett finds that when people try to talk about

abstraction,

> they resort finally to talking about how people,
> especially children, learn. It is hard to avoid
> an analogy between stages of information
> processing that go on in all of us all the time,
> and developmental stages of growth. A curriculum
> sequence based on such an analogy, however, needs
> to be carefully qualified.[12]

In some cases, punctuation may not be needed:

These tasks differ considerably because

> constructing a grammar of a simple text is not
> exactly the same as constructing the grammar of a
> language. Grammars of languages have to account
> not just for the available data in a language, but
> also for the potentially available data, the
> infinite number of sentences that could be
> produced in a language.[13]

Punctuation of Direct Quotations

Quotations should combine logically and grammatically with your own sentences and paragraphs. To incorporate a direct quotation in a research paper, introduce it with an attribution and with an indication of its importance for your arguments. You also need to punctuate it properly, using internal capitalization, quotation marks, ellipses, brackets, and so on, to show the nature of the original source material.

---

[12] James Moffett, *Teaching the Universe of Discourse* (Boston: Houghton Mifflin, 1968), 23.
[13] Elizabeth Closs Traugott and Mary Louise Pratt, *Linguistics for Students of Literature* (New York: Harcourt Brace Jovanovich, 1980), 28.

▪ Capitalization

You may alter the capitalization of a direct quotation to conform to the requirements of your own sentence. You may change a capital letter to low-ercase or a lowercase letter to a capital.

Use lowercase for the first letter (except for proper nouns), regardless of the way it appears in the original, if the quotation forms a grammatical whole with the sentence that encompasses or introduces it, as in this example:

Harrison E. Salisbury has observed that "every war propels

some obscure city or town into the limelight," pointing out

that the identities of Guernica, Coventry, and Stalingrad

emerged largely in connection with wars.[14]

(In the original, *every* is the first word in the sentence.)

Capitalize the first letter, regardless of how it appears in the original, if the quotation is treated as a grammatical whole—that is, if the quotation is formally introduced as a direct quotation or is set by itself as a complete sentence.

William James asks, "How <u>can</u> things so insecure as the

successful experiences of this world afford a stable

anchorage?"[15]

(The original sentence reads, "To begin with, how *can* things so insecure as the successful experiences of this world afford a stable anchorage?")

You may lowercase the first letter of either a run-in or a set-off quotation, even when it is capitalized in the original, as the grammar of your sentence requires.

In the words of H. D. F. Kitto,

> a sense of the wholeness of things is perhaps the
> most typical feature of the Greek mind. . . .
> The modern mind divides, specializes, thinks in
> categories: the Greek instinct was the opposite,
> to take the widest view, to see things as an
> organic whole. The speeches of Cleon and Diodotus
> showed precisely the same thing: the particular
> issue must be generalized.[16]

(The sentence in the original begins with *A.* The ellipsis points indicate the omission of a sentence.)

---

[14]Harrison E. Salisbury, *Behind the Lines—Hanoi* (New York: Bantam, 1967), 84.
[15]William James, *The Varieties of Religious Experience* (New York: Collier, 1961), 120.
[16]H. D. F. Kitto, *The Greeks* (Baltimore: Penguin, 1951), 169.

In the words of H. D. F. Kitto, "a sense of the wholeness of

things is perhaps the most typical feature of the Greek

mind."[16]

MLA style   MLA recommends indicating the capital letter in the original source by enclosing the lowercase letter in brackets.

Harrison E. Salisbury has observed that "[e]very war propels

some obscure city into the limelight," pointing out . . . ·

▪ Quotation Marks

Enclose direct quotations run into the text in double quotation marks. Quotation marks should be placed outside a comma or period and inside a colon or semicolon.

Oscar Wilde wrote that "unselfish people are colourless";

however, most would agree with William Gladstone that

"selfishness is the greatest curse of the human race."[17]

In the case of an exclamation point or question mark, the quotation marks are placed outside when the mark belongs with the quoted material and inside when the mark belongs with the text.

What does Hamlet mean when he tells the players "to hold as

'twere the mirror up to nature"?[18]
(The question mark belongs with the writer's sentence.)

Hamlet asks himself, "Am I a coward?"[19]
(The question mark belongs with the quotation.)

Quotations within run-in quotations   If a portion of the original was enclosed in double quotation marks, change them to single quotation marks in a run-in quotation, as in the following example:

---

[17] Oscar Wilde, *The Picture of Dorian Gray* (New York: Harper and Row, 1965), 68; William Gladstone, speech delivered at Hawarden, 28 May 1890.
[18] William Shakespeare, *Hamlet*, in *The Riverside Shakespeare*, ed. G. Blakemore Evans (Boston: Houghton Mifflin, 1974), act 3, sc. 2, lines 21–22.
[19] *Hamlet* 2.2.571.

Because the French vetoed the European Defense Community,

"the United States was no longer 'pushing on open doors,'

and afterwards Washington conducted itself far more

cautiously."[20]

When quotation marks within single marks are needed, use double marks, and so on, alternating the marks as necessary. This complication is best avoided, however.

Quotations within set-off quotations

When a set-off quotation contains an excerpt that was enclosed in double quotation marks in the original, retain the double quotation marks, as shown below.

Marshall McLuhan points out that the development of print

led to the concept of perspective.

> As the literal or "the letter" later became
> identified with light <u>on</u> rather than light
> <u>through</u> the text, there was also the equivalent
> stress on "point of view" or the <u>fixed</u> position
> of the reader: "from where I am <u>sitting</u>."[21]

■ End Punctuation

End punctuation that may be changed

The punctuation used at the end of a quotation depends on the context into which the quotation is placed. A period in the original, for example, may be changed to a comma or omitted to produce a grammatically correct sentence.

Original   Every man bears the entire form of human nature.[22]

When Montaigne wrote, "Every man bears the entire form of

human nature," he advocated studying the self rather than

others.[22]

---

[20]William Diebold, Jr., *The United States and the Industrial World: American Foreign Economic Policy in the 1970's* (New York: Praeger, 1972), 26.

[21]Marshall McLuhan, *The Gutenberg Galaxy: The Making of Typographic Man* (1962; reprint, New York: Signet, 1969), 138.

[22]Michel de Montaigne, "Of Repentance," in *Selected Essays*, trans. Blanchard Bates (New York: Modern Library, 1949), 285.

```
Montaigne asserted that "every man bears the entire form

of human nature": thus he defended his study of a common

life, his own.22
```

End punctuation that must be retained   Question marks and exclamation marks must accompany the quotations in which they appear. Either of these strong marks of punctuation can take the place of a period. The exclamation mark cannot be excluded even when a colon or semicolon indicates the end of an independent clause or a complete thought.

```
"Give me liberty, or give me death!": Patrick Henry thus

stated his challenge to British rule.
```

The following sentence, though not exclamatory, ends with the exclamation mark of the quotation.

```
It was Patrick Henry who proclaimed, "Give me liberty, or

give me death!"
```
(When considered as a well-known saying, this quotation does not require a note.)

For variations in end punctuation with parenthetical documentation and placement of superscripts after quotations, see Chapters 7, 8, and 9.

▪ Omissions from Quoted Material

You should indicate all omissions from quoted material. To show an ellipsis, use three ellipsis points (periods with one space on either side). The quoted material should read clearly and grammatically without the deleted portion, and the deletion should not alter the meaning or logic of the sentence. Punctuation may be added or deleted if necessary. The following guidelines apply to the use of ellipsis points.

Internal omission   Indicate omission of an internal part of a direct quotation with ellipsis points, separated from the text and from each other by one space. Note the following example:

Original   In the western farm states the Granger movement, organized in 1869 as The Patrons of Husbandry, was able to force regulatory legislation through some state legislatures.[23]

[23]Margaret G. Myers, *A Financial History of the United States* (New York: Columbia University Press, 1970), 226.

Cut version According to Margaret G. Myers, "In the western farm states the Granger movement . . . was able to force regulatory legislation through some state legislatures."[23]

(The original commas are not necessary when the phrase is omitted.)

Omission at beginning of sentence

Ellipsis points are not needed at the beginning of a run-in quotation, regardless of whether it is an incomplete or a complete sentence:

Original As a reactor operates, the fissioning of the uranium nuclei results in the accumulation of radioactive waste—nuclear ashes, so to speak—inside the reactor core.[24]

Cut version Daniel Ford explains that "the fissioning of the uranium nuclei results in the accumulation of radioactive waste . . . inside the reactor core."[24]

When you omit the beginning of the quoted sentence and use the rest of the quotation in a construction requiring a capital letter, the letter may be changed from lowercase to uppercase:

Daniel Ford explains, "The fissioning of the uranium nuclei results in the accumulation of radioactive waste."[24]

In the MLA system the change from lowercase to uppercase is indicated by brackets. A lowercase *t* in brackets [t] would indicate that the original *T* was capitalized; an uppercase *T* in brackets [T] would indicate that the original *t* was lowercase.

MLA system Daniel Ford explains, "[T]he fissioning of the . . .

Omission at end of sentence

Ellipsis points indicate the omission of the end of a sentence only when another sentence of quotation follows immediately. An ellipsis is not necessary in the cut quotation below:

Original A foolish consistency is the hobgoblin of little minds, adored by little statesmen, philosophers and divines.[25]

Cut version Emerson advocated the courage to change one's mind when he said that a "foolish consistency is the hobgoblin of little minds."[25]

---

[24]Daniel Ford, "Three Mile Island—Part 1: Class Nine Accident," A Reporter at Large, *New Yorker*, 6 Apr. 1981, 73.

[25]Ralph Waldo Emerson, "Self-Reliance," in *The American Tradition in Literature*, ed. George Perkins et al., vol. 1, 6th ed. (New York: Random House, 1985), 846.

Ellipsis with original end punctuation

When you wish to retain the original punctuation at the end of either a cut or a full sentence, the appropriate mark of punctuation substitutes for the period preceding the ellipsis points.

Original

Ilse smiled scornfully. "What's it to you? Just because Papa Kremer put us in the same row? You're not jealous of him?"[26]

Cut version

Then Ilse taunts Hans: "What's it to you? . . . You're not

jealous of him?"[26]

Original

From the boy's face one might suppose that sacred emblem to be, in his eyes, the crowning confusion of the great, confused city;—so golden, so high up, so far out of his reach.[27]

Cut version

"From the boy's face one might suppose that sacred emblem to

be, in his eyes, the crowning confusion of the great,

confused city; . . . so far out of his reach."[27]

Period followed by ellipsis

When another sentence follows either a complete or a cut sentence, place a period at the end of the sentence, without an intervening space, and add three ellipsis points. A complete sentence must precede the four dots, and a complete sentence must follow them.

Original

Great advances in the principles of research were made by the ancient Greeks. Building partly upon previous discoveries recorded by the Egyptians and Babylonians, the Greek thinkers delved particularly into astronomy, medicine, physics, and geography, and some of them explored literature and ethics. A few instances will illustrate the scope and the fundamental importance of their contributions to the sum of human learning. Among the earliest whose names we know were Thales and Anaximander (about 600 B.C.), whose principal work was done in astronomy.[28]

Cut version

In a chapter titled "The Role of Research," Tyrus Hillway

points out that "great advances in the principles of

research were made by the ancient Greeks. . . . Greek

thinkers delved particularly into astronomy, medicine,

physics, and geography. . . . Among the earliest whose names

[26]André Schwarz-Bart, *The Last of the Just,* trans. Stephen Becker (New York: Atheneum, 1981), 225.

[27]Charles Dickens, *Bleak House* (New York: Bantam, 1983), 253.

```
we know were Thales and Anaximander . . . whose principal

work was done in astronomy."28
```

(The first ellipsis follows a complete sentence in the original; the second ellipsis follows a cut sentence; the third ellipsis indicates the omission of words within a sentence.)

Omission at beginning of paragraph

In a set-off quotation, indicate the omission of words or sentences at the beginning of a paragraph by starting at the indented margin, without the additional three-space paragraph indention.

Original

The remarkable reduction in fertility that the American population has achieved over the past two centuries is, perhaps, the most obvious cause for the decline in mean household size. As the birthrate fell, the proportion of childless households increased from about 20 percent in 1790 to 48.3 percent in 1950. The effects of the postwar baby boom temporarily reversed this trend, so that only 43.0 percent of all households were childless in 1960. But with the recent decline in fertility, childless households have once again started to increase, accounting for 46.0 percent of the total in 1975.

Increased life expectancy may also have helped to lower the average size of the household. We have seen how the combination of lower fertility and longer life meant that twentieth-century couples were among the first in history who could expect to have a significant number of years together after their children left home. Thus, an increase in childless households and households with one or two children reflects not only lower levels of childbearing, but also more older couples whose children have grown up and left home. For example, in 1970, fully 82.2 percent of all married couples in which the husband's age was between 55 and 64 had no children in their household, a remarkable contrast to the 11.7 percent of couples without children when the husband was 35 to 44.

One other interesting change is the increasing tendency for women to head the households. In part this is directly related to improved life expectancy, although it seems likely that alterations in social attitudes are also involved.[29]

Cut version

```
Berkin and Norton attribute the decline in the size of the

American household to several factors.

        An increase in childless households and households
        with one or two children reflects not only lower
        levels of childbearing, but also more older
        couples whose children have grown up and left
        home.29
```

(The set-off sentence, which is in the second paragraph of the original, begins with *thus*.)

Omission of entire paragraph(s)

Indicate the omission of one or more paragraphs in a prose quotation with an ellipsis at the end of the paragraph immediately preceding the omission. The quoted passages in the following examples come from the excerpt from *Women of America*, cited in footnote 29.

---

[28] Tyrus Hillway, *Introduction to Research* (Boston: Houghton Mifflin, 1956), 15.

[29] Carol Ruth Berkin and Mary Beth Norton, *Women of America: A History* (Boston: Houghton Mifflin, 1979), 29.

Cut version Berkin and Norton attribute the decline in the size of the

American household during the past two hundred years to a

variety of factors.

> The remarkable reduction in fertility that the
> American population has achieved over the past two
> centuries is, perhaps, the most obvious cause for
> the decline in mean household size. . . .
> Increased life expectancy may also have helped to
> lower the average size of the household.[29]

(The ellipsis points after *size* signal the omission of the rest of the sentences in the paragraph; the indention preceding *Increased* indicates that this word starts a new paragraph.)

Omission of more than a few paragraphs Indicate the omission of more than a few paragraphs with a full line of ellipsis points. Some writers prefer to signal the omission of even one complete paragraph in this way.

Berkin and Norton point out that, in addition to an increase

in life expectancy, many other factors account for the

decline in size of the American household:

> The remarkable reduction in fertility that the
> American population has achieved over the past two
> centuries is, perhaps, the most obvious cause for the
> decline in mean household size.

. . . .

> One other interesting change is the increasing
> tendency for women to head the households.[29]

(Here the line of ellipsis points signals the omission of one paragraph.)

Omission of line(s) of poetry Show the omission of one or more lines of poetry with a full line of ellipsis points equal in length to the longest line of the poem, as in this example from Alexander Pope's "An Essay on Criticism."

'Tis with our judgments as our watches: none
Go just alike, yet each believes his own.

. . . .

Authors are partial to their wit, 'tis true,
But are not critics to their judgment too?

▪ Interpolation

Clarifying original
source Except for necessary changes of beginning capitalization and end punctuation, direct quotations should not be altered. However, if you believe that a reader may find a quotation unclear or may miss the point you are trying to make by using the quotation, you may insert explanatory material within the quotation, enclosing it in brackets. Such an addition is called an *interpolation*.

"No society in which these liberties [liberty of conscience,

liberty of pursuits, and freedom to unite] are not, on the

whole, respected, is free, whatever may be its form of

government."[30]

Correcting errors An error in a quotation should be designated in brackets immediately following the error. You may indicate your awareness of an error with the word *sic* (meaning "thus" in Latin) or with a correction.

When the correction would be obvious to your readers, as in most spelling or typographical errors, use *sic*.

Correction with sic John Doe explained, "The results of the 1988 experiment were

quite amasing [sic]"[31]

When the nature of the error might not be readily apparent, supply the correction in brackets.

*Correction in
brackets* Doe added, "The affects [effects] of radiation exceeded our

estimates."[31]

Doe advised that "Smith completed her experiments in 1987

[1986]."[31]

Unless you particularly want to call attention to the inaccuracy or carelessness of a source, you may want to try to avoid quoting sentences with errors.

Indicating source
of italics Indicate the source of italics with an explanatory phrase in brackets when the source might be misinterpreted. Note the following example:

> This is the story of an adolescent whose
> needs are not understood by his father, who thinks
> his son is stupid. The son will not develop
> himself as the father thinks he should, but

---

[30]John Stuart Mill, *On Liberty*, ed. David Spitz (New York: Norton, 1975), 14.
[31]John Doe, letter to author, 19 May 1989.

```
              stubbornly insists on learning instead what he
              [italics in original or original emphasis] thinks
              is of real value.  To achieve his complete self-
              realization, the young man first has to become
              acquainted with his inner being, a process no
              father can prescribe [italics mine or emphasis
              mine] even if he realizes the value of it, as the
              youth's father does not.32
```

(The bracketed material has been interpolated.)

Clarifying
pronoun reference

If the referent of a pronoun in a quotation might be ambiguous or if the pronoun refers to a noun in a previous sentence that is not quoted, supply the noun in brackets.

```
"The scientist refers to it [a datum] as an observation."31
```

```
"This ["The Three Languages"] is the story of an adolescent

whose needs are not understood by his father."32
```

---

[32]Bruno Bettelheim, *The Uses of Enchantment: The Meaning and Importance of Fairy Tales* (New York: Vintage, 1977), 100.

4 Style and Mechanics

Accuracy and clarity in your prose are as essential as precision in taking notes and documenting your sources. If your ideas and conclusions are to make a contribution to knowledge, you must communicate them to as large an audience as possible. For this purpose you need to follow the conventions of style and mechanics readily understood and widely accepted in the academic community.

This chapter surveys the issues of style and mechanics that you are most likely to confront when writing a research paper. For other questions about grammar, diction, mechanics, and usage, you should have at hand and consult frequently a dictionary, a thesaurus, a handbook of grammar, and a textbook on composition and rhetoric. If you are required to follow a local or professional documentation system, you will want to refer to it also.

Style

Style is not mere decoration; it cannot be separated from meaning. Stylistic choices are not made apart from consideration of your ideas and definition of the audience with whom you wish to communicate. Your choices about sentence structure, diction, and tone together create the style of your writing. Because the audience for a research paper is usually the academic community, your writing should be formal in diction and tone.

■ Diction

The diction, or word choice, in a research paper should be formal rather than colloquial. Contractions and abbreviations should be avoided, and in nontechnical papers numbers generally should be spelled out.

▪ Tone

Your tone, or attitude toward your subject, should be serious, not ironic or flippant. Humorous, casual, or conversational approaches are usually inappropriate and ineffective for research papers because they defy your audience's expectations for this kind of writing. Since your purpose in writing is to promote understanding of your subject, you will not want to use a tone that can easily be misinterpreted.

▪ Personal Pronouns

Most research papers should be written in the third person—that is, with nouns or third-person pronouns (*he, she, they,* or *it*) as subjects of the sentences.

Using a first-person pronoun (*I, we, me, us, my, our, mine, ours*) to call attention to the fact that a statement is your opinion often weakens the assertion by implying uncertainty. The reader assumes that statements in your paper, unless otherwise attributed, are your opinion and represent your point of view. The first-person pronoun is appropriate when you relate a personal experience, such as your own process of research, or when you wish to call particular attention to your opinion as distinguished from the views of others. In papers that call for a subjective response to texts, ideas, or situations (some kinds of literary criticism and anthropological studies, for example), you will want to use first-person pronouns. Whatever choice of pronouns you make for the text, you may freely use the first person in the preface and acknowledgments.

Because your reader will assume that you are addressing him or her, second-person pronouns (*you, your*) rarely belong in a research paper. Commands (implied second person, as in "Observe that . . . ," the subject of which is actually *you*) should be avoided. In very informal papers or in creative writing you may address your reader directly.

The edited sentences below demonstrate ways of eliminating unnecessary first- and second-person constructions.

Original   In my opinion, presidential candidates should debate in an uncontrolled forum.

Revised   Presidential candidates should debate in an uncontrolled forum.

Original   I firmly believe that previous researchers have misinterpreted the evidence.

Revised   Previous researchers have misinterpreted the evidence.

Original   Notice that these statistics substantiate the previous

study.

Revised   These statistics substantiate the previous study.

▪ Tense

You should cast verbs in the tense or tenses appropriate to the time of the events under discussion. A few general guidelines apply, however. Events in literary works are discussed in the present tense.

After passing up the opportunity to kill the kneeling

Claudius, Hamlet enters his mother's bedchamber, where he

kills Polonius.

Discussions of literature generally use the present tense.

In <u>What Maisie Knew</u>, Henry James portrays a child . . .

The past tense is appropriate for discussions about works of theory or philosophy.

In his <u>Critique of Pure Reason</u>, Immanuel Kant speculated

that . . .

The present tense, however, may also be used in such discussions to indicate that a given work continues to present the same ideas.

In his <u>Critique of Pure Reason</u>, Kant demonstrates that . . .

When you report the results of research, use the past tense to describe the result of a particular experiment. Use the present tense for generalizations or conclusions.

Scores on standardized tests did not correlate with the

ability to write.
(Reporting the results of a particular study)

Scores on standardized tests do not correlate with the

ability to write.
(Generalization based on one or more studies)

▪ Sentence Structure

Sentences in a research paper should be active, forceful, and varied, reinforcing your meaning. With your sentence structure you will want to explore the full range of possibilities for expressing the logical relationships of ideas. You will want to use compound and complex sentences and parallel constructions, as required by your subject. Because meaning, or content, cannot be separated from its expression in language, weak or inappropriate sentence structure often reveals faulty logic or undeveloped thought. Careful attention to your sentences can help you refine your ideas as you write.

ACTIVE AND PASSIVE VOICE   Active voice is a stronger construction than passive voice. In the active voice, the actor is the subject of the sentence, whereas in the passive voice, the object or receiver of the action is the subject. Sentences should be active except when you specifically want to emphasize that the subject was acted upon, as in "The Lindbergh baby was kidnapped." Changing a sentence from passive to active may result not only in the use of a stronger form of the verb but also in the elimination of wordiness, as in this example:

Passive   The Worldly Philosophers was written by Robert Heilbroner.

Active   Robert Heilbroner wrote The Worldly Philosophers.

POSTPONED SUBJECTS   Expletive constructions—*there are, there is, it is*—result in weak sentences. You can avoid these constructions and both condense and strengthen your sentence by determining the subject of the sentence and supplying a verb.

Original   There is no valid reason for calculating the standard

deviation of such a distribution.

Revised   No valid reason exists for calculating the standard

deviation . . .

Original   It was in the Poetics that Aristotle analyzed Greek tragedy.

Revised   Aristotle analyzed Greek tragedy in the Poetics.

▪ Parallelism

Elements in an outline or list, as well as chapter titles, subtitles, and headings, should be parallel—that is, they should take the same grammatical form. If you use a noun or noun phrase (such as "Effective Regulations") for one chapter title, the next chapter title should also be a noun phrase ("Adequate Screening" rather than, for example, "To Provide Adequate Screening," an infinitive phrase). Similarly, in a sentence outline, all entries must be complete sentences.

The entries in the following outline are not parallel. Entry I is a complete sentence. Entry I.A is a noun phrase. Entry I.B is a participial phrase.

Topic outline with nonparallel entries

   I. Nuclear Opponents Cite Dangers

      A. Nuclear Accidents Involving Leakage

      B. Disposing of Nuclear Waste

      C. Groups That Threaten Sabotage

  II. Protecting against Nuclear Accidents

      A. Sound Design and Construction

      B. Monitoring Systems

      C. Automatic Devices for Correcting Problems

The entries in the following outline are parallel; they are all noun phrases:

Topic outline with parallel entries

   I. Dangers of Nuclear Power Plants

      A. Leakage of Radiation

      B. Disposal of Nuclear Waste

      C. Sabotage by Terrorist Groups

  II. Safety Features of Nuclear Power Plants

      A. Sound Design and Construction

      B. Monitoring Systems

      C. Automatic Correction Devices

You may use other constructions in an outline as long as each entry takes the same form. In the next outline, each entry is a complete sentence.

Sentence outline

   I. Emerson expounded a political theory close to anarchism.

      A. He believed that individuals should govern themselves.

    B. He believed that the state should not be concerned with property.

II. Emerson disapproved of the educational system.

    A. He found fault with methods of instruction.

    B. He criticized the curriculum.

III. Emerson sought to abolish established religion.

■ Logical Consistency

The requirement for parallelism is not exclusively a grammatical one, but a logical one as well. Grammatical inconsistencies often signal problems in logic. Logical consistency requires headings at the same level of an outline to have approximately equivalent importance and to refer to similar categories of ideas. For example, three headings designating historical periods and a fourth at the same level designating procedural difficulties would not be logically consistent. Moreover, each heading at a given level should represent the same degree of generalization and refer to approximately the same kind of information. The following set of headings is logically unbalanced:

Outline without parallel logic

I. U.S. secondary schools during the nineteenth century

II. Changes in secondary school programs in Pennsylvania from 1890 to 1930

III. Nature of secondary school curricular changes from 1930 to 1970

IV. Percentages of teenagers enrolled in high schools

The fourth heading is considerably narrower in focus than the others and calls for purely statistical information rather than interpretation. In addition, the scope of the inquiry changes from national in the first heading to local in the second.

■ Coherence

A paper that is coherent presents ideas, observations, or generalizations in a logical and consistent sequence. Problems with integrating a section of your argument may be a sign that the section belongs somewhere else in the paper or should be omitted.

Transitional expressions

Once you have organized your paper logically, you can use transitional expressions to help your reader see the relationships among sentences and paragraphs. Transitional expressions are words or phrases that indicate contrast (*but, however*), comparison (*similarly, just as*), the introduction of additional information (*also, likewise, in addition*), the presentation of examples (*for example, for instance*), and conclusions (*in short, in conclusion, therefore*). Such words or phrases do not substitute for organizational and logical development. Clear statements of purpose and the demonstration of logical relations with each paragraph, section, and chapter ensure the continuity and coherence of the paper. However, by emphasizing the connections between your sentences and among your ideas, transitional expressions can help the reader follow your argument. You may wish to consult a handbook of grammar for a listing of such expressions and information about how to use them.

▪ Unbiased Language

Most journals and professional organizations have adopted policies requiring that the language in their publications be unbiased: that it neither demean nor exclude any person or group. Avoiding biased language usually demands only minor editing, and most writers consider the goal worthy enough to justify some inconvenience and an occasional infelicity.

Here are a few of the strategies for revising to avoid gender bias.

1. Change a sentence using the generic masculine pronoun from singular to plural.

```
A doctor should know the ethics of his profession.
```

Revision   ```Doctors should know the ethics of their profession.```

Although informal usage now permits linking a singular noun with a plural pronoun, as in "Everyone should hand in their worksheets," this construction is not accepted in formal written usage.

2. Substitute the pronouns *he or she,* as some writers prefer, *she or he,* for *he* used generically.

```
If he is to succeed, a new teacher requires intelligent

supervision.
```

Revision   ```If he or she is to succeed, a new teacher requires . . .```

Because this double pronoun is cumbersome, avoid using it repeatedly, or find a way to edit out the pronoun altogether.

Alternative revision   ```To succeed, a new teacher requires . . .```

3. Use gender-neutral designations for professions and positions.

NEUTRAL	BIASED
flight attendant	stewardess
fire fighter	fireman
chair(person)	chairman
representative, senator	congressman
humanity, humankind	mankind
workers, work force, personnel	manpower

In making revisions to avoid gender bias, you should guard against introducing stylistic or grammatical problems.

The various fields and professions have published their recommendations for avoiding bias and stereotyping:

American Psychological Association. "Guidelines for Nonsexist Language in APA Journals." *American Psychologist* 32 (1977): 487–94.

Frank, Francine Wattman, and Paula A. Treichler. *Language, Gender, and Professional Writing: Theoretical Approaches and Guidelines for Nonsexist Usage.* New York: Modern Language Association, 1989.

International Association of Business Communicators. *Without Bias: A Guidebook for Nondiscriminatory Communication.* 2nd ed. New York: Wiley, 1982.

Mechanics

Correctness in mechanics, which include grammar, punctuation, and other technical matters, is essential to effective communication. This section deals with the problems that arise most frequently during the writing of research papers. You can resolve other questions concerning mechanics and grammar by consulting a grammar handbook or dictionary.

▪ Spelling

When you are in doubt about the spelling of a word or when variant spellings exist, consult a standard dictionary, such as *The American Heritage Dictionary* or *Webster's New Collegiate Dictionary.* Select the preferred American spelling, and use it consistently throughout your paper. For the correct spelling of proper names not found in a dictionary, refer to an authority such as a biographical dictionary or an encyclopedia. If you decide to use an uncommon spelling (such as an archaism or an Anglicism) either once or throughout your paper, you should specify the reason for your decision in a note. When you find a misspelled word in a passage that you wish to quote directly, enter the word exactly as you find it and indicate that the error is not yours by adding *sic* (Latin for "thus") in brackets immediately after the word.

▪ Abbreviations

Do not use abbreviations in the text of a research paper. Exceptions to this general rule include abbreviations of social titles such as *Mr., Messrs., Mrs., Ms.,* and their foreign equivalents; professional and honorary titles such as *Dr., Prof., Rev.,* and *Hon.* preceding proper names; identifications such as *Esq.* (to designate an attorney), *Ph.D., S.T.B.* (Bachelor of Sacred Theology), *Sr.* and *Jr.* following proper names; familiar abbreviations of names of countries (*USSR*), cities (*St. Louis*), and organizations (*UNESCO, YWCA*); and abbreviations for units of time, such as *a.m., p.m., A.D., B.C.* In technical writing, abbreviations of units of measurement such as *mm, cc, ft,* and *in* can be used freely. Names of states, reference works, universities, publishers, and books of the Bible should be spelled out in the text unless you designate an alternative, either in the text or in a note: `(Oxford English Dictionary, hereafter OED)`. Consistently use any abbreviations that you select.

The general warning against abbreviations does not apply to material included in notes, appendixes, bibliographies, and, most particularly, tables and figures, where abbreviations are not only permissible but often preferable and where the accepted style, especially in the sciences and mathematics, allows exceedingly abbreviated forms. Consult your adviser or instructor if you have any questions about the extent to which your subject requires the use of abbreviations.

▪ Hyphenation

Types of compound words

Hyphens are used to create compound words and to indicate the division of a word at the end of a line. Compounds that function as nouns may be open (*school year*), hyphenated (*self-concept*), or closed (*schoolroom*). The current trend is away from the use of the hyphen; generally, it is dropped when a compound becomes common.

The following types of compound words should be hyphenated:

1. Prefixes followed by a capitalized word: *pro-American, post–World War II.*
2. Prefixes followed by a numeral: *post-1980, pre-1900.*
3. Prefixes followed by a hyphenated compound: *pro-city-state.*
4. Compound adjectives preceding nouns (when confusion about which word is the noun might result): *Australian-ballot controversy,* but *a controversy over the Australian ballot; nineteenth-century poet,* but *a poet of the nineteenth century.*
5. Compound adjectives with *self-, half-, quasi-,* and *all-: self-serving, quasi-scientific, all-powerful.*
6. Compounds when mispronunciation might occur without the hyphen: *co-opt, de-emphasize, re-sign* (meaning to sign again, to distinguish it from the word *resign*).
7. Fractional numbers written out: *one-fourth, two and two-thirds.*
8. Combinations of words including a prepositional phrase: *stick-in-the-mud.*
9. Compound nouns with *self-, great-* (relatives), *-in-law,* and *-elect: self-concept, great-grandfather, sister-in-law, president-elect.*

The following combinations of words do not require hyphenation:

1. A compound with an adverb ending in *-ly: broadly conceived plan, widely read book.*
2. A compound with a comparative or superlative adjective: *better built car, higher priced goods.*
3. Foreign phrases used as adjectives: *a priori argument, ad hoc committee.*
4. Uncapitalized words following these prefixes: *after (aftershock); anti (antibiotic); bi (bilingual); co; counter; extra; infra; inter; intra; macro; micro; mid; mini; multi; non; over; post; pre; pro; pseudo; re; semi; sub; super; supra; ultra; un; under.* When the repetition of the final letter of a prefix and the first letter of the subsequent word would double the *i's* or *a's* as in *anti-intellectual,* or would create an unrecognizable word, you should use a hyphen.

Hyphens also indicate the division of a word at the end of a line of typescript. When the division of a word is necessary, the break should come between syllables. See pages 122 through 123 for information on dividing words and lines in typescripts.

▪ Italics

Italic is a typeface in which the letters slant to the right. *This sentence is printed in italic type.* In theses, dissertations, and manuscripts that are going to be published, you should indicate italic with underlining even if your typewriter or printer can produce italics. The underlining of this typed sentence tells a typesetter that the sentence should appear in italics. In desktop publishing and electronic manuscripts, you may wish to use an italic typeface.

Emphasis Italics may be used to provide emphasis within your own work or in direct quotations. This use of italics should be kept to a minimum because an overabundance of emphasized words reduces the impact of them all, as in this sentence:

An hour into the marathon he was in second place, and she

was in last place. Yet she eventually won the race.

When you use italics to add emphasis in direct quotations, indicate your alteration of the original with a note enclosed in brackets: [my emphasis] or [emphasis mine]. Similarly, if you want to point out that the original contains italics, you may do so within brackets: [original emphasis] or [italics in original]. For a detailed discussion of interpolation, see pages 74 and 75 in Chapter 3.

WORDS AS WORDS Italicize references to words as words, letters as letters, and terms you will define for your reader.

She spelled the word laxiflorous.

(Word as word)

That word begins with a capital A.

(Letter as letter)

After you have introduced the definition of a term, you need not continue to italicize it unless you have some other reason for doing so.

The term virgule means slanted line. The virgule is

sometimes called a slash mark.

(Term to be defined)

Foreign words and phrases

Foreign words and phrases should be underlined except when they have become Anglicized, or accepted as English words. Because the status of foreign words changes continually, you will need to consult a current dictionary when you are not certain about italicizing. Some examples of Anglicized foreign words that are no longer italicized are et al., à la carte, Spanish peseta, and joie de vivre. Examples of foreign words that should be italicized include mabinogi, omphalos, and peripeteia.

Genera and species

Italicize the Latin names for the genera and species of plants and animals: Ananas comosus (pineapple); Canis familiaris (dog).

▪ Titles of Works

Punctuation for a title depends on the nature of the source material and the documentation system you follow. Some titles should be underlined to indicate italics; others should be put in quotation marks; some are neither italicized nor put in quotation marks.

ITALICIZED TITLES   The titles of the following types of works should also be italicized—that is, underlined in your typescript—wherever they appear.

Books: Eros and Civilization: A Philosophical Inquiry into Freud

Pamphlets: Regional Dances of Mexico

Journals: Critical Inquiry

Newspapers: Los Angeles Times

Plays: Much Ado about Nothing

Long poems: The Prelude

Magazines: Atlantic Monthly

Films: Field of Dreams

Ballets: Nutcracker

Operas: Don Giovanni

Record albums, tapes, or CDs: André Watts: Live in Tokyo

Paintings: View of Toledo

Sculptures: Pietà

Musical compositions identified by name (rather than by key or type of work): Pastoral Symphony

Legal cases: Truax v. Corrigan

Names of vehicles: HMS Mauretania; space shuttle Atlantis

APA style   The APA style capitalizes titles within the text—like the titles shown in the preceding list—but in bibliographies only the first word is capitalized (see pages 218 and 220 for other rules concerning APA style of capitalization in documenting).

Underline all marks of punctuation and spaces in a title. If a title appears at the end of a sentence, do not underline the final period.

Shakespeare's Proverbial Language: An Index.

Comparative Literature as Academic Discipline: A Statement of Principles, Praxis, Standards.

QUOTATION MARKS WITH TITLES   The titles of the types of works listed below should be put in quotation marks.

Articles in a journal: "The Father and the Bride in Shakespeare"

Articles in a magazine: "The Sporting Scene"

Articles in a newspaper: "Sahara Engulfs Much of Chad"

Articles in an encyclopedia: "Huntington, Collis Potter"

Articles in a compilation: "The Schizophrenic and Language"

Short stories: "The Magic Barrel"

Short poems: "Fern Hill"

Songs: "I Dream of Jeannie"

Chapters in books: "Emergence of the Polis"

Lectures: "Résumé Writing and Effective Interviewing"

Unpublished theses: "The Ambiente of Latin America in Five Novels by Graham Greene"

TITLES WITHOUT UNDERLINING OR QUOTATIONS MARKS
The titles of sacred works, series, editions, and societies and words referring to the divisions of a book are neither underlined nor put in quotation marks.

Sacred writings: Holy Bible, Mark, New Testament, Koran

Series: New Accents, The Brain, Approaches to Teaching Masterpieces of World Literature

Editions: Library of America, Norton Critical Edition

Societies: American Psychological Association, Association of American Petroleum Geologists

Divisions of a book: foreword, preface, introduction, appendix, glossary, chapter, act, volume, scene

TITLES WITHIN TITLES
Titles sometimes include another title. When a title enclosed in quotation marks appears within an italicized title, retain and underline the quotation marks.

Coleridge's "Kubla Khan"
("Kubla Khan" is a short poem included here as part of the title of a book.)

When a title ordinarily enclosed in quotation marks appears within another title that is also ordinarily placed within quotation marks, change the interior quotation marks to single quotation marks.

"A Reading of Coleridge's 'Kubla Khan'"
("Kubla Khan" is a short poem mentioned in the title of an article.)

An underlined title that appears within a title in quotation marks remains underlined.

"A Principle of Unity in Between the Acts"
(*Between the Acts* is a novel mentioned in the title of an article.)

When a title that is ordinarily underlined appears within another underlined title, MLA recommends leaving it without underlining or quotation marks.

Virginia Woolf's The Waves
(*The Waves* is the title of a novel mentioned in the title of another book.)

The Chicago style permits this treatment of underlined titles within underlined titles but favors putting all interior titles, whether normally underlined or quoted, within quotation marks.

Virginia Woolf's "The Waves"

▪ Capitalization

The prose in a research paper follows standard rules and conventions for capitalization.

Titles within the body of the paper

Capitalize the first and last words in titles and all other words with the exception of articles (*a, an, the*), coordinate conjunctions (*and, but, or, for, nor, yet, so*), prepositions (*to, at, before, between,* etc.), and the word *to* in an infinitive. Always capitalize the first and last words of a subtitle, the first word after a colon, and both elements of a hyphenated compound when the second word is a noun or a proper adjective (*Pro-American,* for example). Original capitalization may be changed to conform to these rules. Original spelling and internal punctuation should not be changed.

Titles in documentation

For titles in notes and bibliography, both Chicago and MLA give the same rules for capitalization as those that apply to the body, or text (see paragraph above). APA treats titles in documentation, including parenthetical documentation, differently from those appearing in the text of the research paper. (See pages 217–28.)

Style: An Anti-Text

Two Years before the Mast

The Ship Sails On

Emily Dickinson: The Mind of the Poet

The Roll-Call

Far from the Madding Crowd

"On Actors and Acting"

"The Lotus-Eaters"

College Composition and Communication

University of Toronto Quarterly

References to divisions of research materials or divisions of your paper may be capitalized when they substitute for a title and are followed by a number or letter:

Chapter 7   Section 3   Appendix C

General references to a type of division are not capitalized:

the final chapter   this section   the preface   the glossary

Nearly every foreign language has its own rules for capitalization of titles and names. See *The Chicago Manual of Style,* the *MLA Handbook for Writers of Research Papers,* or a dictionary for the language in question.

▪ Punctuation

Punctuate your writing according to the conventions described in the handbook of grammar you are using. This section of *Form and Style* focuses on the punctuation marks (other than periods and commas) most often required in the text and documentation of research papers: quotation marks, the colon, brackets, parentheses, ellipsis points, and the virgule.

QUOTATION MARKS   Whether in the text, notes, or bibliographical entries, titles of the following types of works should be put in double quotation marks: articles, essays, parts of a collection, newspaper articles, journals and magazine articles, short stories, short poems, unpublished dissertations, and lectures. Single quotation marks indicate the inclusion of one quotation inside another. Quotations that are run into the text should be enclosed in quotation marks. See pages 67 through 68 in Chapter 3 for information about the use of quotation marks for documentation.

THE COLON   Within the text, the colon may be used to introduce quotations, whether long or short, run in or set off. (See pages 62 through 65 in Chapter 3 for information on ways to introduce quotations.) In addition, the colon may follow a complete sentence to introduce material that amplifies or concludes it. Notice that one space follows the colon.

```
In some election years four different political parties may

compete for votes in the state: Democratic, Republican,

Conservative, and Liberal.
```

```
Becker maintains, "None of this is unusual: it is just

interesting gossip about a great man."¹
```

In note and bibliography entries, the colon is used to separate the title from the subtitle and the place of publication from the name of the publisher. One space follows the colon.

BRACKETS   Brackets are used to enclose material interpolated into a direct quotation. Interpolations may be made to clarify the antecedent of a pronoun, indicate the source of an error with the word *sic* (meaning "thus" in Latin), and insert explanatory material within a quotation. (See pages 74 through 75 for a discussion of interpolation.) In addition, brackets within a parenthetical expression function like parentheses, as illustrated on the next page.

---

¹Ernest Becker, *The Denial of Death* (New York: Free Press, 1973), 101.

The moral argument in Elaine Pagels's latest book (<u>Adam,</u>

<u>Eve, and the Serpent</u> [New York: Random House, 1988]) recalls

that of her earlier book on the Gnostic Gospels, according

to one reviewer.

PARENTHESES   Parentheses are used to enclose incidental, explanatory, or qualifying remarks in a sentence. Parenthetical material should not be crucial to the meaning of a sentence; the omission of parenthetical material should leave the meaning of the sentence intact.

Holland reports, "Sam, Saul, Shep, Sebastian, and Sandra (as

I shall call them) all spoke about this 'tableau.'"[2]

Parentheses function like commas in many circumstances but enclose supplemental material more emphatically than do commas. Within the text, parentheses may be used to set off structurally independent elements such as phrases or complete sentences; to set off reference citations within the text; to enclose letters and numbers in enumerations in the text (see page 94); and to enclose or group sets of numbers in mathematical expressions, formulas, and equations. Parentheses also enclose publication information in notes, bibliographies, and lists of works cited.

ELLIPSIS POINTS   Three ellipsis points (space periods) are used to indicate an omission from quoted material. The ellipsis should be preceded and/or followed by punctuation that completes the meaning of the quoted sentence. (See pages 69 through 73 in Chapter 3 for a discussion of the use of ellipsis.) Ellipsis points should not be used in your own writing to extend sentences or to mean *etc*.

THE VIRGULE   A virgule (/), also called a solidus or slant line, with a space on each side is used between lines of poetry that are run into the text.

King Lear immediately gives his youngest daughter another

chance to voice her love for him and thereby receive a

portion of his kingdom: "How, how, Cordelia! Mend your

speech a little, / Lest you may mar your fortunes."[3]

---

[2]Norman N. Holland, *Five Readers Reading* (New Haven: Yale University Press, 1975), 1.
[3]William Shakespeare, *King Lear*, in *The Riverside Shakespeare*, ed. G. Blakemore Evans (Boston: Houghton Mifflin, 1974), act 1, sc. 1, lines 93–94.

The virgule is also used, without space on either side, to indicate alternatives, as in *pass/fail, either/or,* and *and/or.* The virgule also separates elements of a date expressed entirely in numbers, as in *2/20/94.*

▪ Numbers

Numbers expressed in words

In formal nonscientific writing, numbers from one to one hundred and numbers that can be expressed in one or two words—for example, *seventy-five, three thousand, fifteen,* and *seven billion*—should be spelled out. Use numerals for dates; page, street, serial, and telephone numbers; fractions accompanied by a whole number, decimals, and percentages; and quantities combined with abbreviations and symbols. In writing that presents numbers for calculation, express all numbers in numerals.

A sentence should not begin with a numeral. If a number must begin a sentence, spell it out. The word *and* connects a digit in the hundreds to a digit in the tens, as in *two hundred and fifty,* but is omitted above the tens, as in *three thousand fifty* or *two million two hundred thousand.*

If possible, a sentence that starts with a number should be rewritten.

Original
```
Five hundred and seventeen people visited the gallery last
week.
```

Rewritten
```
Last week 517 people visited the gallery.
```

Punctuation of numerals

Numbers consisting of four or more digits have commas inserted at the thousands and millions points. The exceptions are page numbers, street numbers, serial numbers, and numbers to the right of the decimal point. In dates of five digits, insert a comma to mark the thousands.

```
Built in 1916, the elementary school at 10916 Main Street

had a play area comprising 4,729 square feet of concrete and

57,128 square feet of lawn. Maintenance of the yard cost

$56,157 last year.

The illustration is on page 1078.

The fossil dates from 10,000 B.C.

He recorded the serial number as 77266319.

Pi is 3.14592654.
```

Fractions

A fraction should be spelled out in the text when it is not accompanied by a numeral. Fractions are hyphenated when spelled out, as in *two-thirds of the voters.* Numerals in a fraction are separated by a slanted line, as in 2/3 or 27 3/4.

Decimals and percentages

Numbers with decimal points and percentages are written in numerals. The word *percent* (spelled as one word) accompanies the number. In formal nonscientific writing, the percent symbol (%) should be used only in tables and figures. In scientific or technical papers, the use of the percent symbol preceded by a numeral is standard practice. In the absence of a number, the word *percentage* is used.

Sales have increased 37 percent this year.

The current rate of inflation is 2.3 percent.

APA style

APA recommends using the percent symbol in all cases.

The current rate of inflation is 2.3%.

The percentage of nonvoters has increased significantly.

Numbers from mathematical and statistical calculations

Textual reference to numbers derived from mathematical and statistical calculations, including those taken from figures and tables, should be in the form of numerals, even if the numbers might otherwise be written out.

Table 1 indicates that only 2 of the 33 tests were valid.

a ratio of 12:1

in 11% of the cases studied

Numbers with abbreviations

Numbers combined with abbreviations are expressed in numerals: *6 ft*, *27 mm*.

Dates

Dates in the text may be written in one of two ways, depending on your preference:

On 22 July 1989 the group met for the first time.

On July 22, 1989, the group met for the first time.

Notice that commas enclose the year when the month precedes the day, but no commas are needed when the day precedes the month.

When you refer to a month or season and a year, commas to set off the year are optional.

In January 1991 the governor declared a drought emergency.

In January, 1991, the governor declared a drought emergency.

B.C. and A.D.

The abbreviation *B.C.* (meaning "before Christ") follows the year. The abbreviation *A.D.* (*anno Domini* in Latin, or "in the year of our Lord") precedes the year. The designations *B.C.E.* ("before the Christian [or common] era") and *C.E.* (Christian [or common] era) follow the year.

```
Agricultural methods changed little between 1900 B.C. and

A.D. 1400.

Agricultural methods changed little between 1900 B.C.E. and

1400 C.E.
```

Inclusive pages   When citing inclusive pages, enter only the final two digits if all other numbers remain the same: 121–48, 300–07, 1813–16, 23976–78. Enter any numbers that have changed: 2989–3016, 23976–4801. Never use fewer than two digits, except for numbers below ten: 5–8, 1–2, but not 501–2. For numbers below one hundred, enter both digits even if the number in the tens place remains the same: 47–48, 55–69, 70–71.

Inclusive pages: APA   In parenthetical notes and bibliographical entries, APA recommends entering complete page numbers both before and after the hyphen: 121–148, 300–307, 1813–1816, 23976–23978.

Inclusive years   In references to inclusive years, give only the final two digits when the century remains the same: 1975–78, 1939–45, 1901–09, 155–82, 711–17. When the century changes, include the entire set of digits: 1890–1950, 400–1000, 1700–1900, 1994–2004.

Arabic and roman numerals   Current usage discourages roman numerals except for designating individuals in a series, such as Henry VIII, Philip II, and John Smith III, and for numbering outlines. Otherwise, use arabic numerals throughout research papers.

▪ Enumeration

Lists within text   You may wish to give some items special emphasis through enumeration. When the list of items is short enough to be run smoothly into the text, identifying numerals or letters are enclosed in parentheses.

```
The steps in writing a research paper include (1) choosing

a topic, (2) preparing a working bibliography,

(3) outlining the paper, (4) collecting information,

and (5) writing the paper.
```

Such enumeration in the text may also be introduced with a colon.

```
Writing a research paper includes the following steps:

(1) choosing a topic . . .
```

Displayed lists   When the length or number of items to be enumerated would create a cumbersome or confusing sentence if the list were run into the text, set the list off from the text. When the items to be listed are complete sentences, use the following format:

```
The authors made three recommendations for keeping European

markets open:

    1.  Companies must step up their strategic planning in

Europe.

    2.  Business leaders outside Europe must realize that

there is strength in numbers.

    3.  Non-European companies must enlist their

governments' help at the highest levels.
```

If the listed items are words or phrases that are a grammatical part of the lead-in statement, they should be punctuated as a series and a period should be put at the end of the last item.

```
The syllabus for the seminar included sessions on

    1.  new systems of discourse,

    2.  the rhetorical inheritance,

    3.  literacy, and

    4.  measurement of writing ability.
```

When your list of items is subdivided, use either the number-letter sequence or the decimal sequence (see pages 22–23 in Chapter 1).

Displayed outlines   If you need to include an outline within the text, the outline should follow the conventional format and sequence (see pages 22–23). When items enumerated in an outline are longer than one line, align the second and succeeding lines with the first word in the line above.

```
I.  Carol Gilligan attempts to distinguish the moral

    development of women from that of men in In a

    Different Voice.

    A.  Gilligan designates male morality as "the morality

        of justice."

    B.  Gilligan describes female morality as "the morality

        of care."
```

Editing and Proofreading

Your paper should be scholarly and accurate in every way, including style and mechanics. After you have revised your paper, paying attention to the interaction of content and style, you should edit it thoroughly, making corrections in mechanics and grammar, consulting reference books when necessary, and proofreading carefully.

Because writers are often too close to their work to view it objectively, an effective way to measure your audience's reaction is to read the paper to someone else. Reading the paper aloud to yourself can also be helpful. The passages over which you hesitate or stumble probably need revision. Finishing the final draft a few days ahead of your deadline will give you an opportunity to improve your paper. You will be able to read and proofread and then set the paper aside so that you can return to it with a fresh perspective and a keen eye ready to detect rough spots and errors.

5 Tables, Figures, and Computer Materials

Graphic representations of data can help make the results of your research comprehensible to your reader. Tables and figures (the general name for any illustrative material, including graphs, maps, diagrams, and photographs) can buttress your argument by revealing complex relationships in a way that prose alone often cannot. Computers can now be used to generate many types of tables and figures; the principles for presenting them are the same regardless of the medium you use to produce them.

Tables

The data that you collect constitute the evidence on which your inferences and conclusions are based. Large quantities of statistics or numerical data should be tabulated in the interest of both brevity and clarity. Not all statistical matter, however, need be presented in tabular form. If statistics fit smoothly into the text, so much the better. For example, you would not tabulate the following numbers if you had no additional data: "The 607 delegates, representing seventeen nations, voted 402 to 205 in favor of the resolution." A simple array of data may be presented informally in the text:

and the class members were about evenly divided on the

candidates, as is shown in these results:

	Boys	Girls	Total
For Smith	17	16	33
For Brown	13	15	28
Total	30	31	61

Long series of numbers in the body of a paper can interfere with the development of an argument. Readers who are interested more in summaries and conclusions than in details may be distracted by masses of statistics in the text. Although complete and original data should be available in an appendix, tables in the text itself should contain only quantified information such as totals and subtotals, rank-order relationships, and results of statistical analyses.

Clarity and unity in tables

A table should have a unified and clearly stated purpose. It should not try to present too many kinds of data or show too many types of relationships. Of course, a table can be very useful for presenting a large quantity of data, but these data should be organized so that they can be easily assimilated. Normally, tables that duplicate material should be combined.

Tables within the body of the text should be as brief as clarity permits. Very long and complex tables usually belong in an appendix.

▪ Relation of Tables and Text

To help your reader understand the data in a table, you should provide a clear introduction. The introduction might explain the principles governing the table or state the significance of the data. It definitely should explain how the data support your thesis.

Independence of tables and text

Two general rules apply to the relationship between tables and text. First, a table should be so constructed that it may be read and understood with-out reference to the text. For those readers who wish to study only the statistical data, tables should be organized logically and explained fully in a caption, or title. Second, the text should be so complete that readers can follow the argument without referring to the tables. You should incorporate into the body of the paper enough analytical and summary statements derived from each table to provide a coherent and valid report of actual findings.

References to tables

Tables should be placed as close as possible to the discussion of the facts or data in the text. If a table appears within the two or three pages following the first reference to it, only the number of the table need be given in the text ("Table 3 shows . . . "). Tables that are farther away from their initial mention in the text should be referred to by table number and page number ("Table 4 on page 13 shows . . . "). Avoid using imprecise phrases like "in the following table" and "in the table above," which may be confusing when the table is not immediately visible.

▪ Captions

Each table must have a caption, or title, that tells concisely and clearly what the table contains. (The table of contents in the preliminary pages should list tables by number and caption.) The caption should not repeat material from the table column headings or interpret the data presented in the table. Rather, it should be a descriptive phrase:

```
Table 4.   Coastal Vertical Movement of Rocks at Las Cruces
```

not

```
Table 4.   Coastal Vertical Movement of Rocks at Las Cruces
before and after the 3 March 1985 Earthquake
```

(This caption unnecessarily repeats headings from the table.)

Use participial constructions rather than relative clauses.

```
Numbers of Minority Students Attending College, 1980-88
```

not

```
Numbers of Minority Students Who Attended College, 1980-88
```
(This caption contains a wordy construction, the relative clause.)

Even though you may use abbreviations in table columns, you should not use them in captions.

Place the caption above the table. You may use either block style or inverted pyramid style for captions.

Block-style captions The block style places captions flush with the left margin of the table. The rules for the capitalization of such captions are the same as the rules for capitalizing other titles: capitalize the first word, the last word, and all principal words, but lowercase articles (*a, an, the*), coordinate conjunctions (*and, but, or, for, nor, yet, so*), prepositions (for example, *to, at, before, between*), and the word *to* in an infinitive (when these words do not come first or last in the title). The caption should not have end punctuation.

```
Table 7

Distribution of American Tax Dollars among Local, State, and
Federal Governments, 1912 and 1988
```

APA style APA recommends block-style placement of the caption but underlines it.

```
Table 7

Distribution of American Tax Dollars among Local, State, and
Federal Governments, 1912 and 1988
```

Inverted-pyramid captions Captions in the inverted-pyramid format generally follow the same rules of capitalization as block captions; however, all uppercase letters may be used instead. The caption is centered between the left and right margins. Additional lines are centered below the first line.

```
                        Table 7

          Distribution of American Tax Dollars among
             Local, State, and Federal Governments,
                         1912 and 1988
```

or

```
                        TABLE 7

          DISTRIBUTION OF AMERICAN TAX DOLLARS AMONG
             LOCAL, STATE, AND FEDERAL GOVERNMENTS,
                         1912 AND 1988
```

Use the format you adopt throughout your paper.

▪ Numbering

Tables should be numbered with arabic (not roman) numerals. They may be numbered consecutively throughout the paper, including the appendixes. If the last table in the text is Table 23, the first table in Appendix A would be Table 24. Alternatively, tables may be double-numbered by chapter. The numbers, separated by a period, represent the chapter number and the number of the table in that chapter, respectively. Table 3.7 would be the seventh table in Chapter 3; Table 4.1 would be the first table in Chapter 4. This system is particularly useful when you have many tables.

Some individuals and institutions prefer to use all capital letters for the word *table*, as in TABLE 7.

▪ Columns and Rows

The body of a table consists of vertical columns and horizontal rows. Computer programs with the capacity to generate spreadsheets, adjust columns, or generate rules may help you create formats for your tables. If you are using a typewriter, you can devise table formats by using the underline key for horizontal lines and adding vertical lines by hand. If your table can be read easily, vertical rules should be omitted.

APA style APA does not use vertical rules.

Descriptive column headings Columns should have appropriate descriptive headings. Column headings may have subheads, placed in parentheses. If two or more levels of headings are needed, then *decked heads* must be used. In a decked head, two or more related columns are positioned beneath a *spanner head*, a head spanning the width of the columns. A horizontal rule separates the spanner and column heads. In the following example of decked heads, the spanner heads are "Avg. wages in mfg." and "Avg. federal income tax," and the column heads are "Men," "Women," and "Total."

Avg. wages in mfg.			Avg. federal income tax		
Men	Women	Total	Men	Women	Total

Punctuation and capitalization of column heads Capitalize the first word of a table heading, as well as any other word that requires capitalization in a sentence (proper nouns, for example). All other words should be in lowercase. Headings do not take end punctuation. You may use abbreviations, provided their meaning is obvious, to create well-proportioned tables. Possibly ambiguous abbreviations should be clarified with a note or key.

When a table consists of numerous columns or when frequent reference will be made to specific columns, number the columns from left to right. Then in the text you may refer to columns by number.

Horizontal rules   Closely spaced, double horizontal rules (or a single rule) should be placed at the top of the table. A single horizontal rule goes below the column headings—at least one-half space below so as not to look like underlining—and double or single rules go at the bottom of the table. When a table continues on to a second page, the bottom rule appears only at the end of the table, not at the end of each page.

▪ Footnotes for Tables

Tables and figures (see pages 108 through 117) may require footnotes that reveal the source of the data or give explanatory information.

Independent notes for each table   Each table should have an independent series of footnotes, regardless of whether the table is located in the text or in a separate section. Footnotes should be placed at the end of the table, even if the paper contains endnotes. Each table should have a self-contained set of notes.

General notes for entire table   A note that applies to the table as a whole or to the title of the table is indicated by the word *Note* (italicized or underlined), followed by a period and placed flush left below the table. Introduce a note containing bibliographical information with the word *Source(s):* (italicized or underlined), followed by a colon.

Notes to specific items in a table   Designate a note to a specific item, such as a particular heading or statistic, with a superscript. Lowercase letters or standard reference symbols, rather than numbers, should be used as superscripts in tables.

Lowercase letters should begin with [a] and proceed alphabetically, as in superscript[a] and superscript[b]. When superscript letters might be confusing, as in tables consisting of mathematical or chemical equations, standard reference symbols should be used. The customary order of symbols is asterisk (*), dagger (†), double dagger (‡), section mark (§), parallels (||), two asterisks (**), two daggers (††), and so on. If your typewriter or printer does not have these symbols, you may draw them neatly by hand. Symbols should appear as a self-contained series within each table. When tables run more than one page, the list of symbols should be repeated on each page.

APA style   The APA format provides for another type of note, a probability level note, which is used to indicate the probability levels of experimental results. When you have more than one level of probability in a table, use one asterisk for the lowest level, two for the next level, then three, and so on.

$*p < .01.$ $**p < .05.$ $***p < .02.$

If you refer to more than one kind of test, use the sequence of symbols listed earlier: asterisk, dagger, and so on.

Placement of table notes   Group notes together by type; that is, the general notes should form one group, the specific notes another, and the probability notes yet another.

Place all notes flush left, or against the left margin without indention. Depending on the layout of the table, you may want to consider the left side of the table as the left margin, even though it differs from margins within the text.

You may place each note on a separate line, if you have space, or place them consecutively, leaving two spaces after the period for each note before beginning the next.

▪ Oversize Tables

Long tables

Some tables are too large to fit on one page. When tables are too long, you have three options. You may use photography or xerography to reduce the table. (Be sure that the reduced version is legible.) You may divide the table and place sections side by side on a broadside page (see page 111). Or you may spread the table over two or more pages. When a table continues beyond one page, you do not need to repeat the caption. Repeat only the table number, followed by a comma and the word *continued:* `Table 4.7, continued` (see the example on pages 108 and 109). The column headings and subheadings should be repeated on every page. Only the final page of the table should have a bottom rule.

Wide tables

When tables are too wide and cannot be divided into two or more separately numbered tables, you have three options. Preferred practice is to turn a wide table broadside, or lengthwise, on the page, so that the left side of the table is at the bottom of the page and the right side is at the top (see the table on page 111). No text should appear on any page with a broadside table; the page number appears in the usual place.

If the table will not fit broadside, you may present the table across two facing pages. Half of the table goes on a left-hand page, half on a right-hand page (see pages 108 and 109). The right-hand page preceding the first page of the table should be left blank. The horizontal rules at the top of a two-page table should align perfectly across the two pages. If your software or printer cannot generate tables on facing pages, you may want to create the table in two sections and photocopy one section to use in your final copy.

Another option is to fold the page containing an overly wide table, following the instructions on page 105.

Tables too long and too wide

When tables are too long and too wide, you may consider several solutions. Material may be placed broadside and continued onto one or more pages. Material may be reduced photographically or xerographically so that it fits within the standard margins, or six-by-nine inches. Or the page containing the table may be folded (see page 105 for folding instructions).

Figures

The term *figure* usually refers to any kind of graphic representation or illustration, whether in the text or in an appendix. Figures include graphs, charts, drawings, diagrams, maps, photographs, blueprints, and some kinds of computer printouts. Pages containing only photographs may be designated as either plates or figures. If you plan to use illustrations, be sure that you possess or have access to the skills and materials required for a satisfactory finished product. You should investigate the problems and expense of illustrations before you plan a paper around them. Software programs allow you to generate numerous kinds of figures and graphics on a computer. In addition to information and suggestions that may be obtained from commercial advertisers, suppliers, lithographers, and printers, the assistance of faculty in departments such as architecture, computer science, graphic arts, and industrial arts may be valuable.

▪ Relation of Figures and Text

The reader is most likely to understand the concepts and information contained in a figure if you provide an appropriate introduction in the text. The introduction may be a description of the figure or a statement of its significance. You need to show your reader that the content of the figure contributes to your argument.

Independence of figures and text

Like tables, figures should be designed so that they can be read and understood without reference to the text. Captions should be fully descriptive. Moreover, the text should be so complete that the reader can follow the argument without examining the figures. The text, however, should refer to each figure and explain or analyze its content.

References to figures

If a figure appears within the two or three pages following the first reference to it, only the number of the figure need be given in the text ("Figure 4 shows . . ."). When you refer to a figure that is farther away from its initial mention, you should provide both figure number and page number ("Figure 5 on page 19 shows . . .").

▪ Captions

Each figure must have a caption, or title, that tells concisely and clearly what the figure contains. Avoid wordy introductory phrases such as "Graph showing" or "Chart representing." Captions should be placed below the figure. The table of contents should list figures by number and caption.

When you have a typed or printed figure, you may wish to type or print the caption as well. If the figure is a drawing or photograph, you may print the caption in India ink or use transfer letters. The format and punctuation of captions for figures are the same as those for tables (see page 115).

APA style

APA underlines the figure number but not the caption; it places a period after the figure number and after the caption.

▪ Numbering

Like tables, figures should be numbered with arabic (not roman) numerals. Figures, including those that appear in appendixes, may be numbered consecutively throughout the paper. If the last figure in the text is Figure 9, the first figure in Appendix A would be Figure 10. Alternatively, figures, like tables, may be double-numbered by chapter. Figure 1.1 would be the first figure in Chapter 1; Figure 2.2 would be the second figure in Chapter 2.

If the total number of illustrations in your paper is small, then each illustration may be labeled and numbered as a figure regardless of whether it is a map, a graph, a diagram, or whatever. If your paper has more than ten illustrations of any one type (more than ten graphs or more than ten maps, for example), you should identify each type and give it a separate sequence of numbers. A series of maps would be numbered as Map 1, Map 2, . . . , Map 12, and so on. A series of photographs would be numbered as Photo 1, Photo 2; a series of graphs as Graph 1, Graph 2, . . . , Graph 20. (If you number by chapter, the sequences would be Map 1.1, Map 1.2, Map 2.1, Map 2.2, and so on.)

▪ Hand-drawn and Computer-generated Graphs

Line, bar, area, and volume graphs effectively convey quantitative and proportional data. They may be drawn by hand, or generated with computer software.

Line graphs

DESIGN OF GRAPHS   A line graph shows the relationship between two or more variables. The data have a range of some kind, such as time, age, distance, or weight. Line graphs may be plotted on rectangular coordinate paper or generated on a computer. The graphs at the top and bottom of page 114 are line graphs.

Bar graphs

Bar graphs consist of a series of shaded columns or bars arranged to show the relationships among certain data or groups of data (see the middle figure on page 114 and the figure on page 116). Bar graphs may be divided into two categories. One type consists of bars of different lengths and allows direct comparison of quantities or percentages. Each bar may be shaded to show varying degrees of component elements. The other type consists of bars of the same length. The bars usually represent 100 percent or some other unit and are shaded to allow comparison of component elements.

Area and volume graphs

Area and volume graphs show relationships between or among quantities. The so-called pie chart, or circle graph, is the best-known example. The entire pie represents 100 percent, and the size of each slice indicates the appropriate proportion of the whole. A common method of emphasizing one element is to arrange the pie to look as though a slice (the factor to be stressed) has been cut and slightly withdrawn (see the pie charts on page 115).

PRESENTATION OF NUMERICAL DATA IN GRAPHS   Whatever the design or technology you use to generate a graph, you will want to observe the conventions pertaining to the presentation of numerical data.

1. Scales of numerical value read from left to right and usually from bottom to top.
2. If one or both scales have a zero point, it should be indicated, even if a break in the continuity of the scale must be drawn.
3. Scales that are based on percentages should indicate clearly the basis of comparison.
4. Scale values should be placed toward the outside of the figure; normally, this is to the left of the vertical scale and below the horizontal scale.
5. The exact numerical data from which a graph is produced should be included either in the figure or in an accompanying table.
6. A key or legend must be included when symbols or distances are not otherwise explained.

▪ Mounted Illustrations

A photograph, map, or printed form smaller than the regular page should be mounted on thesis paper or on heavier paper, depending on the thickness and weight of the illustration. Use rubber cement or dry mounting tissue and allow the page to dry or set thoroughly.

Plates
Pages consisting of or containing only photographs are frequently referred to as *plates*. The plate number and caption may be placed at the top of the page or, in the case of a full-page photograph, centered on the preceding page. Departmental practice and preference should be followed consistently in the preparation, placement, and labeling of plates. A list of plates ordinarily follows the table of contents in the preliminaries.

Captions
Captions for mounted illustrations may be typed, lettered by hand, or made from dry-transfer letters. Captions should be entered on the page before the illustrations are mounted.

▪ Oversize Figures

Photographic reduction
A figure that is too large to fit on a standard page may be folded or photographically reduced. Reduction is generally preferable as long as the material remains easily readable.

Folding large figures and tables
If you decide to fold an overly wide figure or table, you must make the fold or folds in such a way that the figure cannot be accidentally caught up in the binding. A wide figure should be folded from right to left—that is, the left side should be fixed in the binding and the right side should be folded in. Take the right side of the figure and fold it to the left, placing the right edge one and one-half inches from the left margin. If more than one fold is necessary, bring the next fold over to two and one-half inches from the left side of the page. Additional folds should follow one inch to the right of the previous one.

An overly long figure or table should be folded from bottom to top. Follow the instructions above for horizontal folding. The bottom fold should be at least one inch from the bottom of the other pages in the text. You will need to cut a strip one inch wide from the left side of the folded section so that it will miss the binding.

Avoid folding oversize figures and tables in two directions.

▪ Supplies for Creating Figures

Illustrations pose special problems, so you may want to seek technical advice. Perhaps a college or university duplicating service, an instructional media center, or a department of architecture, art, graphic arts, or industrial arts may be able to assist you.

Paper
The paper you use for figures should be similar in weight to the paper used for the text. Advisers generally want to approve any variation from the prescribed thesis paper. You would not expect objections to the use of full-size photographs or photostats. The inclusion of graphs on cross-ruled paper, however, may not be acceptable. If it is not, the figure may be prepared on graph paper and then photocopied, a process that generally makes the ruling invisible.

If your thesis or dissertation is to be microfilmed, you should investigate the advantages and limitations of various kinds of paper and materials. For example, India ink reproduces far better than ballpoint pen, and blue ink does not reproduce well at all.

Aids for creating figures
In planning for illustrations, you should find out which of the various technical or commercial aids will best suit your needs. You may have to

investigate and decide among one or more of the following: computer-generated material; hand-drawn or commercially prepared symbols and figures; dry-transfer or direct-application tape; translucent or opaque figures or tape; reproducible or nonreproducible copies; and use of thesis paper only or inclusion also of sensitized paper and/or transparent film for the preparation of overlays. Computer-generated graphics can make most kinds of graphs and tables. Dry-transfer lines, shadings, and cross-hatching are readily available from artist supply houses and graphic arts companies (blueprinters, lithographers, printers). Dry-transfer figures and designs are applied directly to the paper by rubbing the upper surface of the material to which they adhere.

You will also have to decide whether the master copies of illustrations are to be photocopied, photostated, or xeroxed for inclusion in each copy of the paper, or whether an original illustration is to be drawn or otherwise prepared for each copy. If only one set of illustrations is to be prepared, the master copies need to be done with paper and ink that reproduce well.

Computer Materials

The increasing use of computers in research requires special attention to the availability of computer programs, as well as formats adapted to presenting computer output.

▪ Computer Programs

If published programs are used, the source note for the figure should not only include a reference to title, author, and publisher but also mention the machine used and the operation system, such as MS-DOS or UNIX. If the program is available only locally or if it was prepared especially for your investigation, it should be reproduced by computer printout (see page 117).

▪ Computer Output

Printouts are the output category of computer material. You will have to decide which tables, figures, and other computer output are to be incorporated into the text and which are best placed in an appendix. Any information added to the printout, such as page numbers, captions, explanations or notes, should be inserted with a typewriter.

TABLES, FIGURES, AND COMPUTER MATERIALS

Sample Pages

Table 13

Accident Reports in Government Shops and in the Iron and
Steel and the Machine-building Industries

Week in which disability terminated	Government shops		Iron and steel (1910)	Machine building (1912)
	Arsenals (1912)	Navy yards (1912)		
(No. of 300-day workers	3,992	15,608	65,147	15,703)

No. of disabilities terminating in specified week

First week	89	535	9,889	7,680
Second week	27	153	4,433	2,048
Third week	57	339	1,915	869
Fourth week	57	257	1,014	512
Fifth week	15	129	807	272
Sixth week and later	55	320	1,251	621
Total	300	1,733	19,309	12,002

Percentages

First week	30	31	51	64
Second week	9	9	23	17
Third week	19	20	10	7
Fourth week	19	15	5	5
Fifth week	5	7	4	2
Sixth week and later	18	18	7	5
Total	100	100	100	100

Table 13, continued

Week in which disability terminated	Government shops		Iron and steel (1910)	Machine building (1912)
	Arsenals (1912)	Navy yards (1912)		

Percentages (excluding all under the third week)

Third week	31	32	39	38
Fourth week	31	25	20	23
Fifth week	8	12	16	12
Sixth week and later	30	31	25	27
Total	100	100	100	100

Accident frequency rates (per 1,000 300-day workers)

First week	22	34	152	66
Second week	7	10	68	18
Third week	14	22	29	8
Fourth week	14	17	16	4
Fifth week	4	8	12	2
Sixth week and later	14	21	19	5
Total	75	112	296	103

Long table on facing pages

Table 3

A Comparison of DAT Subtest Scores and Ninth-
Grade Semester Grades for Algebra

DAT subtest	N	r	Percentage of efficiency	Mean	S.D.
Verbal reasoning	129	.31[a]	4.61	25.85	8.46
Numerical ability	132	.51[a]	13.40	19.10	7.06
Abstract reasoning	124	.29[a]	4.00	34.00	8.44
Space relations	123	.20[b]	2.02	47.85	19.94

[a] Correlation significant at the .01 level.

[b] Correlation significant at the .05 level.

Table 4 shows correlations of the Differential Aptitude Test subtest scores with grades in Spanish. The correlations of .57 (Verbal Reasoning), .43 (Spelling), and .58 (Sentences) were significant at the .01 level.

Table 4

A Comparison of DAT Subtest Scores and Ninth-
Grade Semester Grades for Spanish

DAT subtest	N	r	Percentage of efficiency	Mean	S.D.
Verbal reasoning	74	.57[a]	17.15	22.10	8.46
Spelling	68	.43[a]	9.72	44.95	22.53
Sentences	72	.58[a]	18.54	26.80	13.17

[a] Correlation significant at the .01 level.

Two short tables on a page with text

APPENDIX D

Table 19. Spelling Scores of the DAT and First Semester Grades in Spanish for 68 Freshmen at Roosevelt High School (r = .43)

Raw score	F	D	C	B	A	Total students
90–94						
85–89				1		1
80–84			1	2		3
75–79			1	2	2	5
70–74				1		1
65–69				3	1	4
60–64			4	1	1	6
55–59	1	1		1	2	5
50–54	1	2	1	2		7
45–49			2		1	3
40–44	1		3	1	1	6
35–39		2	1	1		4
30–34		1	3	2		6
25–29	1		1		1	3
20–24		2	1			3
15–19		1		1		2
10–14		1	2			3
5–9	1	1		1		3
0–1	1	2				3

(No. receiving grade of)

Broadside table with doubled-up columns separated by two vertical lines

Table 3

Representative Microprobe Analyses of Amphibole and Chlorite
Weight % oxides

	1	2	3	4	5	6
SiO_2	39.1	41.4	40.8	39.9	33.2	33.58
TiO_2	0.10	0.08	0.32	0.34	0.04	0.064
Al_2O_3	20.8	21.8	14.4	20.0	12.7	13.5
FeO	12.0	15.04	18.4	12.3	4.72	9.21
MnO	0.50	0.45	0.31	0.43	0.07	0.21
MgO	9.20	6.80	7.28	8.83	30.3	28.9
CaO	7.50	7.04	9.90	7.47	0.12	0.18
Na_2O	6.27	6.83	4.37	6.20	0.00	0.002
K2O	0.37	0.49	0.18	0.31	0.08	-
Total	95.8	99.9	95.9	95.7	81.3	85.65

Cations for 23 Oxygens
(24 oxygens for chlorite)

	1	2	3	4	5	6
Si	5.86	5.99	6.30	5.97	5.76	5.66
^{iv}Al	2.14	2.01	1.70	2.03	2.24	2.34
Ti	0.012	0.009	0.037	0.038	0.005	0.009
Al	1.52	1.70	0.92	1.50	0.36	0.35
Fe	1.50	1.82	2.37	1.54	0.68	1.30
Mn	0.064	0.055	0.040	0.054	0.008	0.032
Mg	2.05	1.47	1.68	1.97	7.84	7.26
Sum C	5.15	5.05	5.04	5.10		
Ca	1.20	1.09	1.64	1.20	0.024	0.032
Na_B	0.65	0.86	0.32	0.70	0.000	0.000
Sum B	2.00	2.00	2.00	2.00		
Na_A	1.17	1.06	0.99	1.10		
K	0.070	0.090	0.036	0.060	0.016	
Total	16.24	16.15	16.03	16.16	16.94	16.98

1. magnesio-alumino taramite, MVJ84-9C.
2. alumino taramite, MVJ84-9B.
3. ferroan pargasite, LACMNH 20370.
4. magnesio-alumino taramite, R-15.
5. clinochlore, MVJ84-42-2.
6. clinochlore, R-10.

Computer-generated table

In 1930, Folling discovered that phenylketonuria was actually a
metabolic error. Figure 2 is a pictorial representation of
competition for amino acid uptake into the brain.

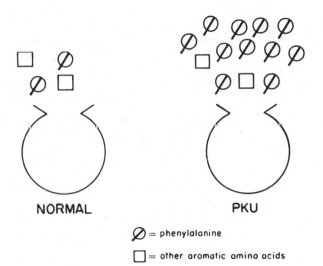

Figure 2

Competition for Uptake of
Amino Acids by Brain

Source: John A. Anderson and Kenneth F. Swaiman, eds., Phenylketonuria
and Allied Metabolic Diseases, U.S., Department of Health, Education,
and Welfare, Children's Bureau (Washington: GPO, 1967), 3.

The drawing at left shows equal amounts of phenylalanine
and other amino acids being taken up into the brain under normal
conditions. If, as shown at right, the system is loaded with
huge amounts of phenylalanine, this reduces the opportunity for
uptake of other amino acids that utilize the same catalytic site.

Hand-drawn illustration on a page with text

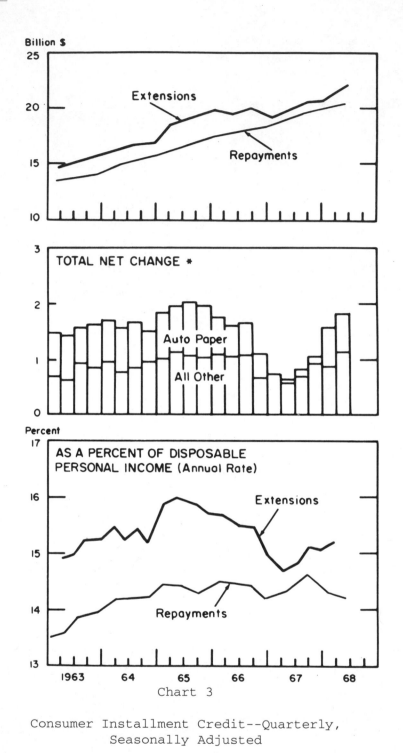

Billion $

Extensions

Repayments

TOTAL NET CHANGE *

Auto Paper

All Other

Percent

AS A PERCENT OF DISPOSABLE
PERSONAL INCOME (Annual Rate)

Extensions

Repayments

1963   64   65   66   67   68

Chart 3

Consumer Installment Credit--Quarterly,
Seasonally Adjusted

*Extensions minus repayments

**Three-part chart (each separate figure in such a composite may
have its own caption or be collectively labeled "Chart" or "Figure"
as here)**

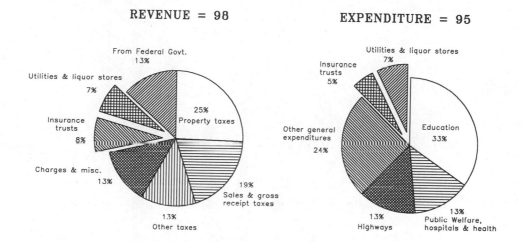

REVENUE = 98

From Federal Govt.
13%

Utilities & liquor stores
7%

Insurance trusts
8%

Charges & misc.
13%

25%
Property taxes

19%
Sales & gross
receipt taxes

13%
Other taxes

EXPENDITURE = 95

Utilities & liquor stores
7%

Insurance trusts
5%

Other general
expenditures
24%

Education
33%

13%
Public Welfare,
hospitals & health

13%
Highways

Figure 2.4

Distribution of State and Local Government
Revenue and Expenditure in 1966
(in Billions of Dollars)

FIGURE 2.4 ·

DISTRIBUTION OF STATE AND LOCAL GOVERNMENT
REVENUE AND EXPENDITURE IN 1966
(IN BILLIONS OF DOLLARS)

Figure 2.4. Distribution of State and Local Government Revenue and
Expenditure in 1966 (in Billions of Dollars)

Figure 2.4
Distribution of State and Local Government Revenue and Expenditure
in 1966 (in Billions of Dollars)

**Computer-generated pie charts with segments separated
for emphasis and sample caption formats**

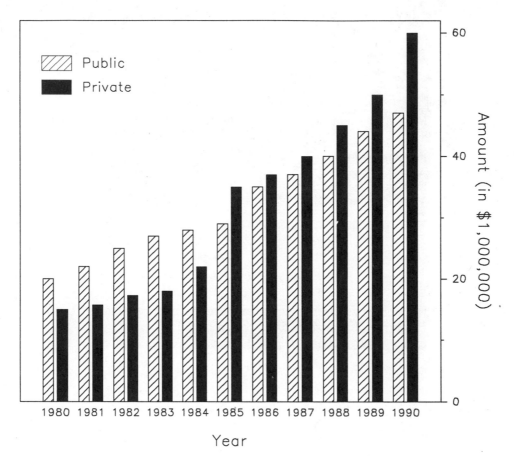

Figure 7.2

Amounts of Scholarship Aid to Students at Bennett University Received

from Public and Private Sources, 1980-90

Computer-generated bar graph

```
        PROGRAM DUST
C       TO CONVERT PARTICLE VOLUME DISTRIBUTION DATA INTO
C       PARTICLE COUNT ESTIMATE PER CHANGE OF STANTON DATA
        REAL*4 AREA(5),VOL(5,8),LABEL(15),SLABEL(15),PART(5,8),
        1 LENGTH(8),WIDTH(5)
        INTEGER*2 IPART(8)
        BYTE FILNAM(15)
        DATA WIDTH,LENGTH/1.5,3.75,7.5,15.0,30.0,1.5,3.75,7.5,15.0,30.0,
        1 60.0,120.0,240.0/
C
        IN=3
        OUT=6
        PI=3.14159
        DO 100 I=1,5
        AREA(I)=PI*(WIDTH(I)*0.5)**2
        DO 100 J=1,8
        VOL(I,J)=AREA(I)*LENGTH(J)
100     CONTINUE
C       OPEN INPUT DATA FILE BY ENTERING FILNAM
105     TYPE 1
1       FORMAT(' INPUT DATA FILE NAME: ',$)
        ACCEPT 2,FILNAM
2       FORMAT(15A1)
        I=ILEN(FILNAM,15)
C       REJECT IF FILNAM IF LENGTH IS 0 OR NEGATIVE
        IF(I.LE.0) GO TO 105
        CALL ASSIGN(IN,FILNAM,I,'OLD','NC')
C
        READ(IN,3) LABEL
3       FORMAT(15A4)
        WRITE(OUT,4) LABEL
4       FORMAT('1',15A4)
        READ(IN,5) ND
5       FORMAT(I3)
        DO 300 M=1,ND
        SUM=0.
        READ(IN,3) SLABEL
        WRITE(OUT,6) SLABEL
6       FORMAT('0',15A4)
        WRITE(OUT,7) LENGTH
7       FORMAT(' AVERAGE LENGTH:',8F13.2/' WIDTH')
        DO 200 I=1,5
        READ(IN,8) IPART
8       FORMAT(10I3)
        DO 200 J=1,8
        DART=IPART(J)/VOL(I,J)
        SUM=SUM+DART
        PART(I,J)=DART
200     CONTINUE
        SUM=100./SUM
        DO 240 I=1,5
        DO 220 J=1,8
        PART(I,J)=PART(I,J)*SUM
220     CONTINUE
        WRITE(OUT,9)WIDTH(I),(PART(I,J),J=1,8)
9       FORMAT(' ',F10.2,6X,8F13.3)
240     CONTINUE
300     CONTINUE
        TYPE 10
10      FORMAT(' ANOTHER DATA SET (1) OR STOP (0)? ',$)
        ACCEPT 5,I
        IF(I.GT.0) GOTO 105
        STOP
        END
```

Oversize computer program reduced photographically to fit on one page

6 The Finished Copy

This chapter provides information about turning the final draft of your research paper into a finished copy that will be accepted by your instructor or institution, or by the publication to which you submit it.

The Final Draft

Before you begin to think about producing the finished copy, you should have a completely accurate, thoroughly polished final draft. The final draft should correctly observe the conventions regarding capitalization, punctuation, spelling, compound words, hyphenation, and paragraphing. It should reveal thoughtful word choices and attention to detail in the use of quotations. Even though your paper is still in draft form, it should follow the format requirements for front and back matter, margins, indention, notes and bibliography, placement of documentation, spacing, and so on. This groundwork is particularly important if someone else will type your paper, but it is also necessary if you plan to type or print the paper yourself. Advisers of theses and dissertations often wish to approve the final draft before you prepare the finished copy.

Equipment and Supplies

The equipment you need to produce the finished copy includes a typewriter or a word processor and printer with appropriate software; the supplies may include paper, a typewriter ribbon, and materials for making corrections. Before you acquire any of these supplies, you should ascertain departmental or institutional requirements.

▪ The Typewriter or Computer Printer

You will want to use a machine that produces clean, clear copy. An electric or electronic typewriter is preferable to a manual machine because it produces a better copy. Computer printers can generally be divided into two classes: dot-matrix printers (of varying qualities, including near-letter quality) and letter-quality printers, such as daisy-wheel, ink-jet, and laser printers. Because this technology has been developing rapidly, requirements and standards for reports, theses, and dissertations likewise have been changing. Dot-matrix printing may not be acceptable, particularly for a dissertation that will be photocopied rather than set into type. It is a good idea to show your adviser some sample pages before you prepare the finished copy.

▪ Type

Most machines allow you to choose between two sizes of type: *elite type*, which contains twelve spaces or letters to the inch, and *pica type*, which contains ten spaces or letters to the inch. Elite type increases by about one-fifth the amount of material that fits on each page. Your choice of type size may depend either on individual or institutional preference.

Some electronic typewriters and computer printers offer smaller or larger type, as well as an array of different typefaces. These should not be used for theses or dissertations, and they rarely are acceptable in reports written for academic credit. For information on creating a facsimile of typeset material with a computer, see *The Art of Desktop Publishing: Using the Personal Computer to Publish It Yourself*, eds. Tony Bove, Cheryl Rhodes, and Wes Thomas, 2nd ed. (Toronto: Bantam, 1987).

▪ Software

If you plan to produce computer graphics or to print your finished copy on a computer printer, you will need appropriate software programmed to send the correct instructions to the printer. If you plan to submit your text on a diskette, you should make certain that your reader has a word-processing program compatible with the one you use. For information on submitting manuscripts on diskettes to publishers, consult *Chicago Guide to Preparing Electronic Manuscripts for Authors and Publishers* (Chicago: University of Chicago Press, 1987).

▪ Special Symbols

Special symbols are a practical necessity in some subjects and professional fields. Special-purpose typewriters are available, and special keys may be purchased for most ordinary typewriters. Some typewriters have interchangeable elements for different languages and disciplines. Similarly, many printers have fonts that allow you to use special letters and symbols. In some cases you must enter instructions in your word-processing program in order to send such symbols to your printer.

Special symbols most often needed, even in general subject matter, include accent marks, both grave (`) and acute (´), and square brackets ([ ]). Most other symbols are particular to a specialized subject. Any symbol not available on your typewriter or printer should be neatly handwritten on the page in black ink.

▪ Ribbon

A black typewriter or printer ribbon should be used. The ribbon may be either cloth or carbon, as appropriate. In cloth ribbons, nylon is preferable to cotton, which smears easily. A cloth ribbon should be changed as often as necessary to produce a consistent copy. A carbon ribbon is used only once.

▪ Paper

Most colleges and universities require the writer to present the original copy of a research paper, thesis, or dissertation on a good-quality bond paper of twenty-pound weight, eight and one-half by eleven inches in size. A rag content of 25 or 50 percent is ordinarily required (the higher the percentage, the more durable the paper). Erasable bond and onion skin generally are not acceptable because they smear easily. These requirements hold whether you use a typewriter or a computer printer.

▪ Copies

Any copies that must be submitted with the original should be photocopies. Keep at least one copy of your paper for yourself in case some mishap befalls the original and other photocopies. All pages of each photocopy should be identical in weight, color, and texture of paper.

▪ Materials for Correction

You can reduce the need for corrections by quickly proofreading each page before removing it from the typewriter or running the computer printer. On a typewriter, simple corrections can usually be made at this time so that they are hardly noticeable. After the sheets have been removed from the machine, the discovery of errors often requires the retyping of the entire page. After retyping, you should proofread again.

Correcting typed copy

Typed letters may be removed with correction fluid (Liquid Paper is one well-known brand), white carbon paper, an erasing ribbon, or correction tape. Whichever material you use, make certain that the letter or word is completely removed or covered before you type over it. If your typewriter has an erasing ribbon, you probably will want to use it. Correction fluid, if applied carefully, can be used to make an acceptable correction.

Correcting on a word processor   You should also proofread carefully when you use a word processor. Some programs include a spell checker, which helps you detect typographical errors, as well as misspelled words; however, it does not pick up an error if you type the wrong word, such as *the* for *he,* but spell it correctly. Once you have located an error in a computer-generated text, you may use the "find-and-replace" function, available in most word-processing programs, to search for and correct all instances of the error.

Typing and Printing Instructions

This section contains instructions for typing the elements of a research paper that apply whether the typist uses a typewriter or a word processor.

▪ Numbering of Pages

All pages of the text of a research paper should be numbered, including the first page. Position numerals in the upper right-hand corner one inch from the top of the page, flush with the right margin.

You may wish to use a running head—a designation of your paper accompanying the page number. Many editors recommend this practice as a means of helping to ensure that one manuscript does not become confused with another. MLA recommends placing the name of the writer before the numeral without intervening punctuation, as in `Jones 2` (optional in a dissertation). Double-space to the first line of the text. For the running head, APA recommends a shortened version of the title, up to a maximum of fifty spaces, including spacing and punctuation, with the page number two spaces below, as in

`Equality of Access`

`5`

for the fifth page of a paper entitled "Equality of Access in Public Higher Education."

In a research paper, the title page and outline should not be numbered or counted as pages. The first page of the text of a research paper is page one.

In a thesis or dissertation, front matter, such as the abstract and the approval sheet, should not be numbered or counted as part of the thesis or dissertation. The title page and copyright page should be counted but not numbered. Use lowercase roman numerals for front matter and arabic numerals running consecutively for the text and the back matter. Front-matter page numbers are placed one inch from the bottom of the page, centered between the margins. Leave at least a double space between the last line of the front-matter text and the page number.

APA style   APA numbers the title page and all succeeding pages with continuous arabic numerals.

If your word-processing program does not allow you to paginate according to these requirements, you may want to consult with your adviser about using another format.

■ Spacing

You should follow whatever policies on spacing you select throughout your paper. Conventions and requirements for spacing exist not to create additional hurdles for you but to make your paper readable.

MARGINS　　Margins should measure one and one-half inches on the left and one inch on the right and at the top and bottom. The wider left margin provides room for binding. Page numbers and running heads should sit one inch from either the top or bottom of the paper. Larger or smaller margins may be required by a local style sheet.

APA style　　APA recommends margins of one and one-half inches on all four sides of the typescript.

Because precision in the spacing of note and bibliographical entries is important, right-hand margins should not be justified—that is, lines should not be spaced out so that the right margin is even. Justification on a typewriter or printer often leaves irregular, unattractive spacing that interferes with reading and distorts the spacing of the documentation.

INDENTION　　Indent the first line of a paragraph five spaces. Bring all subsequent lines to the left margin.

For indention of set-off quotations, see page 125.

CENTERED MATERIAL　　Any material to be centered on a page, such as first-level headings and set-off poetry, should be centered between margins, not between the edges of the page.

Most computer programs and electronic typewriters allow you to center a line automatically by pressing a combination of function keys before or after typing the line.

DIVISION OF WORDS, NUMBERS, AND LINES OF TEXT　　When the division of a word is necessary, the break should come between syllables. Standard dictionaries indicate the proper places to break words. Many word-processing programs hyphenate words automatically.

At the end of a line, one-letter and two-letter divisions, such as *a-ble, a-tone, de-velop, consecrat-ed,* or *entire-ly,* are not acceptable. The word should be written on one line, or another division point should be used—

Compound words　　for example, *conse-crated.* As a general rule, compound words should be divided between the elements that make up the compound—for example, *volley-ball* rather than *vol-leyball.* When the appearance of a part of a word would lead to confusion about pronunciation (as in *wo-men*), the word

Hyphenated words　　should not be broken. Divide words that are already hyphenated only at the hyphen.

The writer must indicate for the typist the nature of hyphens at the end of lines in the draft. In some cases, the hyphen at the end of a line should be omitted when the word is typed on one line. In the case of a hyphenated word, however, the hyphen at the end of the line should be retained when the word is typed on one line; the retention of the hyphen is indicated by a small line drawn just below the hyphen.

```
                                                        volley-
ball
```

(Word typed on one line: *volleyball*)

```
                                                          self=
centered
```

(Word typed on one line: *self-centered*)

Indivisible elements ·The following elements should never be divided: letters that are the names of radio or television stations, government agencies, institutions, or companies; the name of the month and the day; years; hours of the day; monetary expressions; and parts of an equation.

```
KWLZ        RFC    March 2     6x + 4y = 27
```

$$C + O_2 = CO_2 \qquad \$1,378.50 \qquad 525 \ B.C. \qquad 4{:}00 \ a.m.$$

In the case of proper names, the given name and surname or initials and surname should be on the same line when possible; very long names are an exception.

Long formulas and equations Very long formulas or equations may be set on centered lines by themselves, if necessary, to avoid breaking. If an equation is so long and complex that it must be run over to another line, the break should come if possible before the equality sign (in algebraic equations) or after the arrow (chemical equations).

When a word cannot be included in its entirety or properly divided and hyphenated within the established margin, the entire word should be placed on the next line. No more than two successive lines should end with **Divisions between pages** hyphenated words. Words should not be broken between pages. Avoid carrying over just one line of a paragraph to the following page.

ALIGNMENT OF NUMERALS When numerals are arranged in vertical lists, both arabic and roman numerals should be aligned on the right side. This alignment makes the left side uneven, but it is the accepted form. Due allowance must be made when starting a column to provide space for the longest number to be listed. Columns of figures should appear as follows:

```
        I.              1
       II.              7
      III.             18
      XIV.            296
   XXXIII.         26,173
  XXXVIII.      1,008,957
```

Numbers with decimals are aligned on the decimal points.

```
  7.9

123.657

 54.4

  7.3333
```

PUNCTUATION   Periods, colons, commas, question marks, and semi-colons follow the previous letter without spacing. Two spaces follow a period. One space follows a colon, a semicolon, and a comma. Dashes are indicated by two consecutive hyphens (--). Neither hyphens nor dashes have space on either side of them.

```
She needs the following materials: one saw, one hammer,

and one nail.
```
(One space after a colon in text)

```
New York: Random House
```
(One space after a colon in facts of publication)

```
Writing the Research Paper: A Guide and Sourcebook
```
(One space after a colon between title and subtitle)

```
To err is human; to forgive, divine.

1976; New York: Holt, 1983.
```
(One space after semicolon, whether in text or notes)

```
The stock--American Can--was selling above par.
```
(No space on either side of a dash)

```
Two-thirds of the members attended.
```
(No space on either side of a hyphen)

LEADERS   On pages containing the table of contents and the list of tables and figures, you may wish to use leaders, or spaced periods. They must be arranged so that the periods are aligned perpendicularly and will end at the same point on the right-hand side—usually about two or three spaces before the material to which the leader guides the reader's eye. A simple way to accomplish this alignment is to place all the periods on the even numbers of the typing scale.

▪ Quotations

SUPERSCRIPTS   Within the text, a superscript should be placed without any intervening space after the end punctuation. In notes, the superscript should be indented five spaces and followed by one space. If you use a word-processing program that does not produce superscripts, check with an adviser about an acceptable alternative, such as placing the number in parentheses.

RUN-IN PROSE QUOTATIONS   Run short prose quotations (fewer than four typed lines, or about forty words) into the text and enclose them in double quotation marks. If the original excerpt contains a direct quotation, change the double quotation marks around the internal quotation to single quotation marks.

SET-OFF PROSE QUOTATIONS   Set off long quotations (more than four typed lines) in indented, block-style paragraphs. Unlike run-in quotations, quotations that are set off are not enclosed in quotation marks.

Set-off quotations may be single- or double-spaced. Single-spacing is often preferred for theses and dissertations to save space and to make the finished paper resemble a book. MLA and APA formats call for double-spacing set-off quotations, particularly in materials that are to be set by a printer. Whichever spacing you select should be used consistently throughout the paper. Indicate omissions, alterations, and corrections of quoted material as specified on pages 69 through 73.

Set-off quotations, whether single- or double-spaced, should be separated from the text by one double space both above and below, and they should be indented ten spaces from the left margin. Indent three spaces within set-off material to indicate indentions in the original.

APA spacing   Indent set-off material five spaces from the left margin, and indent five spaces to indicate indentions in the original.

POETRY   Short excerpts of poetry (less than two lines) should be run into the text and enclosed in double quotation marks. Separate each line of poetry by a virgule, or solidus, with a space on either side of it. Excerpts of three or more lines should be set off and may be single- or double-spaced. (See the discussion of spacing in the preceding section.) Double-space between stanzas. Indent poetry ten spaces from the left margin; indention may be five spaces when the line would otherwise have to be broken. Lines of poetry extending beyond one typescript line should be indented five spaces, broken, and indented ten spaces on the next line. Alignment and spacing within the set-off quotation should follow the original as closely as possible.

EPIGRAPHS   Direct quotations that precede an entire text or a chapter should be aligned twenty spaces from the left margin and continue to the right margin. Double-space from the chapter title to the epigraph. Single-space the epigraph itself. Indention in the original is indicated with an additional three-space indention. The spacing suffices to indicate that the epigraph is a direct quotation; quotation marks are not needed. Single-space to the attribution of the quotation, which appears below the epigraph, flush with the right margin. Begin the attribution approximately at the middle of the page. Double-space to the first line of text.

ELLIPSIS   Indicate the omission of any portion of a quoted excerpt with three ellipsis points (three spaced dots). When an ellipsis is used within a sentence, leave a space before the first dot and after the third. Use four dots (a period plus three ellipsis points) to signify the omission of any of the following: (1) the end of a quoted sentence, (2) the beginning of the following sentence, (3) one or more sentences, and (4) one or more paragraphs. Place the first of the four dots, with no intervening space, immediately after the last quoted word. The omission of the end of a sentence and the omission of one or more subsequent sentences are indicated in the same way. A complete sentence must precede the four dots, and another complete sentence must follow them.

When you retain the original punctuation at the end of a cut or a complete sentence, that mark of punctuation (question mark, exclamation point, semicolon, colon, comma) takes the place of the period. (See examples and explanations on pages 69–73.)

A full line of ellipsis points can signal the omission of an entire paragraph and should be used when more than a few paragraphs are omitted. In quotations of poetry, a full line of ellipsis points running the length of the longest line indicates the omission of one or more lines of the poem. When a line of ellipsis points is used to indicate the omission of a line or paragraph, the dots run between the margins of the indented material.

BRACKETS   Enclose in square brackets ([ ]) corrections, clarifications, and editorial comments inserted in direct quotations. If your typewriter or printer does not have brackets, insert them neatly in black ink. Do not substitute parentheses or any other typographical symbol.

END PUNCTUATION WITH DOCUMENTATION   For placement of end punctuation with superscripts or parenthetical documentation, see Chapter 7, pages 143 and 149. If you are using MLA or APA style, see the appropriate section.

QUOTATIONS IN NOTES   Run in all direct quotations in both footnotes and endnotes, regardless of the length of the quotation. Use single- or double-spacing consistent with other entries. If the quotation consists of more than one paragraph, begin each paragraph at the left margin without indention. Place quotation marks at the beginning of each paragraph and at the beginning and end of the entire quotation. Provide any necessary bibliographical information for the quotation within parentheses directly after the quotation. Poetry in notes should be blocked and indented, as in the text.

▪ Endnotes and Footnotes

PLACEMENT OF THE SUPERSCRIPT IN THE TEXT   Leave no space between the superscript (note number) in the text and the word or mark of punctuation that it follows. Place the superscript before a dash, but after all other marks of punctuation.

SEQUENCE OF NOTE NUMBERS   The numbering of endnotes or footnotes should run consecutively through each chapter. Some institutions may want notes to run consecutively throughout the entire dissertation. You should check with your graduate office or adviser about the numbering of notes.

LOCATION OF FOOTNOTES   Place every footnote at the bottom of the page on which the citation appears. Type a one-and-one-half-inch line with the underline key, starting from the left margin, one double space below the last line of the text. Place the first footnote one double space below the line.

SPACING OF FOOTNOTES   Indent the first line of each note five spaces. Subsequent lines start at the left margin. Place the superscript one-half space above the line and leave one space between the superscript and the first letter in the note. Single-space within footnotes, and double-space between them.

CONTINUED FOOTNOTES   When a footnote cannot be included without running into the bottom margin (one inch) and cannot be omitted without making the page noticeably short, the footnote may be split and carried over to the next page. Conclude the footnote without indention, ahead of the next footnote in the series.

LOCATION OF ENDNOTES   Endnotes should be placed in a separate section entitled "Notes" (not "Endnotes") either at the end of the entire paper immediately preceding the bibliography or at the end of each chapter. Endnotes should be numbered consecutively throughout each chapter or throughout the entire paper, as local regulations specify.

SPACING OF ENDNOTES   Indent the first line of each note five spaces. Subsequent lines start at the left margin. Place the superscript one-half space above the line, and leave one space between the superscript and the first word of the note. Double-space throughout, both within and between entries.

▪ Headings within Chapters

Space the headings you decide to use within the text (see pages 45 through 46 in Chapter 2) as follows:

First Level within the Text

Double-space above and below centered headings. Capitalize the first letter of each word except articles, conjunctions, and prepositions, unless they are the first or last word in the heading. Underscore with a solid line. Do not number unless local guidelines so specify, in which case use arabic numerals. If a heading is more than four inches long (forty-eight elite or forty pica spaces), use a double-spaced inverted-pyramid format. The title should not have terminal punctuation, unless it ends with a question mark or an exclamation point.

Second Level within the Text

Leave a double space above and below freestanding side headings; align with the left margin. Capitalize and punctuate as you would centered headings. If a side heading is more than about two and one-half inches long (thirty elite or twenty-five pica spaces), divide the heading, placing the second line a double space below, with a two-space hanging indention.

Third Level within the Text.   The text begins here.

Double-space to paragraph headings, indent five spaces, and under-score each heading with a solid line. Capitalize the first word and proper nouns and adjectives only. End the heading with a period and begin the text on the same line.

▪ Tables and Figures

PLACEMENT   The following guidelines apply to the placement of tables and figures in the text:

1. Confine each table or figure to one page if possible. Leave the usual margins.
2. Include textual material on the page with a table or figure that occupies no more than half the page (but see item 4 below). The page should begin with text. Leave a quadruple space both above and below a table or figure.
3. Place a table or figure between complete paragraphs. Avoid inserting a table or figure into the middle of a paragraph, even if you have to leave some extra space on the page.
4. Some tables and figures may be placed on separate pages. These include materials that must be increased or reduced in scale and those that require special artwork. When you generate a table or figure on software other than your word-processing program, you may want to enter it on a separate page. Placing a table or figure on a separate page makes revision easy because retyping or reprinting the text

does not affect the material. A series of small tables or figures discussed together in the text may be grouped together on one page (see page 114).

5. For tables too large to fit on one page, follow the instructions on page 102 for placing tables broadside and dividing them. If an oversize figure cannot be reduced photographically, fold it according to instructions on page 105.

PAGINATION   Place the assigned page number (and any running head) in the usual position in the upper right-hand corner on all pages containing tables and figures. If the margins have been decreased, adjust the placement of the page number accordingly. Type or print the page number on a folded figure after the page has been folded.

MARGINS   If a table or figure is less than six inches wide, center it between the margins. Try to leave at least one-inch margins; three-fourths of an inch should be the absolute minimum. Remember that a one-and-one-half-inch margin must be maintained on the left.

Tables **CAPTIONS**   Determine your department's preference for table captions (see pages 98–99 for styles of captions) and then use the chosen format consistently. Double-space (or, if necessary because of lack of space, single-space) captions and place them *above* the table. Block-style captions begin flush with the left margin of the table, which might not coincide with the left margin of other pages. Inverted-pyramid captions should be centered between margins.

Double-space from the caption to the top rule of the table. Begin the table with a single horizontal rule or with two closely spaced horizontal rules extending the width of the table.

Figures   Place the caption one quadruple space *below* the figure. Otherwise, follow the instructions given above for table captions.

Tables **FOOTNOTES**   Double-space below the bottom rule of the table or, if the table continues on to additional pages, below the last line of material. Indent footnotes five spaces from the left margin of the table. Space them as you space footnotes in the text.

Figures   Double-space below the caption. Indent footnotes five spaces from the left margin of the figure. Space them as you space footnotes in the text. Alternatively, you may place a footnote in an open space within the figure, as long as the footnote does not interfere with the clear presentation of your illustration.

SPACING IN TABLES   The spacing and proportion of a table should be designed to contribute to clarity and readability of the table.

Column headings   These guidelines apply to the spacing of column headings.

1. Leave a blank space above and below all column headings; single-space within headings; and leave at least one space on either side of the longest heading.

2. Center headings between the vertical rules that enclose them or, if there are no vertical rules, in the space allowed for each column. Enclose sub-headings in parentheses and center them below the main heading.
3. Align the bottom lines of all column headings on the same plane.
4. Type or print a horizontal rule (use the underscore key) one single space below the column headings.
5. If you number the columns, place the numerals in parentheses on the next line below the lowest order of column headings.

Table body   Follow these guidelines for spacing items in the body of a table:

1. Leave enough space between columns so that each entry stands out as a separate item that can be read easily.
2. If columns are divided by vertical rules, leave at least one space on each side of the longest entry.
3. Align columns of words on the left.
4. Align columns of numbers on their decimal points.

```
Number of samples included      324
Number of titrations made         6
Average of findings             32.6
Mean variation of findings       2.456
```

5. In mixed columns of numbers and other items, align the numbers on their decimal points and center other items in the column.
6. Single-space within items and use one and one-half spaces or a double space between items, unless space availability or restrictions indicate a more desirable spacing.

▪ Chapter Numbers and Titles

Type the word CHAPTER in full caps, use an arabic numeral (CHAPTER 1; CHAPTER 5), and position these one inch from the top of the page, centered between the margins. Type the title in uppercase and lowercase letters one double space below the chapter number. Center the title between the margins. Double-space titles of two or more lines, using an inverted-pyramid style. The title should not have terminal punctuation unless it ends with a question mark or an exclamation point. Double-space below the title to the first line of the text.

▪ Part-Title Pages

If a work is divided into parts, each part may be introduced with a page bearing the part title. This page should be numbered and counted like any other page of the text. Type the part number and title slightly above the center of the page with double-spacing as follows:

```
PART 2

From the Renaissance to Hume
```

When a chapter title follows the part title without intervening text, the chapter title should be placed on the following page. When text follows the part title, it should begin one double space below the title.

▪ Bibliographies and Lists of Works Cited

TITLE   Type `Bibliography`, `Works Cited`, `References`, or another appropriate heading a double space from your name and the page number, centered between margins and without end punctuation. Double-space to the first entry or heading. Any subheadings should be placed as in the text: first level, centered and underlined; second level, flush with the left margin and underlined; third level, indented five spaces, underlined, and followed by a period.

SPACING   Bibliographies and works cited lists may be double-spaced or single-spaced. Double spacing is generally preferred; single-spacing may be required for dissertations to save space. Double-spaced entries should be double-spaced both within and between entries. Single-spaced bibliographies and works cited lists should be single-spaced within entries and double-spaced between entries. (See the sample bibliography and works cited pages at the end of Chapter 1.)

Use a hanging indention. Begin each entry at the left margin, and indent succeeding lines in the entry five spaces. If there are two or more entries by one author, type three hyphens (followed by a period or a comma, as appropriate) in place of the name for the second and following listings.

PUNCTUATION   Periods mark the end of the author, title, and facts of publication sections. Two spaces follow each period; one space follows commas and colons. Be careful to insert only one space after the colon (old styles required two spaces).

ANNOTATIONS   Begin annotations either immediately after the end of an entry or on the next line, indented ten spaces. In either case, indent succeeding lines five spaces from the left margin.

▪ Front Matter for a Thesis or Dissertation

ABSTRACT   Type the word `Abstract` (*or* `ABSTRACT`) one inch from the top of the page, centered between the margins. Double-space to the full title of your thesis or dissertation as it appears on the title page, either in uppercase or in uppercase and lowercase letters. Double-space to your full legal name, which should be centered in uppercase and lowercase letters. Double-space to the text of the abstract, which should be double-spaced. The abstract page(s) are neither counted nor numbered.

Because requirements for the format and placement of the abstract vary greatly among institutions, be certain to consult your graduate office about its requirements.

TITLE PAGE   Use an approved title-page format, either selected from the examples on pages 49 and 50 or as specified by local policy. The title may appear entirely in capital letters or in uppercase and lowercase letters. The title page is counted but not numbered.

COPYRIGHT PAGE   The copyright notice, if any, appears on a separate page following the title page. Center the notice, and position the last line one inch from the bottom of the page. Circle a lowercase c next to the year; type your full legal name a double space below; center the words ALL RIGHTS RESERVED a double space below your name. (See the sample copyright page on page 51.) The copyright page is counted but not numbered.

TABLE OF CONTENTS   Words designating elements of the paper, such as the preface and bibliography, should be typed in uppercase and lowercase (Table of Contents), following the rules for capitalization of titles. An alternative format places such titles entirely in capital letters (TABLE OF CONTENTS).

Type Table of Contents (*or* TABLE OF CONTENTS) one inch from the top of the page, centered between the margins. No terminal punctuation follows the heading of any line of the table of contents. Type Chapter flush with the left-hand margin and Page flush with the right-hand margin. Position Page a double space below the heading and place Chapter after the listing of the preliminaries. See Chapter 4 for the alignment of *period leaders* (spaced periods leading from the chapter title or heading on the left to the page number on the right).

Indent one-digit chapter numbers five spaces, and position numbers of two digits or more by aligning the numerals in the right-hand column. The wording, capitalization, and punctuation of titles and headings should be typed exactly as they appear in the text. Headings and subheadings underlined in the text should not be underlined in the table of contents. Use a two-space hanging indention (that is, the first line at the margin and subsequent lines indented) within headings and between successive levels. Type the names for the reference materials (Bibliography, Appendix, etc.) flush with the left margin; place the page number of the first page of each section in the column at the right. With separate appendixes, list each by letter (A, B, C, etc.) and title, if any.

For a partially condensed version of the above, single-space between the second- and third-level headings.

For an even more condensed version, you may run in second- and third-level heads, use period leaders only with chapter titles, and double-space only between chapters.

LIST OF TABLES   Type Tables *or* List of Tables (TABLES *or* LIST OF TABLES) one inch from the top of the page, centered between the margins and without terminal punctuation. Double-space to the labels Table and Page, which should be placed flush with the left and right margins, respectively. Indent and space captions for tables, following the guidelines for the Table of Contents on page 41.

LIST OF FIGURES   Type `Figures` *or* `List of Figures` (`FIGURES` *or* `LIST OF FIGURES`) one inch from the top of the page, centered between the margins and without terminal punctuation. Place column headings, captions, and page numbers as in a list of tables.

ACKNOWLEDGMENTS OR PREFACE   Type `Acknowledgments` *or* `Preface` (`ACKNOWLEDGMENTS` *or* `PREFACE`) one inch from the top of the page. The title should be centered between the margins and should have no terminal punctuation. Double-space to the first line of the text.

▪ Back Matter for a Thesis or Dissertation

APPENDIX   Type `Appendix` (*or* `APPENDIX`), along with its appropriate letter, one inch from the top of the page, centered between the margins. Double-space to the text of the appendix, which should be double-spaced.

GLOSSARY   Type `Glossary` (*or* `GLOSSARY`) one inch from the top of the page, centered between the margins. Double-space to the glossary. Double-space any preliminary explanation of the glossary, and arrange the words along the left margin and their definitions along the right margin. Your spacing should allow readers to find the meanings readily. The format for the glossary will vary with the length and type of terms.

ENDNOTES AND BIBLIOGRAPHY OR LIST OF WORKS CITED
See page 127 in this chapter for information about endnotes and page 131 in this chapter for information about bibliographies and lists of works cited.

INDEX   Type `Index` (*or* `INDEX`) one inch from the top of the page, centered between the margins. The index should be double-spaced, one column to a page. Indent subheadings five spaces. Entries are followed by a comma and the page number(s) on which the reference to the subject appears.

II Systems of Documentation

General Information on Documentation

Documentation, either through notes or through parenthetical references and an accompanying bibliography or list of works cited, serves to acknowledge the sources of ideas and information in your paper. The authority or source for both facts and opinions—whether quoted directly or indirectly or derived from primary or from secondary sources—must be cited to provide your reader with an accurate account of the materials on which you base your conclusions. Omission of full and precise documentation can result in inaccurate and invalid research or in plagiarism (see Chapter 3).

The two basic types of systems for documenting materials from other sources are the note-bibliography system and the parenthetical-reference system. The note-bibliography format involves presentation of bibliographical information in footnotes or endnotes and in a bibliography. This system has been widely used for undergraduate and graduate research papers in the humanities and the social sciences and for papers in many of the professions. The parenthetical-reference system, which may use either author's name and page number (MLA) or author's name and date of the work cited (APA) within parentheses, entails including documentation in parentheses within the text and in a list of works cited. In the MLA system, this list is entitled "Works Cited"; in the APA system, it is entitled "References."

This book provides instructions for using both of these systems. The note-bibliography system here is based on *The Chicago Manual of Style*, 14th edition (see pages 142–97). The parenthetical reference systems are (1) Modern Language Association style (see pages 198–212) and (2) American Psychological Association style (see pages 213–28). A section on legal citation, which uses notes only, appears in Appendix B.

Your choice among these systems of documentation might be governed by the conventions of your field of study, the suggestions of your adviser, the requirements of your university, or your personal taste. If you plan to enter a field or profession that uses either MLA or APA style in its journals, you probably will want to begin using that style as soon as possible. You should select a format in the beginning stages of research and follow it consistently throughout the process of preparing your paper.

Purposes of Notes and Parenthetical References

Notes and parenthetical references may serve one or more purposes: to acknowledge indebtedness, to establish the validity of evidence, to indicate cross-references within the paper, to amplify ideas in the text, and to provide additional bibliographical information.

▪ Acknowledging Indebtedness

All material gathered from sources, whether quoted directly or indirectly, requires documentation in a research paper. Information that qualifies as common knowledge (see page 55) does not need to be documented except when it is quoted directly. When the audience for a paper is very specialized, the amount of material that constitutes common knowledge may be greater than it is for a research paper directed to a general audience. The citation of sources, then, sometimes requires making judgments about whether a piece of information is common knowledge and about the degree of your dependence on a source for the information. When you are in doubt about whether to document something, it is wise to do so, particularly in undergraduate papers.

▪ Establishing the Validity of Evidence

Citation of sources of information gives readers a way to establish the accuracy of direct or indirect quotations and to verify the validity of your interpretation and use of sources.

Even if you use a parenthetical reference system, you may occasionally use notes for some kinds of documentation. These notes should be complete in themselves, and they should read as additional information that can be removed without changing the meaning of the text. The paper should read logically and coherently without the notes. Essential ideas and information should be presented in the text; unimportant and peripheral information should be omitted.

▪ Providing Cross-References within the Paper

Notes referring readers to materials in other parts of the paper or in the appendixes can help readers establish the proper relationships among ideas and concepts.

▪ Amplifying Ideas

Informational notes can provide discussion or amplification of points in the text. They should be used only when such discussion cannot be included in the text without interrupting or complicating the development. Material such as technical discussions or definitions, incidental comments, corollaries, additional information, and reconciliation of conflicting views might be presented in an informational note.

An example of an informational note follows:

Informational note

1 Sophocles, _Antigone_, trans. Elizabeth Wyckoff, in _The Complete Greek Tragedies: Sophocles I_, ed. David Green and Richmond Lattimore (Chicago: University of Chicago Press,

```
1954).  The authorship of these lines has long been
disputed, and difference of opinion remains though modern
critics tend to accept them, as did Aristotle.  Bernard Knox
explains the scene as a solitary moment of self-discovery
for Antigone: "She can at last identify the driving force
behind her action, the private, irrational imperative. . . .
It is her fanatical devotion to one particular family, her
own, the doomed, incestuous, accursed house of Oedipus."
Sophocles, The Three Theban Plays, trans. Robert Fagles and
ed. Bernard Knox (New York: Viking, 1982), 33.
```

▪ Providing Additional Bibliography

Bibliographical notes can allow you to mention sources indirectly relevant to your paper that you have not cited yourself but that another researcher might wish to pursue.

An example of a bibliographical note follows:

**Bibliographical
note**

```
     2 For differing explanations of the causes of Mill's
breakdown, see William Albert Levi, "The `Mental Crisis' of
John Stuart Mill," Psychoanalytic Review 23 (1945): 86-101;
John Durham, "The Influence of John Stuart Mill's Mental
Crisis on His Thoughts," American Imago 20 (1963): 369-84.
```

Bibliographies

The concluding section of a research paper, thesis, or dissertation is usually an alphabetical listing of source materials. This list is generally entitled "Bibliography" with note-bibliography format, "Works Cited" with MLA format, and "Reference List" with APA parenthetical documentation. This listing serves several functions. It allows the reader to observe the scope of the research behind the paper or to see if a particular work has been used. When parenthetical documentation is the chosen format, the list of works cited permits a reader to locate full bibliographical information for materials referred to in parenthetical notes. The bibliography may also provide the reader with a foundation for further research.

It is wise to prepare a draft of the bibliography or list of works cited before you begin to write. If you have working bibliography cards written out in the correct form and arranged in alphabetical order, you can easily create a bibliography or list of works cited from them. Having a draft of a bibliography will allow you to make notes or parenthetical references quickly and accurately. For note-bibliography format, you will have all the information you need for first references. For parenthetical documentation, you will be able to make sound judgments about ways of introducing direct and indirect quotations to minimize parenthetical documentation in the text. If, after writing the paper, you find that you have not referred to one or more works, you can eliminate them from your list of works cited before typing the final copy.

▪ Alphabetization of Entries

Entries in a bibliography and works cited list are alphabetized by the last name of the author or the first word, excluding articles, of a group or corporate author. An entry for which the author is unknown, such as a newspaper article or unsigned review, is alphabetized by the first word of the title, excluding *A*, *An*, and *The*. The entry for an anonymous work is alphabetized by the first word of the title, excluding articles. *Anonymous* is never used as an author entry. Letter-by-letter alphabetizing is generally preferred to word-by-word alphabetizing for research papers and dissertations. (See page 10 for an explanation of the difference between word-by-word and letter-by-letter systems of alphabetization.) The following list shows letter-by-letter alphabetizing:

```
Barzun, Jacques.  The Modern Researcher . . .


Bazerman, Charles.  The Informed Writer . . .


"Breakdown in Communication" . . .


Break of Day


Business Books in Print . . .


"Businesses Tighten Accounting Procedures" . . .


"The Businesswoman and the Corporation" . . .
```

The entry for a work by two or more authors is alphabetized by the surname of the author who is listed first on the title page, regardless of whether the names on the title page are in alphabetical order.

```
Smith, B. Othanel, William O. Stanley, and J. Harlan Shores.
     Fundamentals of Curriculum Development.  2nd ed. . . .
```

▪ Referring to More Than One Work

When you have two or more works by the same author, entries after the first begin with three hyphens positioned flush with the left margin and followed by a period and two spaces.

```
Burke, Kenneth.  A Grammar of Motives.  Englewood Cliffs:
     Prentice-Hall, 1954.


---.  A Rhetoric of Motives.  Englewood Cliffs: Prentice-
     Hall, 1950.
```

The hyphens stand for the same author or authors named in the preceding entry. If the person named served as editor, translator, or compiler, place a comma and the appropriate abbreviation after the hyphens. When an author listed alone is listed later as a coauthor, you must spell out the full author entry.

An author entry precedes an entry for the same person as an editor, which precedes an entry for the same person as a coeditor or coauthor.

```
Good, Carter V.  The Basics of Research in Education.  N.p.:
     Hill, 1960.


---.  Essentials of Educational Research.  New York:
     Appleton-Century-Crofts, 1966.


---, ed.  Dictionary of Education.  3rd ed.  New York:
     McGraw-Hill, 1973.


Good, Carter V., and Douglas E. Scates.  Methods of
     Research.  New York: Appleton-Century-Crofts, 1954.
```

APA style   APA lists the name of the author in every entry.

```
Good, C. V. (1960).  The Basics of Research in Education.
     N.p.: Hill.


Good, C. V. (1966).  Essentials of Educational Research.
     New York: Appleton-Century-Crofts.


Good, C. V., ed. (1973).  Dictionary of Education.  3rd ed.
     New York: McGraw-Hill.


Good, C. V., & Scates, D. E. (1954).  Methods of Research.
     New York: Appleton-Century-Crofts.
```

▪ Types of Bibliographies

A bibliography may be one of several types, depending on the requirements of the assignment or the logic of the subject. The type most frequently required for both undergraduate and graduate research papers is a list of the works cited. Another type of bibliography goes beyond works actually cited in a paper and includes all the works used in preparation for writing the paper. (Such a list is titled "Works Consulted" or "Bibliography.") A third type, a comprehensive compilation of works on a subject (entitled "Bibliography"), may be desirable for some subjects. Finally, there is the annotated bibliography—each entry is accompanied by a short descriptive or evaluative statement—which assesses the nature or value of the material (see sample on page 36).

You may wish to classify the entries in a long bibliography according to one of these categories: form of publication; subject or chapters of the paper;

or primary and secondary sources. Lists of works cited should not be divided. Short research papers and reports usually do not require classified bibliographies.

Classification by form of publication

Grouping references according to their form of publication often facilitates the use of a bibliography; for example, books may be listed in one group, periodicals in a second group, and government publications in still another. A general guideline for this sort of classification is to divide bibliographies of more than thirty entries, to divide bibliographies of twenty to thirty items only if the nature or variety of the entries warrants classification, and to use a single alphabetical listing for fewer than twenty entries.

Classification by subject or chapter

A bibliography may also be divided by subject or chapter. A study of the history of religious education in the United States might have bibliography entries grouped by denominations or by period, such as decades or centuries.

Classification by primary and secondary sources

The distinction between primary sources and secondary sources is often used as a basis of classification, especially in the humanities and social sciences (see page 37 for a sample). The distinction is an important one in investigations that rely on documents. Original documents and accounts, or exact copies of them, are generally superior to secondary sources in satisfying criteria of scholarship. Furthermore, a writer reflects a standard of scholarship in making an accurate distinction between the two kinds of sources in the bibliographical listing. The writer of the history of a university, for example, might want to distinguish between primary sources (such as minutes of meetings, university catalogs, financial records, and students' diaries) and secondary sources (such as previous historical accounts).

When you have decided which of the three systems of documentation you will use, turn to the appropriate chapter.

7 *Chicago Manual* Style

This chapter presents a note-bibliography system based on *The Chicago Manual of Style,* 14th edition. Readers of the last edition of *Form and Style* will notice some minor changes in the entries, many of which have been occasioned by publication of the 14th edition of *The Chicago Manual of Style,* 1993.

Endnotes and Footnotes

The citation of a source in the note-bibliography system is indicated in the text with a superscript (raised number), which refers to a note providing information about the source. The notes are called *footnotes* when they appear at the bottom of the page and *endnotes* when they are collected in a section at the end of each chapter or at the end of the entire paper. Dissertations to be microfilmed should have footnotes, because turning back to endnotes on a microfilm reader can be distracting. Most other papers have endnotes.

■ Designation of Notes in the Text

A note is indicated in the text by a raised arabic numeral. The superscript should be raised one-half space (never a full space) above the line and should be placed directly after the material (without a space) for which the corresponding note provides the source. The best placement of the number is at the end of a sentence or, if that would cause confusion or inaccuracy, at the end of a clause. The number goes outside all punctuation except the dash, and it should not be underlined, circled, or followed by a period. The examples given below demonstrate correct and incorrect placement of the superscript.

Correct Mina P. Shaughnessy points out that "the beginning writer

does not know how writers behave."[1]

Incorrect Mina P. Shaughnessy[1] points out . . . .

Incorrect Mina P. Shaughnessy points out that "the beginning writer

does not know how writers behave."[1]

Correct Mina P. Shaughnessy speculated that the inexperienced writer

is handicapped by lack of knowledge about the process of

writing.[1]

Correct "The beginning writer does not know how writers behave"[1]--

all of the research points to this conclusion.

Numbering of notes Both endnotes and footnotes are usually numbered consecutively within a chapter, starting at number one in each new chapter. Some institutions recommend beginning the numbering afresh on each page when footnotes are used or numbering throughout the entire thesis when endnotes are used.

See Chapter 5 for the placement and numbering of notes in figures and tables.

■ First Reference and Subsequent Reference

First reference The first time you cite a source in the notes give a complete entry in the correct format for the bibliographical style you are using throughout the paper. For a book, a complete entry includes the following information (if applicable): complete name of the author; title of the book; editor,

---

[1]Mina P. Shaughnessy, *Errors and Expectations: A Guide for the Teacher of Basic Writing* (New York: Oxford University Press, 1977), 79.

compiler, or translator; series and number; edition (other than first); number of volumes; city and state of publication; publisher; date of publication; volume number; page number(s). For an article in a periodical, a complete entry usually includes the following: complete name of the author; title of the article; name of the periodical; volume and/or number of the issue; date; page number(s). (See the first-reference forms for numerous types of sources on the "Footnotes and Endnotes" pages, the even-numbered pages from 170 through 196.)

Subsequent reference   After the first complete reference note, you should use a shortened format for subsequent references to the same work. In most cases, the last name of the author and the page number serve to identify the work. When you have more than one work by the same author, you will need to use the author's name, the title (abbreviated if it is lengthy) of the work, and the page number, as the examples below illustrate. Subsequent reference notes should provide enough information to allow the reader to locate the original note or the bibliography entry, but they should not be longer than necessary.

LAST NAME OF THE AUTHOR   Subsequent references in the note-bibliography system usually consist of the last name of the author, the page number(s), and any other information required for identification of the source.

[2] Leonard Shatzkin, In Cold Type: Overcoming the Book Crisis (Boston: Houghton Mifflin, 1982), 45.

[3] Benjamin Woolley, Virtual Worlds: A Journey in Hype and Hyperreality (Cambridge, England: Blackwell, 1992), 100.

[4] Shatzkin, 45-47.

[5] Woolley, 81.

[6] Shatzkin, 45.

Subsequent references to work without author   When an article or book does not have a named author, the subsequent reference includes the title of the article or book (shortened when the title is long) and the page number(s).

Shortening titles   Shortened titles should include significant identifying words. Abbreviations should not be used, and the original word order should not be changed. *Chicago Manual* does not advise shortening a title of fewer than five words except for the omission of an initial article. Subtitles should always be omitted in subsequent references.

ORIGINAL TITLE	**SHORTENED VERSION**
Teaching and Learning English as a Foreign Language	Teaching and Learning English
When Literacy Empowers: Navajo Language in Print	When Literacy Empowers

First reference   [7] "Student-built Shelter Used in Hurricane Relief," Chronicle of Higher Education, 14 Oct. 1992, A5.

Intervening note   [8] Morgan, 14.

Subsequent reference

9 "Student-built Shelter," A5.

Subsequent references to more than one work by an author

When more than one work by an author is cited, each subsequent reference must include not only the name of the author, but also the title of the article or book (again, shortened when the title is long).

First references

10 Václav Havel, Keeping the Faith: Summer Meditations (New York: Knopf, 1990), 15.

11 Václav Havel, Living in Truth (New York: Knopf, 1987), 43.

Subsequent references

12 Havel, Keeping the Faith, 43.

13 Havel, Living in Truth, 72.

Subsequent references to work with more than one author

For a work with multiple authors, give the last names of up to three authors. When a work has four or more authors, give the name of the first author followed by *et al.* (the abbreviation for *et alii*, "and others").

First reference

14 Cleanth Brooks and Robert Penn Warren, Modern Rhetoric, 4th ed. (New York: Harcourt, 1979), 56.

Subsequent reference

15 Brooks and Warren, 89.

First reference

16 Janice M. Lauer et al., Four Worlds of Writing (New York: Harper and Row, 1981), 77.

(The book has four authors.)

Subsequent reference

17 Lauer et al., 80.

Authors with the same last name

When you have more than one author with the same last name, include first names or initials in subsequent references:

First references

18 Helen C. White, The Mysticism of William Blake (New York: Russell, 1964), 75.

19 E. B. White, Charlotte's Web (New York: Harper, 1952), 67.

Subsequent references

20 Helen C. White, 77.

21 E. B. White, 95.

Works with name of editor, compiler, or translator in place of name of author

Some works have the name of an editor, compiler, or translator in place of the name of an author. In subsequent references, you should list the name or names of an editor, compiler, or translator without the accompanying abbreviation *ed.*, *comp.*, or *trans.*), which should appear in the bibliography:

First reference

22 Henry Brandon, ed., In Search of a New World Order: The Future of U.S.-European Relations (Washington, D.C.: Brookings, 1992), 231.

Subsequent reference

²³ Brandon, 17.

Text

Many of the articles in Research on Composing advocate further exploration of the motivation for writing.²⁴

First reference

²⁴ Charles R. Cooper and Lee Odell, eds. Research on Composing: Points of Departure (Urbana: NCTE, 1978), xi-xviii.

Subsequent reference

²⁵ Cooper and Odell, xi-xviii.

Multivolume works

If a multivolume work has one general title, each subsequent citation must include the volume number:

First reference

²⁶ Gerhard von Rad, Old Testament Theology, trans. D. M. G. Stalker, 2 vols. (New York: Harper and Row, 1962-65).

(This initial citation refers to the complete work rather than to any specific page within a volume.)

Subsequent reference

²⁷ Rad, 1:76.

(This citation refers to material on page 76 of volume 1.)

When each volume in a multivolume work has a separate title, however, the title of the volume serves as identification:

²⁸ James C. Crutchfield, ed., The Fisheries: Problems in Resource Management, vol. 1 of Studies on Public Policy Issues in Resource Management (Seattle: University of Washington Press, 1965), 61.

²⁹ Crutchfield, Fisheries, 62.

Indirect citation

A note should indicate the source to which you are indebted for a piece of information, whether the source is primary (the original work, document, or manuscript) or secondary (a quoted excerpt or paraphrase of one source in another work). Your authority is the work you actually consulted, and that work should be cited in the notes and in the bibliography. Try to work from original sources whenever possible and appropriate, but if the original source is not available and you must quote from another, you must indicate the secondary nature of the reference. This kind of note provides an honest statement of the nature and scope of your research; should the secondary work have misquoted or misrepresented the original, you account for the sources of your error.

Depending on whether the emphasis in your text is on the cited source or the original source of the material, an indirect citation may take one of two forms, as is illustrated below for a reference to material from Matthew Josephson that the writer located in a work by Ron Chernow.

Emphasis on the cited source

³⁰ Ron Chernow, The House of Morgan (New York: Simon & Schuster, Touchstone, 1990), 47, citing [or quoting] Matthew Josephson, The Robber Barons (New York: Harcourt, Brace, 1934), 338.

Emphasis on the original source

³¹ Matthew Josephson, The Robber Barons (New York: Harcourt, Brace, 1934, 338, cited [or quoted] in Ron Chernow, The House of Morgan (New York: Simon & Schuster, Touchstone, 1990), 47.

Only the work you actually consulted appears in the bibliography.

MULTIPLE NOTES   When you wish to list more than one source for a sentence, you may wish to use a multiple note. Each part of the note should take the appropriate form for either the first or subsequent reference: the two forms may be used together in one note. Separate each reference in the series with a semicolon.

³² David Bromwich, Politics by Other Means: Higher Education and Group Thinking (New Haven: Yale University Press, 1993), 45; Smith, ibid., 17; Francis Oakley, Community of Learning: The American College and the Liberal Arts Tradition (London: Oxford University Press, 1993), 57–62.

LATIN ABBREVIATIONS   Latin abbreviations for subsequent references are now rarely used, and they should not be used at all with MLA and APA systems.

Ibid.   In consecutive references to the same source, the abbreviation *ibid.* ("in the same place"), the only Latin abbreviation acceptable for bibliographical information, may be used to avoid repetition. If the second reference is to the same page as the initial reference, *ibid.* is used alone. It may also be used with a page number, to indicate a different page in the same source.

³³ Robert C. Solomon, Ethics and Excellence (Oxford: Oxford University Press, 1992), 179.

³⁴ Ibid.

³⁵ Ibid., 100.

Ibid. may be used to refer to a second article by the same author in the same book or issue of a periodical, but not to a different book by the same author. The following examples illustrate references to two contributions by the same author to a book of readings.

³⁶ John Drury, "Luke," in The Literary Guide to the Bible, ed. Robert Alter and Frank Kermode (Cambridge: Harvard University Press), 418.

³⁷ Drury, "Mark," ibid., 402.

Ibid. should not be used to refer to a work in an immediately preceding multiple note, and in footnotes *ibid.* should not be used more than two pages after the original citation. Most writers who do use the Latin forms treat them as Anglicized words and therefore do not underline them to indicate italics; previously, these abbreviations were italicized.

TITLE ONLY: WORKS OF LITERATURE   Although the first reference to a work of literature gives full details on the author, title, and facts of publication, subsequent references may be considerably abbreviated, sometimes leaving out the name of the author and shortening the title of the work when it is well known. Abbreviations should be used to designate the parts of a literary work: volume (vol.), part (pt.), number (no.), numbers (nos.), book (bk.), chapter (chap.). No abbreviation for lines should be used.

³⁸ John Milton, <u>Paradise Lost</u>, ed. Merritt Y. Hughes (New York: Odyssey, 1962), bk. 9, lines 342–75.

Abbreviated references After you have indicated the kinds of sections to which your numbers refer, as is done in note 28 with *bk.* and *lines,* you may omit the designations in following citations. Subsequent references to well-known works need not include the author's name:

³⁹ <u>Paradise Lost</u> 3.1–55.

Citations for a play should include the numbers of acts, scenes, and lines in arabic numerals. These numerals should be separated by periods without spacing:

⁴⁰ <u>Othello</u> 3.2.1–5.

You may wish to shorten the title even further. See the *MLA Handbook* for acceptable abbreviations of the works of Shakespeare and Chaucer.

⁴¹ <u>Oth</u>. 3.2.1–5.

Subsequent references to less well known works of literature may include the last name of the author (particularly for audiences outside the field of literature or in the case of obscure works). If the reader will understand the reference, subsequent citations may be reduced to a shortened version of the title and designation of the sections:

⁴² Robert Browning, "Soliloquy of the Spanish Cloister," in <u>The Norton Anthology of English Literature</u>, ed. M. H. Abrams et al., 4th ed. (New York: Norton, 1986), stanza 4, lines 25–32.

⁴³ Browning, "Soliloquy" 7.49–52.

or

⁴⁴ "Soliloquy" 7.49–52.

When a work has other types of divisions or when the meaning of a sequence of numbers might not be clear, an explanatory note identifying each element of a citation allows you to abbreviate the note in subsequent references:

⁴⁵ Jane Austen, <u>Emma</u>, ed. Stephen M. Parrish (New York: Norton, 1972). Subsequent references to this edition will appear as <u>E</u>. The first number of each citation refers to

the volume, the second to the chapter, and the third to the page.

> ⁴⁶ E 2.12.75.

Even when a page number would suffice to identify a passage, you should try to designate passages in works of literature by names and numbers of sections because readers often use many different editions of widely reprinted works.

Sacred writing References to the Bible and other sacred writings begin with the particular chapter or book you wish to cite. The version or translation appears only in the bibliographical entry (see page 185). Titles of the books of the Bible should be abbreviated; chapters and verses are expressed in arabic numerals separated by a colon without spacing. See *The Chicago Manual of Style* or the *MLA Handbook* for accepted abbreviations of books of the Bible.

> ⁴⁷ 1 Sam. 14:6-9.

Classical works Refer to classical works by title and main divisions—volume, book, chapter, pages, sections, or lines, as appropriate—in subsequent references. Numerals should be separated by periods without spacing. The initial citation must name the translator and editor. This is important information about any work, but it is essential for classical works, where the translator's task can involve restoring the text or applying new theories about the meaning of particular words.

First reference
> ⁴⁸ Aristotle, Poetics, trans. S. H. Butcher, ed. Francis Fergusson (New York: Hill and Wang, 1961), bk. 7, chap. 2.

Subsequent references to the classics omit the name of the author:

> ⁴⁹ Poetics 8.1.

PARENTHETICAL REFERENCES IN THE TEXT Even when you have chosen the note-bibliography format, you may wish to use some parenthetical references, particularly when, as in a paper on literature, you have multiple references to the same work. Parenthetical references should consist of short entries giving the last name of the author (or an abbreviated title), followed by a comma when the author's name is used, and the page number(s). Final punctuation follows the parentheses.

First reference
In 1680 the Pueblo Indians rebelled swiftly and ferociously. In just a few weeks they accomplished what no other Indians were able to do: they drove the invaders from their land, decisively and completely.⁵⁰

> ⁵⁰ Alvin M. Josephy, Jr., The Patriot Chiefs (1961; reprint, New York: Viking, 1969), 65-66.

Subsequent reference

The subsequent reference may appear in the text:

```
The guiding force and catalyst in the revolt was an

Indian medicine doctor who had been denied the right to

conduct his rituals (Josephy, 87).
```

After the first reference, information such as act, scene, and line; part, verse, and line; and book, chapter, and page number may be included in parentheses after the quotation, whether it is run in or set off. When such a parenthetical reference follows a direct quotation, the punctuation for the sentence follows the parentheses. Particularly in a paper involving several works by one author, abbreviations may be substituted for the title:

```
Indeed, the truth about Jim's affair is so elusive

that even after innumerable evenings spent spinning out

the story on verandahs all over the Pacific, Marlow knows

that "the last word is not said--probably shall never be

said" (LJ 137).
```

(After the edition is cited in the first reference, the novel *Lord Jim* is indicated in subsequent parenthetical references with the abbreviation *LJ*.)

When the quotation is set off, the parenthetical reference appears after the period marking the end of the quotation, without a subsequent period.

```
Marlow mocks Jim's self-assurance:

      The tumult and the menace of wind and sea now appeared
      very contemptible to Jim, increasing the regret of his
      awe at their inefficient menace.  Now he knew what to
      think of it.  It seemed to him he cared nothing for
      the gale.  He could affront greater perils.  (LJ 6)
```

Bibliographies

Three categories of information are needed for each bibliography entry: author, title, and facts of publication. Each of these categories may contain more than one piece of information. A book may have more than one author, and the facts of publication for some materials may be complicated. A period follows each category of information in a bibliography entry—that is, a period follows the author's name, the title, and the facts of publication. Because an entry in a bibliography (unlike an entry in a note) refers to the complete work rather than to a specific passage, a bibliography entry does not include page numbers. A bibliography entry for an article lists the inclusive pages of the entire article rather than the specific pages from which material was selected for citation. (See pages 138–41.)

▪ Books

The author category for a book may include one or more authors, editors, compilers, and translators, or a corporate author or institution. The title category includes the title and subtitle. The facts of publication category identifies the series in which the work appears, the number of volumes in a multivolume work or the particular number of a volume, the edition if it is other than the first, the city of publication (the state is generally omitted), the name of the publisher, and the year of publication.

The basic form of a bibliography entry for a book reads as follows:

Basic bibliography form

Henderson, Hazel. _Paradigms in Progress: Life beyond Economics_. Indianapolis: Knowledge Systems, 1992.

Notice that periods mark the end of the author, title, and facts of publication sections. Two spaces follow each period; one space follows commas and colons. Be careful to insert only one space after each colon (old styles required two spaces).

NAME OF AUTHOR In a bibliography entry, the name of the author appears with the last name first for purposes of alphabetization. When there are two or three authors, the names are listed in the order in which they appear on the title page, whether or not that order is alphabetical. Only the name of the first author appears in inverted order. A comma separates the first name of the first author from succeeding names:

Two (or three) authors

Simonds, Wendy, and Barbara Katz Rothman. _Centuries of Solace: Grief in Popular Literature_. Philadelphia: Temple University Press, 1992.

More than three authors

If a book has more than three authors, list each of their names in the bibliography:

McPherson, William, Stephen Lehmann, Craig Likness, and Marcia Pankake. _English and American Literature: Sources and Strategies for Collection Development_. Chicago: American Library Association, 1987.

In the note form, use only the name of the author listed first on the title page, followed by _et al_.

Two authors with same last name

When two authors have the same last name, the name should be repeated:

Price, Richard, and Sally Price. _Equatoria_. New York: Routledge, 1992.

Pseudonyms

When an author's name as given on the title page is a pseudonym (pen name), the bibliography entry begins with the pseudonym and continues with the author's real name in brackets. If the author's real name is unknown, the abbreviation _pseud._ within brackets follows the name.

Green, Hannah [Joanne Greenberg]. _I Never Promised You a Rose Garden_. New York: Holt, Rinehart and Winston, 1964.

Well-known pseudonyms, such as George Eliot and Mark Twain, do not require the insertion of the writer's real name.

Anonymous works

When no author's name appears on a work or when the title page lists *Anonymous* as the author, the work is listed in the bibliography by title alone. If the author's name is known, it may be put in brackets and the work may be listed in the bibliography under the author's name. *Anonymous* is not used as an author entry.

[Scarborough, Dorothy]. The Wind. New York: Harper, 1925.

or

The Wind. New York: Harper, 1925.

Group or corporation as author

When the author is a group or corporation, the publication is listed under the name of the organization:

Bicycling Magazine. Reconditioning the Bicycle. New York: Rodale, 1989.

When the corporate author is also the publisher, the name does not need to be repeated with the other facts of publication:

Metropolitan Musem of Art. Guide to the Metropolitan Museum of Art. 4th ed. New York, 1987.

Edited volume or compilation

Compilations, or books consisting of discrete selections by one or more authors, may be listed either by the editor or compiler or by the author of an individual article. References to the book as a whole place the name of the compiler or editor first, with the abbreviation *comp.* or *ed.*, as appropriate.

Baum, Robert, ed. Reform and Reaction in Post-Mao China: The Road through Tiananmen. New York: Routledge, 1992.

Emphasis on author of one article

When you want to emphasize an article or chapter in the collection, place the name of the author of the article or chapter first.

Burghardt, Gordon M. "On the Origins of Play." In Play in Animals and Humans, ed. Peter K. Smith, 5-42. Oxford: Basil Blackwell, 1984.

Compilation of material previously published elsewhere

When a compilation consists of material previously published elsewhere, a complete entry gives the original facts of publication as well as the information concerning the compilation.

Ten, C. L. "Mill on Self-Regarding Actions." In John Stuart Mill, On Liberty, ed. David Spitz, 238-46. Norton Critical Edition. New York: Norton, 1972. Originally published in Philosophy 43 (1968): 29-37.

When a compilation reprints an article under a title different from the original title, indicate that the title has been changed or another title added in the later collection.

Langer, Suzanne. "The Great Dramatic Forms: The Comic
    Rhythm." In Comedy: Plays, Theory, and Criticism,
    ed. Marvin Feldheim, 241-53. New York: Harcourt, 1962.
    Originally published as a chapter of Feeling and Form.
    New York: Scribner's, 1953.

In the note form, you need cite only the edition you actually used.

Emphasis on writer of introduction

When you want to cite the introduction or foreword to a book in your bibliography, place the name of the author of this section first.

David H. Rosen. Introduction to Integrity in Depth, by John
    Beebe. College Station: Texas A&M University Press,
    1992.

Translation or edition of work

When a work has been translated or edited by a person other than the author, you must decide under which name you should alphabetize the work. If the emphasis of your investigation or analysis is on the author, the author's name precedes the title and a period follows the title. The appropriate abbreviation and one or more names to indicate compiler, editor, or translator follow. Use *comp.* (compiled by), *ed.* (edited by), and *trans.* (translated by).

Appelfeld, Aharon. Katerina. Trans. Jeffrey Green. New
    York: Random House, 1992.

Emphasis on editor or translator

If the emphasis in your research is on the work of the editor or translator, that name, followed by a comma, the appropriate abbreviation, and a period, precedes the title. The names of the author and the title form a unit: the author's name follows the title in the first name–last name order preceded by a comma, one space, and the word *by*.

Jeffrey Green, trans. Katerina, by Aharon Appelfeld. New
    York: Random House, 1992.

When a bibliography entry begins with three or more editors, compilers, or translators, follow the rules for works with three or more authors. The plural form of the appropriate abbreviation (*eds.*, *comps.*, *trans.*) follows the names.

TITLE The title of a book should appear in the bibliography exactly as it is on the title page. Capitalization, however, may be changed to conform to principles outlined in Chapter 4 or in any style sheet you use. Any subtitle should be separated from the main title by a colon followed by one space. In notes the subtitle is optional, but it must appear in the bibliography entry. The full title should be underlined.

McCannell, Dean. Empty Meeting Grounds: The Tourist Papers.
    New York: Routledge, 1992.

Titles of articles or chapters within a book should be placed within double quotation marks. Names of series and manuscript collections are not underlined.

Edition other than the first

When the edition you use is not the first, the number of the edition, as well as its date of publication, should be provided. Unless you have a particular reason for using an earlier edition, refer to the latest edition of a work. Additional editions may have a variety of designations, such as *2nd rev. ed.* (second revised edition), or *3rd enl. and rev. ed.* (third enlarged and revised edition), and these should be recorded as they appear on the title page. Ordinal numbers are used to designate editions: *2nd, 3rd, 4th*, and so on.

Trimmer, Joseph F. Writing with a Purpose. 10th ed.
     Boston: Houghton Mifflin, 1992.

Previously published with another title

If a book was previously published with another title, whether a different title in English or a title in a foreign language, you may give the original title within parentheses. In the following example, the French title is included because it differs considerably from the title chosen for the English translation:

Foucault, Michel. The Order of Things: An Archaeology of
     the Human Sciences (Les mots et les choses). New
     York: Vintage, 1973.

(Words in the original title are capitalized according to rules for titles in French.)

FACTS OF PUBLICATION   The facts of publication are the place of publication, the name of the publishing house, and the date of publication. The city name alone (without the state name) serves as the place of publication except when it might be confused with another city of the same name. When a publisher lists several cities, select the first as the place of publication. When a book is published simultaneously by two companies, name either the first publisher mentioned on the title page or both publishers, separating the names with a semicolon.

Shortening the name of the publisher

The name of the publisher may be shortened as long as its identity remains clear. Abbreviations such as *Inc., Co.,* and *Ltd.* and an initial *The* should be omitted. *The Chicago Manual* preserves the rest of the name, as in *Holt, Rinehart and Winston* and *University* (or *Univ.*) *of Chicago Press.*
You should decide on a policy for shortening names of publishers and use it consistently throughout your paper. When you cannot find an unambiguous or widely accepted way to shorten a name, it is best to write out the full name.

Date of publication

The date of publication for any work other than an article in a periodical is the year alone, without the month or day. This date generally appears on the title page or on the copyright page. When various printings are listed, the date of the first printing is used in the bibliography or list of works cited. A printing is a press run of a book. An edition is a new version of a text. The most recent edition of a book should be cited unless there is some reason to cite a previous edition.

When the publisher is a division of a publishing company, that information should appear in the entry. In the following entry, Basic Books is a division of HarperCollins.

Bell, Derrick. Faces at the Bottom of the Well: The
     Permanence of Racism. New York: HarperCollins, Basic
     Books, 1992.

Work out of print An entry for a work that was out of print but has been republished should indicate the original date of publication and the fact that the work is a reprint.

```
Markham, Beryl. West with the Night. 1942. Reprint,
     Berkeley: North Point Press, 1983.
```

Paperbound editions When a paperbound book is an original edition, it is listed just as any other book would be.

```
Van Ness, Peter H. Spirituality, Diversion, and Decadence:
     The Contemporary Predicament. Binghamton: State
     University of New York Press, 1992.
```

When a paperbound book is a reprint of the original hardcover edition, the entry indicates the date of publication of the hardcover edition. This information generally appears on the copyright page of the paperbound book.

```
Gaines, Ernest J. In My Father's House. 1978. Reprint,
     New York: Vintage Contemporaries, 1992.
```

Missing information When you cannot locate one or more pieces of information concerning publication, you should use one of the following abbreviations in the appropriate place in the entry:

No place: n.p.
No publisher: n.p.
No date: n.d.
No page: n.pag. *or* unpaginated

Capitalize the abbreviation only when it begins a section of the entry.

```
Eliot, George. Felix Holt. Edinburgh: William Blackwood,
     n.d.
```

```
Eliot, George. Felix Holt. N.p.: William Blackwood, n.d.
```

▪ Multivolume Works and Series

A multivolume work consists of two or more volumes under one general title. Each separate volume may either have its own title or be identified by volume number only.

Reference to complete multivolume work When you wish to refer to a complete multivolume work rather than to any specific volume, the bibliography entry should include the total number of volumes and the inclusive dates of publication, if applicable.

```
Bowsky, William M., ed. Studies in Medieval and Renaissance
     History. 4 vols. Lincoln: University of Nebraska
     Press, 1963-67.
```

The entry for the date indicates that the first volume was published in 1963 and the fourth volume in 1967. It is not necessary to specify intermediate dates. Your note or parenthetical reference will specify the particular volume cited in each instance.

Reference to volume with individual title

When each volume in a multivolume work has an individual title, the entry takes the following form:

```
Freehling, William W.  The Road to Disunion.  Vol. 1 of
     Secessionists at Bay, 1776-1854.  New York: Oxford
     University Press, 1992.
```

Independent works in a series

A series consists of works independent of each other but numbered as belonging to a particular series. The name of the series follows the title and is not underlined.

```
Eiser, J. Richard, ed.  Attitudinal Judgment.  Springer
     Series in Social Psychology, no. 11.  New York and
     Berlin: Springer-Verlag, 1990.
```

■ Periodicals

Any publication that comes out at regular intervals is a periodical. Periodicals for an academic or professional audience are usually called *journals*; periodicals intended for the general public are often called *magazines*. The bibliography entry for periodicals includes the author's complete name, the title of the article, and the facts of publication, which include the name of the periodical, the number of the volume, the date of the volume or the issue number, and the inclusive page numbers for the entire article. (See Chapter 4 for rules regarding inclusive page numbers.)

JOURNALS   Most journals paginate continuously through each volume; that is, each issue continues the numbering of the previous issue rather than beginning anew with page 1. Two spaces follow the author and title entries; one space separates the elements of the facts of publication section. The basic format for an entry referring to such a continuously paginated journal is the following:

Basic form for periodical article

```
Gingrich, Owen.  "Astronomy in the Age of Columbus."
     Scientific American 267 (Nov. 1992): 100-05.
```

Anonymous periodical article

```
"Distant Deposits Hint at Huge Eruption."  Science News 142
     (17 Oct. 1992): 260.
```

Abbreviations

When the season or month of the issue is necessary for identification, as in a journal that does not use issue numbers and begins new pagination with each issue, or when you wish to indicate the month or season, that information should precede the date within the parentheses. Months should be abbreviated as follows: *Jan., Feb., Mar., Apr., Aug., Sept., Oct., Nov.,* and *Dec.* The months May, June, and July are not abbreviated. Some journals use seasons to identify the volume. Seasons (fall or autumn, winter, spring, summer) should not be abbreviated or capitalized (previously *Chicago Manual* did capitalize the seasons in documentation).

In some fields, abbreviations for titles of periodicals are used. If you want to use such abbreviations, follow an authoritative source as a guide to acceptable forms. Many indexes, such as the *Applied Science and Technology Index*, the *Cumulated Index Medicus*, the *Education Index*, the *MLA International Bibliography*, and the *Music Index*, contain glossaries of journal abbreviations used in their compilations.

When a journal begins each issue in a volume with page 1, you need to include the number of the issue, as follows:

Gardner, Thomas. "An Interview with Jorie Graham." <u>Denver Quarterly</u> 26, no. 4 (spring 1992): 79-104.

Designation of series Include a series number or designation in citing periodicals that have been published in more than one series. *Old series* or *original series* is indicated by o.s.; *new series* is identified by n.s. Numbered series are indicated by ordinal numbers, for example, 3rd ser., preceding the volume number.

Dwork, Bernard M. "On the Zeta Function of a Hypersurface." <u>Annals of Mathematics</u>, 2nd ser., 83 (1966): 518-19.

Quotation within titles When double quotation marks appear within the title of an article, they should be changed to single quotation marks.

Sanders, Charles. "'The Waste Land': The Last Minstrel Show?" <u>Journal of Modern Literature</u> 8 (1980): 23-28.

When another mark of punctuation, such as the question mark in the example above, comes at the end of the title, it takes the place of the period.

MAGAZINES Issues of magazines are most often identified by date only, even when they have volume numbers. Page numbers are separated from the date by a comma (rather than a colon, as in journal entries). When magazine articles run on discontinuous pages, enter the page numbers on which the article actually appears, as in the Kinoshita entry below: 38–45, 50, 53–57, for an article that begins on page 38 and ends on page 57 but is interrupted by other material. A comma between page numbers indicates discontinuous pagination. An alternative for indicating discontinuous pages is to cite the first and final pages only, just as one would in continuous pagination.

Kinoshita, June. "The Mapping of the Mind." <u>New York Times Magazine</u>, 18 Oct. 1992, 44-46, 48, 50, 52, 54. (*or* 44-54.)

Kleppner, Daniel. "About Benjamin Thompson." <u>Physics Today</u>, Sept. 1992, 9-10.

"The Bard of Betrayal." <u>Observer Magazine</u>, 27 Sept. 1992, 44-46.

When a magazine article is included in a section with a title, include that title after the name of the article.

"Drummer." The Talk of the Town. <u>New Yorker</u>, 27 Oct. 1980, 45.

NEWSPAPERS   The bibliography entry for a newspaper should include the name of the author (if available), the title of the article (headline) in quotation marks, and the name of the newspaper underlined.

Basic entry   Rasky, Susan F. "Senate Calls for Revisions in New Tax for Health Care." <u>New York Times</u>, 8 June 1989, A20.

Section numbers   When a newspaper has more than one section, enter the number or the letter of the section along with the page number. When the section carries a number, use the abbreviation *sec.* When a page number follows a section number, insert the abbreviation *p.* or *pp.* for *page* or *pages* to avoid confusion. (See examples below.)

Interpolation of city and state   If the name of the newspaper does not indicate its place of publication, the name of the city, state, or nation must be interpolated in brackets before or after the title. Nationally circulated newspapers, such as the *Christian Science Monitor,* do not require the addition of the place of publication.

State interpolated   "Unknown Author of Wind Answers Crane Criticism." <u>Sweetwater (Texas) Daily Reporter</u>, 15 Dec. 1925, 6.

City interpolated   <u>Observer</u> (London), 17 Oct. 1990, sec. 2, pp. 5, 8.

(When the name of the city or state is added after the title, it is not italicized.)

More than one edition   If a newspaper prints more than one edition (for example, the late city edition, the Long Island edition), the edition cited is designated after the date.

Green, Wayne E. "Cold-Fusion Development Spurs Hot Race for Patents." <u>Wall Street Journal</u>, 9 June 1989, eastern ed., B1.

Special types of articles   Editorials and other special classes of articles should be designated.

"Potomac Yard Decision." Editorial. <u>Washington Post</u>, 16 Oct. 1992, A24.

Lightfoot, Frederick S. Letter. <u>New York Times</u>, 21 Oct. 1992, A22.

BOOK REVIEWS   An entry for a book review begins with the name of the reviewer, includes the title (if any) of the review, gives the name of the author and the work being reviewed, and ends with the name of the periodical in which the review appeared, together with the volume number (if applicable), date, and page(s). If the review is unsigned and untitled, the entry begins with *Review* or *Rev.* Examples of three types of review entries follow.

Moore, Walter. "Great Physicist, Great Guy." Review of
<u>Genius: The Life and Science of Richard Feynman</u>, by
James Gleick. <u>New York Times Book Review</u>, 11 Oct.
1992, 3.

Lott, Robert E. Review of <u>Emilia Pardo Bazán</u>, by Walter T.
Pattison. <u>Symposium</u> 28 (1974): 382.

Review of <u>Married to Genius</u>, by Jeffrey Meyers. <u>Journal of
Modern Literature</u> 7 (1979): 579-80.

▪ Works of Literature

The bibliography entry for a book-length work of literature should
follow the principles of creating an entry for a book. For a short work
included in a book or periodical, the entry follows the form for an article in
a collection.

Basic form When the entry refers to the work in an edition without editing or
commentary, the basic form for a book is used.

Tan, Amy. <u>The Joy Luck Club</u>. New York: Ballantine, Ivy,
1989.

When the entry refers to a particular edition or translation of a work,
the name of the editor or translator should be supplied. When the emphasis is on the work rather than the editor, the note begins with the name of
the author.

Conrad, Joseph. <u>Lord Jim</u>. Ed. Thomas C. Moser. New York:
Norton, 1968.

**Emphasis on
translator** When the editor or translator has most importance, that name begins
the entry.

Bergin, Thomas G., trans. and ed. <u>The Divine Comedy</u>, by
Dante Alighieri. New York: Appleton-Century-Crofts,
1955.

**Emphasis on
writer of
introduction** When the emphasis is on the author of the introduction to a particular
edition, the entry may begin with that name.

Daiches, David. Introduction to <u>Pride and Prejudice</u>, by
Jane Austen. New York: Random House, Modern Library,
1950.

Titles of full-length works, including novels, plays, and long poems,
are underlined in bibliography and note entries. Titles of parts of books,
such as chapters, short poems, short stories, and essays, are placed within
quotation marks. (See Chapter 4 for further information on capitalization
of titles.)

SACRED WORKS   The title of the version or translation that you use goes into the bibliography. The titles of sacred works should not be underlined. The name of the translation or version generally suffices without further facts of publication.

The Bible.   Revised Standard Version.

The Book of Mormon.

CLASSICAL WORKS   Give full information in the bibliography concerning the edition. If your subsequent reference notes or parenthetical reference will cite the name of the classical author, that name should appear first in the bibliography entry.

Aristotle.   <u>Poetics</u>.   Trans. S. H. Butcher and ed. Francis
    Fergusson.   New York: Hill and Wang, 1961.

Plato.   <u>The Republic</u>.   Trans. Desmond Lee.   Harmondsworth:
    Penguin, 1955.

▪ Reference Works

Entries for widely known reference works, such as dictionaries, encyclopedias, atlases, and yearbooks, need not include the facts of publication. The edition number or the year suffices for identification of the work. The article or entry appears within quotation marks, and the title of the reference work is underlined.

Encyclopedia entry   "Vicksburg Campaign."   <u>Encyclopaedia Britannica</u>.   1973 ed.

Dictionary entry   "Advertisement."   <u>Webster's Third International Dictionary</u>.
(Because the number of the edition appears in the title, the date is not necessary.)

Atlas entry   "World Climatology."   <u>Times Atlas of the World</u>.   1990 ed.

Signed entry   When an article or entry is signed, the name of the author may be included. When only the initials of the author are given, the full name, if you can locate it in a list of contributors for the work, should be supplied in brackets.

Holman, Harriet R.   "Page, Thomas Nelson."   <u>Collier's
    Encyclopedia</u>.   1987 ed.

B[utler], J[ames] H[armon].   "Amphitheatre."   <u>Encyclopaedia
    Britannica</u>.   1973 ed.

Specialized reference works   Entries for little-known or specialized reference works should include the full facts of publication.

```
Ealwell, John, Murray Millgate, and Peter Newman.  The New
     Palgrave: A Dictionary of Economics.  London:
     Macmillan, 1987.
```

When you cite a particular author in a specialized reference work, your bibliography entry should begin with the name of the author(s) of the article.

```
Brasingly, C. Reginald.  "Birth Order."  In Encyclopedia of
     Psychology, ed. Raymond J. Corsini.  New York: Wiley,
     1984.
```

▪ Public Documents

A publication authorized or printed by a government entity, such as a nation, state, or city, is called a *public document*. Public documents take a wide variety of forms: records of meetings and proceedings, regulations, reports of research, guidelines for industries, and statistics on current and future trends. The *Monthly Catalog of U.S. Government Publications*, 1930–, provides a full listing of the publications of various branches of government in the United States. Many states and cities also publish such listings. In addition, the federal government regularly publishes a *Checklist of United States Public Documents*.

Bibliographical entries for public documents, like those for other kinds of works, consist of three parts—author, title and facts of publication—each of which may contain several elements. Each part ends with a period, followed by two spaces.

Because there are many types and sources of documents, it may be difficult to know where to place all the information. When you cannot follow the rules given below, use your judgment about presenting the information in a way that allows your reader to locate the document.

Author entry   The author entry may include several elements, presented in this order:

1. The governing body—such as nation, state, county, or city—in order of size and importance
2. The identity of the division of government—such as Congress, Senate, or Department of State
3. The name of any particular committee and subcommittee within the division

The author entry for a document prepared by a subcommittee of the United States Senate Committee on Agriculture would read as follows:

```
U.S. Senate.  Committee on Agriculture.  Subcommittee on
     Loans.
```

Even when the name of an individual author appears on the title page, in most cases the author of a document is still considered to be the governing body that commissioned and published the work. The personal names of individual authors usually follow the title.

Chicago Style

Title entry The title entry for a public document includes the following:

1. The name of the publication, underlined
2. The name of any individual authors (or editors or compilers)
3. A designation of the document's identity—such as *Hearing, Proclamation, Executive Order, Report,* or *Document*—when applicable
4. Information about the date or origin, such as the session of Congress or the number of the document

Within the title entry, you may use abbreviations: *S.* for Senate, *H.* for House, *Cong.* for Congress, *res.* for resolution, *doc.* for document, *sess.* for session. The title entry for a document that has an individual author would read as follows:

Precedents, Decisions on Points of Order, with Phraseology, in the United States Senate. Report prepared by Henry Gilfry. 62nd Cong., 2nd sess., 1938. S. Doc. 1123.

Alternatively, if the name of the author seems to be more important than the name of the government body, either for the purposes of your research or for accurate attribution of the work, you may begin the entry with the name of the individual author:

Gates, Jane Potter. Educational and Training Opportunities in Sustainable Agriculture. U.S. Department of Agriculture. Beltsville, Md.: National Agricultural Library, 1991.

Facts of publication The facts of publication include the following:

1. The city of publication
2. The publisher
3. The date of publication, as distinct from the date of the session of Congress that produced the information

The publisher of most United States government documents is the Government Printing Office, abbreviated *GPO*, located in Washington, D.C. The usual facts of publication for a U.S. government document read as follows: Washington: GPO, 19XX. These facts of publication may be omitted in citations to congressional and other documents that already contain detailed identifying information. When a document has another publisher, follow the general rules for the facts of publication.

Enter the page number, following the rules for a book or article, as appropriate. When a page number follows the number for a part or section, introduce it with the abbreviation *p.* or *pp.* to avoid confusion.

A bibliography entry for a document with author, title, and facts of publication, then, reads as follows:

U.S. Congress. House. Committee on Agriculture. Subcommittee on Dairy and Poultry. Federal Loan for Poultry Processing Plant in New Castle, Pa. Hearing. 89th Cong., 1st sess., 19 Oct. 1965. Washington: GPO, 1966.

Congressional Record Because the *Congressional Record* is widely known and often cited, it may be entered without the author entry or the facts of publication:

Congressional Record. 89th Cong., 2nd sess., 1966. Vol. 72, pt. 5, pp. 12161–214.

Although you may encounter numerous kinds of documents, the most frequently used may be categorized as follows.

Constitution of the United States A bibliography entry for the Constitution of the United States should contain only the name:

Constitution of the United States.

(The note or parenthetical reference should include the article or amendment and section, as well as the clause, if appropriate.)

Congressional documents An entry for a hearing, a transcript of the testimony of witnesses before congressional committees, should include the name of the committee to which testimony was presented:

U.S. Congress. Senate. Committee on Environment and Public Works. Construction and Repair Programs to Alleviate Unemployment. Hearing. 97th Cong., 2nd sess., 1 Dec. 1982. Washington: GPO, 1983.

Individual acts of Congress are published separately after passage. These separate publications should be cited as documents:

U.S. Congress. Senate. Committee on Commerce, Science, and Transportation. Subcommittee on Surface Transportation. Household Goods Transportation Act of 1980. Washington: GPO, 1983.

After the laws have been compiled in the *Statutes at Large*, they should be cited as laws (see the discussion of legal citation in Appendix B).

Entries for reports prepared by Congress should follow the basic form for a document:

U.S. Congress. House. Committee on Post Office and Civil Service. Background on the Civil Service Retirement System. Report prepared by the Congressional Research Service. Washington: GPO, 1983.

Executive documents The executive branch issues presidential proclamations, executive orders, and reports of executive departments and bureaus.

U.S. President. Proclamation. Martin Luther King Day. 15 Jan. 1988.

U.S. Department of Commerce. Bureau of the Census. Aircraft Propellers. Washington: Bureau, 1979.

Treaties made by the United States since 1950 have been published in *United States Treaties and Other International Agreements*. Entries for treaties, as well as for other kinds of documents published in books, include the title of the collection.

```
U.S. Department of State. "Nuclear Weapons Test Ban," 15
    Aug. 1992, TIAS no. 1943. United States Treaties and
    Other International Agreements, vol. 34.
```

Entries for documents published by states and cities, as well as by other nations, follow the same principles for note and bibliography entries.

Unpublished documents Unpublished documents, or those published for a small audience, often do not include all of the information necessary for a complete bibliography entry. When that is the case, you will fill in the entry with descriptions of the material sufficient to enable the reader to locate it. Titles of unpublished materials are placed within quotation marks rather than underlined, as in the following examples:

```
"Automobile, Aerospace and Agricultural Implement Workers of
    America: International Union, United, AFL-CIO, and the
    Ford Motor Company, Agreement between." 20 Oct. 1961.
```

```
Stone Cutters Association of North America. Journeymen.
    "Constitution and By-Laws." 1926.
```

▪ Unpublished Sources

In the citation of unpublished sources, improvisation is occasionally necessary. You may encounter sources that do not provide all of the usual information. When that is the case, include any other piece of information essential for locating the source according to the principles of the style you are using.

If the source has an individual or corporate author, list the name as in any author entry. Titles of unpublished works are not underlined but are enclosed in double quotation marks. If you have to supply a title for the source, that title is neither underlined nor quoted. The facts of publication include the origin or location of the source and the date.

Manuscript materials A citation to manuscript materials—such as letters, scrapbooks, diaries, sermons, financial records, minutes of meetings, and legal transactions—includes the name of the author, the name of the collection and the library, the location of the library, the nature of the materials, and any other relevant information.

An entry for a letter gives the names of the sender and addressee, the date, and the location.

```
Cockburn, Robert. Letter to Lord Melville. 17 May 1819.
    Group 125, Manuscript Collection. Rutgers University,
    New Brunswick, N.J.
```

For a letter cited from a published volume, the entry follows the format for citation of a book or a collection, as appropriate.

The nature of the manuscript materials should be indicated in the entry.

Towne, Zaccheus. Diary. July 1776–Feb. 1777. Group 615, Manuscript Collection. Rutgers University, New Brunswick, N.J.

Supplied titles　When a manuscript does not have an author or a title, the writer supplies a description of the materials so they can be identified and located. Supplied titles and descriptions are neither underlined nor enclosed in quotation marks.

Papers on Industrial Espionage. Report of Agent 106. 17 July 1919. University of Washington, Seattle.

Manuscript: MS　A manuscript—a handwritten copy—is indicated by the abbreviation *MS*.

Scarborough, Dorothy. "The Wind." MS. Dorothy Scarborough Papers. The Texas Collection, Baylor University, Waco, Tex.

Typescript: TS　A typescript—a typewritten copy of a work or a transcription of an oral source such as interview—is designated with the abbreviation *TS*.

The Oral Memoirs of J. R. Smith. TS. Oral History Division. Butler College, Butler, N.Y.

Photocopied material　The form of a work duplicated by photocopying machine, mimeograph, or ditto should be indicated in the citation.

Yaffe, James. "A Report on the [University of Nebraska] Summer Writing Institute: 1979." Lincoln: Department of English, n.d. Photocopy.

▪ Dissertations

When dissertations and theses are cited as unpublished sources, their titles appear within quotation marks.

Virgili, Carmen. "Literature of the Spanish Civil War." Ph.D. diss., New York University, 1990.

A dissertation published by a microfilm service should be entered in a bibliography according to the guidelines for a book, with the title appearing in italics.

Moskop, William W. The Prudent Politician: An Extension of Aristotle's Ethical Theory. Ph.D. diss., George Washington University, 1984. Ann Arbor, UMI, 1985. 85-13289.

When you cite the abstract for a dissertation, follow the above format, but include also a reference to *Dissertation Abstracts International (DAI)*, published until 1969 as Dissertation Abstracts (DAI).

Stone, James Clement. <u>The Evolution of Civil War Novels for Children</u> (Ph.D. diss., University of Cincinnati, 1991), abstract in <u>Dissertation Abstracts International</u> 51 (1991): 2299A.

▪ Nonprint Sources

With nonprint sources, as with unpublished sources, use your judgment about supplying the information a reader would need to locate the source.

Films
In an entry for a film, the writer, producer, or director may take the position of author, depending on the relative importance of each. The title of the film is underlined, and the entry should include the company and the year of release.

Robinson, Phil Alden, dir. <u>Field of Dreams</u>. With Kevin Costner, Amy Madigan, and James Earl Jones. Universal, 1989.

Performances
Performances of music, ballet, or drama should be identified by the author, director, conductor, choreographer, and/or the principal participants, depending on your emphasis. The entry should include the name of the theater, the city, and the date.

Robbins, Jerome, dir. and chor. <u>Jerome Robbins' Broadway</u>. Imperial Theatre, New York, 14 June 1989.

Mehta, Zubin, dir. New York Philharmonic. Avery Fisher Hall, Lincoln Center, New York, 25 Nov. 1980.

Kylian, Jiri. <u>Return to the Strange Land</u>. With Cynthia Anderson and Michael Bjerknes. Joffrey Ballet. City Center, New York, 19 Nov. 1980.

Parker, Stewart. <u>Pentecost</u>. Dir. Kevin Kinley. Round House Theatre, Washington, D.C., 25 Oct. 1992.

Musical compositions
When musical compositions are identified by the type or key of the work, they are not underlined. When the composition is normally given another title, that title is underlined.

Mozart, Wolfgang Amadeus. Piano Concerto in B-flat major, K. 595.

Schubert, Franz. Symphony No. 8 (<u>Unfinished</u>).

Recordings
References to recordings should give the name of the composer and/or the performer(s), the title of the piece or of the recording, the record label, the catalog number, the year of release, and the nature of the material.

Monteverdi, Claudio. L'Orfeo. Dir. Nikolaus Harnoncourt.
    With Lajos Kozma. Concentus Musicus Wien. Telefunken,
    SKH 21/1-3, n.d. Compact disk.

Karajan, Herbert von, cond. Brahms's Symphony No. 1 in
    C minor, op. 68. Vienna Philharmonic Orchestra.
    London Records, STS 15194, 1960. Recording.

(This title, which normally would not be italicized, is italicized here as the title of a recording.)

The Beatles. "The Long and Winding Road." Let It Be.
    Apple Records, n.d. Recording.

Thomas, Dylan. "Fern Hill." Dylan Thomas Reading. Vol. 1.
    Caedmon, TC 1102, n.d. Compact disk.

Tapes and cassettes   Citations for tape recordings, audiocassettes, or videocassettes should
follow the format for recordings. Specify the nature of the material.

Paolucci, Anne. Dante and Machiavelli. Deland, Fla.:
    Everett/Edwards, n.d. Audiocassette.

Shepherd, Jean, Leigh Brown, and Bob Clark. A Christmas
    Story. Culver City: MGM/UA, 1984. Videocassette.

Works of art   Titles of works of art are underlined and the works of art are identified
by their location, either in a museum or other collection or institution or in
a book with reproductions.

Gainsborough, Thomas. The Morning Walk. National Gallery,
    London.

Vallayer-Coster, Anne. The White Soup Bowl. Private
    Collection, Paris. Plate 52 in Women Artists:
    1550-1950, by Ann Sutherland Harris and Linda
    Nochlin. New York: Knopf, 1977.

Television and radio programs   Citations for television and radio programs should include any of the
following information: title of the segment in quotation marks; name of the
series underlined; producer, director, and/or writer; actors or performers;
the name of the broadcasting corporation; and the date of the broadcast.

Jonathan: The Boy Nobody Wanted. With JoBeth Williams and
    Chris Burke. WNBC, New York, 19 Oct. 1992.

"The Best of Friends." Masterpiece Theatre. WNET, Newark,
    N.J., 18 Oct. 1992.

Personal contact with sources   Personal contact between the writer and another scholar or expert in
the field might include interviews, lectures, telephone conversations, and

letters. All of these are treated in notes and bibliography as unpublished sources. When you cite such a source, you must obtain permission to use it, unless, as in the case of a speech or an address, general permission for recording has been granted.

```
Smith, John.  Letters to author.  7 Feb. to 22 Mar. 1992.
```

```
Purcell, Thomas.  Telephone interview by author.  25 Oct.
     1990.
```

```
Teller, Edward.  Interview by author.  12 July 1962.
```

Speeches   References to a speech or paper delivered at a meeting should include the name of the speaker, the title of the speech or paper, the name of the group, and the date and location of the meeting.

```
Jochens, Jenny.  "Gender Equality in Law?: The Case of
     Medieval Iceland."  Paper presented at the Center for
     Medieval and Early Renaissance Studies, 26th Annual
     Conference.  Binghamton, N.Y., 15 Oct. 1992.
```

Information services   Entries for materials available in microform—microfilm, microfiche, or any other type of film reproduction—should follow the format for the type of material reproduced in the author and title entries. Facts of publication may include the name of the information service supplying the microfilm, such as Educational Resources Information Center (ERIC), Congressional Information Service (CIS), or National Technical Information Service (NTIS), along with identifying numbers or dates. The names of well-known information services, such as those just mentioned, may be abbreviated.

```
Groark, James J.  Utilization of Library Resources by
     Students in Non-residential Degree Programs.  ERIC,
     1974, ED 121 236.
```

When the nature of the reproduction may not be apparent, the type of microform may be specified in the entry.

```
Nicoll, Allardyce, and George Freeley, eds.  American
     Drama of the Nineteenth Century.  New York: Readex
     Microprint, 1965-.  Micro-opaque.
```

▪ Computer Materials

A bibliography entry for computer software, such as programs, languages, and systems, should include the following information, if it is available: the title (underlined), identification of the version or date, the company owning the copyright and the city in which the company is located, numbers necessary for identification of the software, and the physical nature of the item. Because the information available for these relatively unstandardized materials differs greatly, in many cases it will be necessary to follow the principles for creating bibliography entries rather than to use any specific bibliography form. The entry below refers to the program for checking spelling that accompanies the word-processing program *Visiword*.

Computer programs

```
Microsoft Windows.  Computer software.  Version 3.1.
     MacIntosh.  Redmond, Wash.: Microsoft, 1990.
```

(A manual for computer software should be treated like a book.)

Material from electronic databases

Material received from a computer retrieval service should be treated like other printed material of the same type, for example, articles or encyclopedia entries. When you refer to a particular entry, give the name of the service and the numbers identifying the document.

```
Books Out-of-Print Plus.  New York: Bowker, 1979-.  CD-ROM.
```

```
Laroche, Jacques M.  Typology of Instructional Theories.
     DIALOG, PsycINFO, 72-03548.
```

Examples of Footnote and Endnote Forms and Bibliography Forms

The following pages show examples of note forms and bibliography forms in *Chicago Manual* style. The form for notes is on the left-hand page; the corresponding form for the bibliography (or the list of works cited) is on the right.

FOOTNOTES AND ENDNOTES

Books

Basic form

¹ Hazel Henderson, <u>Paradigms in Progress: Life beyond Economics</u> (Indianapolis: Knowledge Systems, 1992), 62.

(The subtitle is optional in the note.)

Two authors

² Wendy Simonds and Barbara Katz Rothman, <u>Centuries of Solace: Grief in Popular Literature</u> (Philadelphia: Temple University Press, 1992), 35.

More than three authors

³ William McPherson et al., <u>English and American Literature: Sources and Strategies for Collection Development</u> (Chicago: American Library Association, 1987), 67.

Two authors with same last name

⁴ Richard Price and Sally Price, <u>Equatoria</u> (New York: Routledge, 1992), 75–77.

Pseudonym (real name supplied)

⁵ Hannah Green [Joanne Greenberg], <u>I Never Promised You a Rose Garden</u> (New York: Holt, Rinehart and Winston, 1964), 15.

Author's name missing

⁶ [Dorothy Scarborough], <u>The Wind</u> (New York: Harper, 1925), 27.

or

⁷ <u>The Wind</u> (New York: Harper, 1925), 27.

Group or corporation as author

⁸ Bicycling Magazine, <u>Reconditioning the Bicycle</u> (New York: Rodale, 1989), 25.

Group or corporation as author and publisher

⁹ Metropolitan Museum of Art, <u>Guide to the Metropolitan Museum of Art</u>, 4th ed. (New York, 1987), 63–66.

Edited work or compilation

¹⁰ Robert Baum, ed., <u>Reform and Reaction in Post-Mao China: The Road through Tiananmen</u> (New York: Routledge, 1992).

BIBLIOGRAPHY

Books

Henderson, Hazel. <u>Paradigms in Progress: Life beyond Economics</u>. Indianapolis: Knowledge Systems, 1992.

Simonds, Wendy, and Barbara Katz Rothman. <u>Centuries of Solace: Grief in Popular Literature</u>. Philadelphia: Temple University Press, 1992.

McPherson, William, Stephen Lehmann, Craig Likness, and Marcia Pankake. <u>English and American Literature: Sources and Strategies for Collection Development</u>. Chicago: American Library Association, 1987.

Price, Richard, and Sally Price. <u>Equatoria</u>. New York: Routledge, 1992.

Green, Hannah [Joanne Greenberg]. <u>I Never Promised You a Rose Garden</u>. New York: Holt, Rinehart and Winston, 1964.

[Scarborough, Dorothy]. <u>The Wind</u>. New York: Harper, 1925.

or

<u>The Wind</u>. New York: Harper, 1925.

Bicycling Magazine. <u>Reconditioning the Bicycle</u>. New York: Rodale, 1989.

Metropolitan Museum of Art. <u>Guide to the Metropolitan Museum of Art</u>. 4th ed. New York, 1987.

Baum, Robert, ed. <u>Reform and Reaction in Post-Mao China: The Road through Tiananmen</u>. New York: Routledge, 1992.

FOOTNOTES AND ENDNOTES

Books

Two editors

11 Evelyn Fox Keller and Elizabeth A. Lloyd, eds., Keywords in Evolutionary Biology (Cambridge: Harvard University Press, 1992), 15.

Edited volume, emphasis on author of one article

12 Gordon H. Burghardt, "On the Origins of Play," in Play in Animals and Humans, ed. Peter K. Smith (Oxford: Basil Blackwell, 1984), 5-42.

Reprint of an article in an edited volume

13 C. L. Ten, "Mill on Self-Regarding Actions," in John Stuart Mill, On Liberty, ed. David Spitz, Norton Critical Edition (New York: Norton, 1972), 239.

Reprint with change of title

14 Suzanne Langer, "The Great Dramatic Forms: The Comic Rhythm" in Comedy: Plays, Theory, and Criticism, ed. Marvin Feldheim (New York: Harcourt, 1962), 242.

Emphasis on author of introduction, afterword, or preface

15 David H. Rosen, introduction to Integrity in Depth, by John Beebe (College Station: Texas A&M University Press, 1992), x-xiii.

Translation, emphasis on author

16 Aharon Appelfeld, Katerina, trans. Jeffrey Green (New York: Random House, 1992), 67.

Translation, emphasis on translator

17 Jeffrey Green, trans., Katerina, by Aharon Appelfeld (New York: Random House, 1992).

Indirect citation, emphasis on cited source

18 Ron Chernow, The House of Morgan (New York: Simon & Schuster, Touchstone, 1990), 47, citing [or quoting] Matthew Josephson, The Robber Barons (New York: Harcourt, Brace, 1934), 338.

Indirect citation, emphasis on original source

19 Matthew Josephson, The Robber Barons (New York: Harcourt, Brace, 1934), 338, cited [or quoted] in Ron Chernow, The House of Morgan (New York: Simon & Schuster, Touchstone, 1990), 47.

BIBLIOGRAPHY

Books

Keller, Evelyn Fox, and Elizabeth A. Lloyd, eds. Keywords in Evolutionary Biology. Cambridge: Harvard University Press, 1992.

Burghardt, Gordon M., ed. "On the Origins of Play." In Play in Animals and Humans, ed. Peter K. Smith, 5-42. Oxford: Basil Blackwell, 1984.

Ten, C. L. "Mill on Self-Regarding Actions." In John Stuart Mill, On Liberty, ed. David Spitz, 238-46. Norton Critical Edition. New York: Norton, 1972. Originally published in Philosophy 43 (1968): 29-37.

Langer, Suzanne. "The Great Dramatic Forms: The Comic Rhythm." In Comedy: Plays, Theory, and Criticism, ed. Marvin Feldheim, 241-53. New York: Harcourt, 1962. Originally published as a chapter of Feeling and Form. New York: Scribner's, 1953.

Rosen, David H. Introduction to Integrity in Depth, by John Beebe. College Station: Texas A&M University Press, 1992.

Appelfeld, Aharon. Katerina. Trans. Jeffrey Green. New York: Random House, 1992.

Green, Jeffrey, trans. Katerina, by Aharon Appelfeld. New York: Random House, 1992.

Chernow, Ron. The House of Morgan: An American Banking Dynasty and the Rise of Modern Finance. New York: Simon and Schuster, Touchstone, 1990.

Chicago Style

FOOTNOTES AND ENDNOTES

Books

Book, edition other than the first

> ²⁰ Joseph F. Trimmer, <u>Writing with a Purpose</u>, 10th ed. (Boston: Houghton Mifflin, 1992), 167.

Work originally published with a different title

> ²¹ Michel Foucault, <u>The Order of Things: An Archaeology of the Human Sciences (Les mots et les choses)</u> (New York: Vintage, 1973), 100.
>
> (When the original title is in a foreign language, follow the rules for capitalization of titles in that language.)

Book, publication by division of a publisher

> ²² Derrick Bell, <u>Faces at the Bottom of the Well: The Permanence of Racism</u> (New York: HarperCollins, Basic Books, 1992), 124.

Republished work

> ²³ Beryl Markham, <u>West with the Night</u> (1942; reprint, Berkeley: North Point Press, 1983), 17.

Book originally published paperbound

> ²⁴ Peter H. Van Ness, <u>Spirituality, Diversion, and Decadence: The Contemporary Predicament</u> (Binghamton: State University of New York Press), 1992, 333.

Paperbound book, reprinted edition

> ²⁵ Ernest J. Gaines, <u>In My Father's House</u> (1978; reprint, New York: Vintage Contemporaries, 1992), 32.

Facts of publication missing

> ²⁶ George Eliot, <u>Felix Holt</u> (Edinburgh: William Blackwood, n.d.), 17.
>
> (In the position of the date, n.d. means "no date.")
>
> ²⁷ George Eliot, <u>Felix Holt</u> (N.p.: William Blackwood, n.d.), 17.
>
> (In the position of the place of publication, n.p. means "no place.")
>
> ²⁸ George Eliot, <u>Felix Holt</u> (Edinburgh: n.p., n.d.), 17.
>
> (In the position of the publisher, n.p. means "no publisher."
>
> ²⁹ George Eliot, <u>Felix Holt</u> (Edinburgh: William Blackwood, n.d.), n. pag. (**or** unpaginated).

Chicago Style

BIBLIOGRAPHY

Books

Trimmer, Joseph F. Writing with a Purpose. 10th ed. Boston: Houghton Mifflin, 1992.

Foucault, Michel. The Order of Things: An Archaeology of the Human Sciences (Les mots et les choses). New York: Vintage, 1973.
(When the original title is in a foreign language, follow the rules for capitalization of titles in that language.)

Bell, Derrick. Faces at the Bottom of the Well: The Permanence of Racism. New York: HarperCollins, Basic Books, 1992.

Markham, Beryl. West with the Night. 1942. Reprint, Berkeley: North Point Press, 1983.

Van Ness, Peter H. Spirituality, Diversion, and Decadence: The Contemporary Predicament. Binghamton: State University of New York Press, 1992.

Gaines, Ernest J. In My Father's House. 1978. Reprint, New York: Vintage Contemporaries, 1992.

Eliot, George. Felix Holt. Edinburgh: William Blackwood, n.d.

Eliot, George. Felix Holt. N.p.: William Blackwood, n.d.

Eliot, George. Felix Holt. Edinburgh: n.p., n.d.

Eliot, George. Felix Holt. Edinburgh: William Blackwood, n.d.
(Indication that a work is unpaginated is not necessary in a bibliography. An entry in a list of works cited would add *n. pag.* or *Unpaginated* at the end, followed by a period.)

Chicago Style

FOOTNOTES AND ENDNOTES

Multivolume Works and Series

Multivolume work, general title, reference to a particular volume

³⁰ William M. Bowsky, ed., <u>Studies in Medieval and Renaissance History</u>, 4 vols. (Lincoln: University of Nebraska Press, 1963–67), 2:273–96.

Multivolume work, individual titles

³¹ William W. Freehling, <u>The Road to Disunion</u>, vol. 1 of <u>Secessionists at Bay, 1776–1854</u> (New York: Oxford University Press, 1992), 23.

Work in a series

³² J. Richard Eiser, ed., <u>Attitudinal Judgment</u>, Springer Series in Social Psychology, no. 11 (New York and Berlin: Springer-Verlag, 1990), 45.

Work in a series, proceedings

³³ Walter L. Smith and William E. Wilkinson, eds., <u>Proceedings of the Symposium on Congestion Theory</u>, Probability and Statistics Monograph Series, no. 2 (Chapel Hill: Univ. of North Carolina Press, 1965), 401.

Work in a series, author and editor

³⁴ Henry Eno, <u>Twenty Years on the Pacific Slope: Letters of Henry Eno from California and Nevada, 1848–1871</u>, ed. W. Turrentine Jackson, Yale Western Americana Series, vol. 8 (New Haven: Yale University Press, 1965), 14–44.

Work in a series, translator and editor

³⁵ Jack F. Kilpatrick and Anna Gritts Kilpatrick, trans. and eds., <u>The Shadow of Sequoyah: Social Documents of the Cherokees, 1862–1964</u>, Civilization of the American Indian Series, no. 81 (Norman: University of Oklahoma Press, 1965), 47–54.

Journals

Basic form

³⁶ Owen Gingrich, "Astronomy in the Age of Columbus," <u>Scientific American</u> 267 (Nov. 1992): 100–05.

Unsigned article

³⁷ "Distant Deposits Hint at Huge Eruption," <u>Science News</u> 142 (17 Oct. 1992): 260.

Chicago Style

BIBLIOGRAPHY

Multivolume Works and Series

Bowsky, William M., ed. <u>Studies in Medieval and Renaissance History</u>. 4 vols. Lincoln: University of Nebraska Press, 1963–67.

Freehling, William W. <u>The Road to Disunion</u>. Vol. 1 of <u>Secessionists at Bay, 1776–1854</u>. New York: Oxford University Press, 1992.

Eiser, J. Richard, ed. <u>Attitudinal Judgment</u>. Springer Series in Social Psychology, no. 11. New York and Berlin: Springer-Verlag, 1990.

Smith, Walter L. and William E. Wilkinson, eds. <u>Proceedings of the Symposium on Congestion Theory</u>. Probability and Statistics Monograph Series, no. 2. Chapel Hill: University of North Carolina Press, 1965.

Eno, Henry. <u>Twenty Years on the Pacific Slope: Letters of Henry Eno from California and Nevada, 1848–1871</u>. Ed. W. Turrentine Jackson. Yale Western Americana Series, vol. 8. New Haven: Yale University Press, 1965.

Kilpatrick, Jack F., and Anna Gritts Kilpatrick, trans. and eds. <u>The Shadow of Sequoyah: Social Documents of the Cherokees, 1862–1964</u>. Civilization of the American Indian Series, no. 81. Norman: University of Oklahoma Press, 1965.

Journals

Gingrich, Owen. "Astronomy in the Age of Columbus." <u>Scientific American</u> 267 (Nov. 1992): 100–05.

"Distant Deposits Hint at Huge Eruption." <u>Science News</u> 142 (17 Oct. 1992): 260.

FOOTNOTES AND ENDNOTES

Journals

Season or month necessary for identification

38 Thomas Gardner, "An Interview with Jorie Graham," Denver Quarterly 26, no. 4 (spring 1992): 79–104.

Issues with numbers only

39 C. E. Nwezeh, "The Comparative Approach to Modern African Literature," Yearbook of General and Comparative Literature, no. 28 (1979): 22.

Series designation

40 Bernard M. Dwork, "On the Zeta Function of a Hypersurface," Annals of Mathematics, 2nd ser., 83 (1966): 518.

Magazines

Weekly

41 June Kinoshita, "The Mapping of the Mind," New York Times Magazine, 18 Oct. 1992, 44.

Monthly

42 Daniel Kleppner, "About Benjamin Thompson," Physics Today, Sept. 1992, 9.

Unsigned article

43 "The Bard of Betrayal," Observer Magazine, 27 Sept. 1992, 44.

Weekly column item

44 "Drummer," The Talk of the Town, New Yorker, 27 Oct. 1980, 45.

Newspapers

Basic form

45 Susan F. Rasky, "Senate Calls for Revisions in New Tax for Health Care," New York Times, 8 June 1989, A20.

State interpolated

46 "Unknown Author of Wind Answers Crane Criticism," Sweetwater (Texas) Daily Reporter, 15 Dec. 1925, 6.

BIBLIOGRAPHY

Journals

Gardner, Thomas. "An Interview with Jorie Graham." Denver Quarterly 26, no. 4 (spring 1992): 79-104.

Nwezeh, C. E. "The Comparative Approach to Modern African Literature." Yearbook of General and Comparative Literature, no. 28 (1979): 22.

Dwork, Bernard M. "On the Zeta Function of a Hypersurface." Annals of Mathematics, 2nd ser., 83 (1966): 518-19.

Magazines

Kinoshita, June. "The Mapping of the Mind." New York Times Magazine, 18 Oct. 1992, 44-46, 48, 50, 52, 54. (or 44-54.)

Kleppner, Daniel. "About Benjamin Thompson." Physics Today, Sept. 1992, 9-10.

"The Bard of Betrayal." Observer Magazine, 27 Sept. 1992, 44-46.

"Drummer." The Talk of the Town. New Yorker, 27 Oct. 1980, 45.

Newspapers

Rasky, Susan F. "Senate Calls for Revisions in New Tax for Health Care." New York Times, 8 June 1989, A20.

"Unknown Author of Wind Answers Crane Criticism." Sweetwater (Texas) Daily Reporter, 15 Dec. 1925, 6.

FOOTNOTES AND ENDNOTES

Newspapers

City interpolated, with section number

47 Observer (London), 17 Oct. 1990, sec. 2, p. 5.

Author, title, edition

48 Wayne E. Green, "Cold-Fusion Development Spurs Hot Race for Patents," Wall Street Journal, 9 June 1989, eastern ed., B1.

Editorial

49 "Potomac Yard Decision," editorial, Washington Post, 16 Oct. 1992, A24.

Letter

50 Frederick S. Lightfoot, letter, New York Times, 21 Oct. 1992, A22.

Numbered section, columns indicated, no title or author

51 San Francisco Sunday Examiner & Chronicle, 26 June 1990, sec. 2, p. 4, cols. 1–3.

Reviews

Signed, with title, in magazine

52 Walter Moore, "Great Physicist, Great Guy," review of Genius: The Life and Science of Richard Feynman, by James Gleick, New York Times Book Review, 11 Oct. 1992, 3.

Signed, untitled, in journal

53 Gail M. Kienitz, review of Tennyson and the Doom of Romanticism, by Herbert F. Tucker, Religion and Literature 24 (Spring 1992): 87–90.

Unsigned, untitled, in journal

54 Review of Married to Genius, by Jeffrey Meyers, Journal of Modern Literature 7 (1979): 579.

Works of Literature

Without editing or commentary

55 Amy Tan, The Joy Luck Club (New York: Ballantine, Ivy, 1989), 125.

BIBLIOGRAPHY

Newspapers

Observer (London), 17 Oct. 1990, sec. 2, pp. 5, 8.

Green, Wayne E. "Cold-Fusion Development Spurs Hot Race for
    Patents." Wall Street Journal, 9 June 1989, eastern ed., B1.

"Potomac Yard Decision." Editorial. Washington Post, 16 Oct. 1992,
    A24.

Lightfoot, Frederick S. Letter. New York Times, 21 Oct. 1992, A22.

San Francisco Sunday Examiner & Chronicle. 26 June 1990, sec. 2, p.
    4, cols. 1-3.

Reviews

Moore, Walter. "Great Physicist, Great Guy." Review of Genius: The
    Life and Science of Richard Feynman, by James Gleick. New York
    Times Book Review, 11 Oct. 1992, 3.

Kienitz, Gail M. Review of Tennyson and the Doom of Romanticism, by
    Herbert F. Tucker. Religion and Literature 24 (Spring 1992):
    87-90.

Review of Married to Genius, by Jeffrey Meyers. Journal of Modern
    Literature 7 (1979): 579-80.

Works of Literature

Tan, Amy. The Joy Luck Club. New York: Ballantine, Ivy, 1989.

FOOTNOTES AND ENDNOTES

Works of Literature

Edited, emphasis on author

> 56 Joseph Conrad, Lord Jim, ed. Thomas C. Moser (New York: Norton, 1968), 65.

Edited, emphasis on editor or translator

> 57 Thomas G. Bergin, trans. and ed., The Divine Comedy, by Dante Alighieri (New York: Appleton-Century-Crofts, 1955), 19.

Edited, emphasis on writer of introduction

> 58 David Daiches, introduction to Pride and Prejudice, by Jane Austen (New York: Modern Library, Random House, 1950), vii.

Play: act, scene, line

> 59 William Shakespeare, Othello, in Shakespeare: Twenty-three Plays and the Sonnets, ed. Thomas Marc Parrott, 2nd ed. (New York: Scribner's, 1953), act 3, sc. 2, lines 1–5.
>
> (First reference)
>
> 60 Othello 3.2.1–5.
>
> (Subsequent reference, either in notes or within parentheses in the text)
>
> *or*
>
> 61 Oth. 4.1.5–17.

Long poem: book or canto, line

> 62 John Milton, Paradise Lost, ed. Merritt Y. Hughes (New York: Odyssey, 1962), bk. 9, lines 342–75.
>
> (First reference)
>
> 63 Paradise Lost 3.1–55.
>
> (Subsequent reference, either in notes or within parentheses in the text)
>
> *or*
>
> 64 PL 3.1–55.

Short poem: stanza, line

> 65 Walt Whitman, "Song of Myself," in The American Tradition in Literature, ed. George Perkins et al., vol. 2, 6th ed. (New York: Norton, 1985), sec. 6, lines 131–35.
>
> (First reference)
>
> 66 "Song of Myself" 7.145–48.
>
> (Subsequent reference)

BIBLIOGRAPHY

Works of Literature

Conrad, Joseph. <u>Lord Jim</u>. Ed. Thomas C. Moser. New York: Norton,
   1968.

Bergin, Thomas G., trans. and ed. <u>The Divine Comedy</u>, by Dante
   Alighieri. New York: Appleton-Century-Crofts, 1955.

Daiches, David. Introduction to Pride and <u>Prejudice</u>, by Jane Austen.
   New York: Modern Library, 1950.

Parrott, Thomas Marc, ed. <u>Shakespeare: Twenty-three Plays and the
   Sonnets</u>. 2nd ed. New York: Scribner's, 1953.

(The bibliography entry specifies the edition or version of the play being cited in the notes or the
text. In a list of works cited, the entry begins with the author, followed by the title.)

Milton, John. <u>Paradise Lost</u>. Ed. Merritt Y. Hughes. New York:
   Odyssey, 1962.

Perkins, George, Sculley Bradley, Richmond Croom Beatty, and
   E. Hudson Long, eds. <u>The American Tradition in Literature</u>.
   2 vols. 6th ed. New York: Norton, 1985.

FOOTNOTES AND ENDNOTES

Works of Literature

Biblical citation, chapter, verse

    ⁶⁷ 1 Sam. 14:6-9.

Classical translation: book, chapter

    ⁶⁸ Aristotle, Poetics, trans. S. H. Butcher, ed. Francis Fergusson (New York: Hill and Wang, 1961), bk. 7, chap. 2.
(First reference)

    ⁶⁹ Poetics 7.2.
(Subsequent reference)

Classical translation: numbered divisions

    ⁷⁰ Plato, The Republic, trans. Desmond Lee (Harmondsworth: Penguin, 1955), 562E-C.
(First reference)

    ⁷¹ Republic 562E-C.
(Subsequent reference)

Reference Works

Encyclopedia entry, unsigned

    ⁷² "Vicksburg Campaign," Encyclopaedia Britannica, 1973 ed.

Dictionary entry

    ⁷³ "Advertisement," Webster's Third International Dictionary.

Atlas entry

    ⁷⁴ "World Climatology," Times Atlas of the World, 1990 ed.

General encyclopedia, signed entry

    ⁷⁵ Harriet R. Holman, "Page, Thomas Nelson," Collier's Encyclopedia, 1987 ed.

General encyclopedia, initialed article, name supplied

    ⁷⁶ J[ames] H[armon] B[utler], "Amphitheatre," Encyclopaedia Britannica, 1973 ed.

Chicago Style

BIBLIOGRAPHY

Works of Literature

The Bible. Revised Standard Version.

Aristotle. Poetics. Trans. S. H. Butcher and ed. Francis Fergusson.
    New York: Hill and Wang, 1961.

Plato. The Republic. Trans. Desmond Lee. Harmondsworth: Penguin,
    1955.

Reference Works

"Vicksburg Campaign." Encyclopaedia Britannica. 1973 ed.

"Advertisement." Webster's Third International Dictionary.
(Because the number of the edition appears in the title, the date is not needed.)

"World Climatology." Times Atlas of the World. 1990 ed.

Holman, Harriet R. "Page, Thomas Nelson." Collier's Encyclopedia.
    1987 ed.

B[Butler], J[ames] H[armon]. "Amphitheatre." Encyclopaedia
    Britannica. 1973 ed.

FOOTNOTES AND ENDNOTES

Reference Works

Dictionary not widely known

77 John Ealwell, Murray Millgate, and Peter Newman, The New Palgrave: A Dictionary of Economics (London: Macmillan, 1987), 177.

Reference work not widely known, signed article

78 C. Reginald Brasingly, "Birth Order," in Encyclopedia of Psychology, ed. Raymond J. Corsini (New York: Wiley, 1984).

Public Documents

Document with author and title

79 Jane Potter Gates, Educational and Training Opportunities in Sustainable Agriculture, U.S. Department of Agriculture (Beltsville, Md.: National Agricultural Library, 1991), 23.

Congressional hearing, House

80 Congress, House, Committee on Agriculture, Subcommittee on Dairy and Poultry, Federal Loan for Poultry Processing Plant in New Castle, Pa., hearing, 89th Cong., 1st sess., 19 Oct. 1965 (Washington: GPO, 1966), 47.

Congressional Record

81 Congressional Record, 89th Cong., 2nd sess., 1966, vol. 72, pt. 5, p. 12161.

Constitution

82 Constitution of the United States, art. 3, sec. 1.

Congressional hearing

83 Congress, Senate, Committee on Environment and Public Works, Construction and Repair Programs to Alleviate Unemployment, hearing, 97th Cong., 2nd sess., 1 Dec. 1982 (Washington: GPO, 1983), 8.

Act of Congress

84 Congress, Senate, Committee on Commerce, Science, and Transportation, Subcommittee on Surface Transportation, Household Goods Transportation Act of 1980 (Washington: GPO, 1983), 2.

BIBLIOGRAPHY

Reference Works

Ealwell, John, Murray Millgate, and Peter Newman. The New Palgrave: A Dictionary of Economics. London: Macmillan, 1987.

Brasingly, C. Reginald. "Birth Order." In Encyclopedia of Psychology, ed. Raymond J. Corsini. New York: Wiley, 1984.

Public Documents

Gates, Jane Potter. Educational and Training Opportunities in Sustainable Agriculture. U.S. Department of Agriculture. Beltsville, Md.: National Agricultural Library, 1991.

U.S. Congress. House. Committee on Agriculture. Subcommittee on Dairy and Poultry. Federal Loan for Poultry Processing Plant in New Castle, Pa. Hearing. 89th Cong., 1st sess., 19 Oct. 1965. Washington: GPO, 1966.

Congressional Record, 89th Cong., 2nd sess., 1966. Vol. 72, pt. 5, pp. 12161–214.

Constitution of the United States.

U.S. Congress. Senate. Committee on Environment and Public Works. Construction and Repair Programs to Alleviate Unemployment. Hearing, 97th Cong., 2nd sess., 1 Dec. 1982. Washington: GPO, 1983.

U.S. Congress. Senate. Committee on Commerce, Science, and Transportation. Subcommittee on Surface Transportation. Household Goods Transportation Act of 1980. Washington: GPO, 1983.

FOOTNOTES AND ENDNOTES

Public Documents

Congressional report prepared by another agency

85 Congress, House, Committee on Post Office and Civil Service, <u>Background on the Civil Service Retirement System</u>, report prepared by the Congressional Research Service (Washington: GPO, 1983), 17.

Executive document

86 President, proclamation, <u>Martin Luther King Day</u>, 15 Jan. 1988.

Executive report

87 Department of Commerce, Bureau of the Census, <u>Aircraft Propellers</u> (Washington: Bureau, 1979), 13.

Treaty

88 Department of State, "Nuclear Weapons Test Ban," 15 Aug. 1990, TIAS no. 1943, <u>United States Treaties and Other International Agreements</u>, vol. 34, pt. 6, p. 7.

Labor union agreement, unpublished

89 "Automobile, Aerospace and Agricultural Implement Workers of America: International Union, United, AFL-CIO, and the Ford Motor Company, Agreement between," 20 Oct. 1961, 184–85.

Labor union document, untitled, unpublished

90 Stone Cutters Association of North America, Journeymen, "Constitution and By-Laws," 1926, 4.

Convention proceedings

91 Longshoremen's and Warehousemen's Union, International, CIO, <u>Proceedings of the Seventh Biennial Convention of San Francisco, 7 Apr. to 11 Apr. 1947</u> (San Francisco: Trade Pressroom, n.d.), 83.

State statutes

92 California, <u>Education Code</u>, Sec. 13444(1990).

Unpublished Sources

Manuscript, letter

93 Robert Cockburn, letter to Lord Melville, 17 May 1819, Manuscript Collection, Rutgers University, New Brunswick, N.J., group 125.

BIBLIOGRAPHY

Public Documents

U.S. Congress. House. Committee on Post Office and Civil Service. Background on the Civil Service Retirement System. Report prepared by the Congressional Research Service. Washington: GPO, 1983.

U.S. President. Proclamation. Martin Luther King Day. 15 Jan. 1988.

U.S. Department of Commerce. Bureau of the Census. Aircraft Propellers. Washington: Bureau, 1979.

U.S. Department of State. "Nuclear Weapons Test Ban," 15 Aug. 1990, TIAS no. 1943. United States Treaties and Other International Agreements, vol. 34.

"Automobile, Aerospace and Agricultural Implement Workers of America: International Union, United, AFL-CIO, and the Ford Motor Company, Agreement between." 20 Oct. 1961.

Stone Cutters Association of North America. Journeymen. "Constitution and By-Laws." 1926.

Longshoremen's and Warehousemen's Union, International, CIO. Proceedings of the Seventh Biennial Convention of San Francisco, 7 Apr. to 11 Apr. 1947. San Francisco: Trade Pressroom, n.d.

California. Education Code. 1990.

Unpublished Sources

Cockburn, Robert. Letter to Lord Melville. 17 May 1819. Group 125, Manuscript Collection. Rutgers University, New Brunswick, N.J.

FOOTNOTES AND ENDNOTES

Unpublished Sources

Manuscript, nature identified

94 Zaccheus Towne, diary, July 1776–Feb. 1777, Manuscript Collection, Rutgers University, New Brunswick, N.J., group 615.

Manuscript, title supplied

95 Papers on Industrial Espionage, Report of Agent 106, 17 July 1919, University of Washington, Seattle.

Manuscript, handwritten

96 Dorothy Scarborough, "The Wind," MS, Dorothy Scarborough Papers, The Texas Collection, Baylor University, Waco, Tex., 2.

Typescript

97 The Oral Memoirs of J. R. Smith, TS, Oral History Division, Butler College, Butler, N.Y., 75.

Photocopied work

98 James Yaffe, "A Report on the [University of Nebraska] Summer Writing Institute: 1979" (Lincoln: Department of English, n.d.), 4.

Dissertations

Dissertation, typescript

99 Carmen Virgili, "Literature of the Spanish Civil War" (Ph.D. diss., New York University, 1990), 22.

Dissertation published by microfilm service

100 William W. Moskop, The Prudent Politician: An Extension of Aristotle's Ethical Theory, Ph.D. diss., George Washington University, 1984 (Ann Arbor, UMI, 1985), 79.

Abstract of dissertation

101 James Clement Stone, The Evolution of Civil War Novels for Children. (Ph.D. diss., University of Cincinnati, 1991), abstract in Dissertation Abstracts International 51 (1991): 2299A.

Nonprint Sources

Film

102 Phil Alden Robinson, dir., Field of Dreams, with Kevin Costner, Amy Madigan, and James Earl Jones, Universal, 1989.

BIBLIOGRAPHY

Unpublished Sources

Towne, Zaccheus. Diary. July 1776-Feb. 1777. Group 615, Manuscript
    Collection, Rutgers University, New Brunswick, N.J.

Papers on Industrial Espionage. Report of Agent 106. 17 July 1919.
    University of Washington, Seattle.

Scarborough, Dorothy. "The Wind." MS. Dorothy Scarborough Papers.
    The Texas Collection. Baylor University, Waco, Tex.

The Oral Memoirs of J. R. Smith. TS. Oral History Division. Butler
    College, Butler, N.Y.

Yaffe, James. "A Report on the [University of Nebraska] Summer
    Writing Institute: 1979." Lincoln: Department of English, n.d.
    Photocopy.

Dissertations

Virgili, Carmen. "Literature of the Spanish Civil War." Ph.D.
    diss., New York University, 1990.

Moskop, William W. The Prudent Politician: An Extension of
    Aristotle's Ethical Theory. Ph.D. diss., George Washington
    University, 1984. Ann Arbor, UMI, 1985. 85-13289.

Stone, James Clement. The Evolution of Civil War Novels for Children.
    Ph.D. diss., University of Cincinnati, 1991. Abstract in
    Dissertation Abstracts International 51 (1991): 2299A.

Nonprint Sources

Robinson, Phil Alden, dir. Field of Dreams. With Kevin Costner, Amy
    Madigan, and James Earl Jones. Universal, 1989.

FOOTNOTES AND ENDNOTES

Nonprint Sources

Performance, musical theater

103 Jerome Robbins, dir. and chor., <u>Jerome Robbins' Broadway</u>, Imperial Theatre, New York, 14 June 1989.

Performance, orchestra

104 Zubin Mehta, dir., New York Philharmonic, Avery Fisher Hall, Lincoln Center, New York, 25 Nov. 1980.

Performance, ballet

105 Jiri Kylian, <u>Return to the Strange Land</u>, with Cynthia Anderson and Michael Bjerknes, Joffrey Ballet, City Center, New York, 19 Nov. 1980.

Performance, drama, emphasis on author of play

106 Stewart Parker, <u>Pentecost</u>, dir. Kevin Kinley, Round House Theatre, Washington, D.C., 25 Oct. 1992.

Musical composition

107 Wolfgang Amadeus Mozart, Piano Concerto in B-flat major, K. 595.

Musical composition, with title

108 Franz Schubert, Symphony No. 8 (<u>Unfinished</u>).

Recording, emphasis on composer

109 Claudio Monteverdi, <u>L'Orfeo</u>, dir. Nikolaus Harnoncourt, with Lajos Kozma, Concentus Musicus Wien, Telefunken, SKH 21/1-3 n.d.

Recording, emphasis on conductor

110 Herbert von Karajan, cond., <u>Brahms's Symphony No. 1 in C minor, op. 68</u>, Vienna Philharmonic Orchestra, London Records, STS 15194, 1960.

Recording, emphasis on performer

111 The Beatles, "The Long and Winding Road," <u>Let It Be</u>, Apple Records, n.d.

Recording, spoken

112 Dylan Thomas, "Fern Hill," <u>Dylan Thomas Reading</u>, vol. 1, Caedmon, TC 1102, n.d.

Audiocassette

113 Anne Paolucci, <u>Dante and Machiavelli</u> (Deland, Fla.: Everett/Edwards, n.d.), audiocassette.

BIBLIOGRAPHY

Nonprint Sources

Robbins, Jerome, dir. and chor. Jerome Robbins' Broadway. Imperial
    Theatre, New York, 14 June 1989.

Mehta, Zubin, dir. New York Philharmonic. Avery Fisher Hall,
    Lincoln Center, New York, 25 Nov. 1980.

Kylian, Jiri. Return to the Strange Land. With Cynthia Anderson and
    Michael Bjerknes. Joffrey Ballet. City Center, New York, 19
    Nov. 1980.

Parker, Stewart. Pentecost. Dir. Kevin Kinley. Round House
    Theatre, Washington, D.C., 25 Oct. 1992.

Mozart, Wolfgang Amadeus. Piano Concerto in B-flat major, K. 595.

Schubert, Franz. Symphony No. 8 (Unfinished).

Monteverdi, Claudio. L'Orfeo. Dir. Nikolaus Harnoncourt. With Lajos
    Kozma. Concentus Musicus Wien. Telefunken, SKH 21/1-3, n.d.

Karajan, Herbert von, cond. Brahms's Symphony No. 1 in C minor, op.
    68. Vienna Philharmonic Orchestra. London Records, STS 15194,
    1960.

The Beatles. "The Long and Winding Road." Let It Be. Apple
    Records, n.d.

Thomas, Dylan. "Fern Hill." Dylan Thomas Reading. Vol. 1.
    Caedmon, TC 1102, n.d.

Paolucci, Anne. Dante and Machiavelli. Deland, Fla.:
    Everett/Edwards, n.d. Audiocassette.

FOOTNOTES AND ENDNOTES

Nonprint Sources

Videocassette

114 Jean Shepherd, Leigh Brown, and Bob Clark, A Christmas Story (Culver City: MGM/UA, 1984), videocassette.

Work of art

.115 Thomas Gainsborough, The Morning Walk, National Gallery, London.

Work of art, reproduction in book

116 Anne Vallayer-Coster, The White Soup Bowl, private collection, Paris; plate 52 in Women Artists: 1550–1950, by Ann Sutherland Harris and Linda Nochlin (New York: Knopf, 1977), 82.

Television program

117 Jonathan: The Boy Nobody Wanted, with JoBeth Williams and Chris Burke, WNBC, 19 Oct. 1992.

Television program, episode in series

118 "The Best of Friends," Masterpiece Theatre, WNET, Newark, N.J., 18 Oct. 1992.

Letter to author

119 John Smith, letters to author, 7 Feb. to 22 Mar. 1992.

Interview, telephone

120 Thomas Purcell, telephone interview by author, 25 Oct. 1990.

Interview, in person

121 Julia Kristeva, interview by author, 20 Oct. 1992.

Paper read at a meeting

122 Jenny Jochens, "Gender Equality in Law?: The Case of Medieval Iceland," paper presented at the Center for Medieval and Early Renaissance Studies, 26th Annual Conference, Binghamton, N.Y., 15 Oct. 1992.

Microform Materials

Information service

123 James J. Groark, Utilization of Library Resources by Students in Non-residential Degree Programs (ERIC, ED 121 236, 1974), 7.

BIBLIOGRAPHY

Nonprint Sources

Shepherd, Jean, Leigh Brown, and Bob Clark. A Christmas Story. Culver City: MGM/UA, 1984. Videocassette.

Gainsborough, Thomas. The Morning Walk. National Gallery, London.

Vallayer-Coster, Anne. The White Soup Bowl. Private collection, Paris. Plate 52 in Women Artists: 1550-1950, by Ann Sutherland Harris and Linda Nochlin. New York: Knopf, 1977.

Jonathan: The Boy Nobody Wanted. With JoBeth Williams and Chris Burke. WNBC, New York, 19 Oct. 1992.

"The Best of Friends." Masterpiece Theatre. WNET, Newark, N.J., 18 Oct. 1992.

Smith, John. Letters to author. 7 Feb. to 22 Mar. 1992.

Purcell, Thomas. Telephone interview by author. 25 Oct. 1990.

Kristeva, Julia. Interview by author. 20 Oct. 1992.

Jochens, Jenny. "Gender Equality in Law?: The Case of Medieval Iceland." Paper presented at the Center for Medieval and Early Renaissance Studies, 26th Annual Conference. Binghamton, N.Y., 15 Oct. 1992.

Microform Materials

Groark, James J. Utilization of Library Resources by Students in Non-residential Degree Programs. ERIC, 1974, ED 121 236.

FOOTNOTES AND ENDNOTES

Microform Materials

Microform, identification of type

124 Allardyce Nicoll and George Freeley, eds., American Drama of the Nineteenth Century (New York: Readex Microprint, 1965-), micro-opaque.

Computer Materials

Computer software

125 Microsoft Windows, computer software, version 3.1. MacIntosh. (Redmond, Wash.: Microsoft, 1990).

Electronic database, CD-ROM

126 Books Out-of-Print Plus (New York: Bowker, 1979-), CD-ROM.

Electronic database

127 Jacques M. Laroche. Typology of Instructional Theories, 1984, DIALOG, PsycINFO, 72-03548.

BIBLIOGRAPHY

Microform Materials

Nicoll, Allardyce, and George Freeley, eds. American Drama of
the Nineteenth Century. New York: Readex Microprint, 1965-.
Micro-opaque.

Computer Materials

Microsoft Windows. Computer software. Version 3.1. MacIntosh.
Redmond, Wash.: Microsoft, 1990.

Books Out-of-Print Plus. New York: Bowker, 1979-. CD-ROM.

Laroche, Jacques M. Typology of Instructional Theories. 1984.
DIALOG, PsycINFO, 72-03548.

8 Modern Language Association Style

Modern Language Association format (MLA) requires citation within the text rather than endnotes or footnotes. Citation in the text provides information, usually the name of the author and the page number(s), to lead the reader to the accompanying bibliographical entry; if necessary, it may also give other information, such as the volume number, for locating the material. Complete information about each source cited in the text is supplied in a listing of works cited, which is placed at the end of the research paper. For an example of such a list, see the List of Works Cited on pages 203 and 204, which provides bibliographical information for the works used to illustrate the nature of parenthetical citation.

Content of Parenthetical Citations

When you cite a source, using either direct quotation or a summary, include within the text enough information, but no more than is necessary, to identify the source. Most parenthetical citations include the name of the author and the page number, without an intervening comma. When the author's name appears in the introduction to the material, you need not repeat the name within parentheses, as the following examples indicate:

Author not cited in text

At least one other educator has recently quarreled with the tradition division of the curriculum into discrete subjects (Moffett 5-10).

Author cited in text

Moffett has identified public narrative as one kind of discourse (42-44).

Work with more than one author

When a work has two or three authors, include all the names within parentheses:

One textbook defines rhetoric as "the art of using language effectively" (Brooks and Warren 5).

Brooks and Warren define rhetoric as "the art of using language effectively" (5).

Work with four or more authors

When a work has four or more authors, give only the last name of the first author followed by *et al.* (the abbreviation for *et alii*, "and others"):

The authors of Four Worlds of Writing begin with the premise that "writing represents a way of making meaning of our experience" (Lauer et al. 2).

More than one author with same last name

When you have more than one author with the same last name, include first names in subsequent references. Subsequent references to Helen C. White's *The Mysticism of William Blake* and E. B. White's *Charlotte's Web* would read as follows: (Helen C. White 75) and (E. B. White 67).

List the names of an editor, compiler, or translator without the accompanying abbreviation that appears in the list of works cited:

Many of the articles in Research on Composing advocate further exploration of the motivation for writing (Cooper and Odell).

Work listed by title only

When you have a work listed only by title in your works cited section, use a shortened version of the title in parentheses.

The prime ministers of four Caribbean nations attended the installation of the new parliament in Grenada ("New Parliament" 5).

Corporate author

When you have a corporate author, use the name of the organization, abbreviated if it is lengthy, in place of the name of the author:

```
The faculty handbook emphasized this point (Columbia

University 123-24).
```

Works cited by author or by author and title

When you cite an entire work by the name of the author alone or by author and title, you do not need a parenthetical reference. A reader will be able to find bibliographical information by looking up the author's name in your list of works cited:

```
Murray's book allows a beginner to share the experience of a

professional writer.

Shaughnessy's study of her students' papers has inspired a

generation of teachers.
```

Multivolume works

To cite an entire volume of a multivolume work, use the author's name and the abbreviation *vol.*:

```
This valuable reference work surveys the major operas of

Mozart and Puccini (Newman, vol. 2).
```

To cite a portion of a volume of a multivolume work, use an arabic numeral to indicate the volume followed by a colon and the page number(s):

```
Newman discusses the controversy surrounding the quality of

Mozart's The Magic Flute (2: 104-05).
```

If the author's name were not in the text, the parenthetical reference would read (Newman 2: 104–05).

Two or more works by same author

When you have two works or more by the same author, use a shortened version of the title in each reference:

```
Shaughnessy points out that "the beginning writer does not

know how writers behave" (Errors 79).

Teachers applauded Shaughnessy's assertion that "teaching

them [beginning writers] to write well is not only suitable

but challenging work for those who would be teachers and

scholars in a democracy" ("Diving In" 68).
```

Material cited in another source

When you refer to material cited in a source other than the original, use the abbreviation *qtd. in* to indicate where you actually found the quotation:

Goethe wrote that "it takes more culture to perceive the

virtues of The Magic Flute than to point out its defects"

(qtd. in Newman 2: 104).

Multiple citations   When you wish to include more than one work in a parenthetical citation, separate entries with a semicolon:

(Errors 79; "Diving In" 68; Brooks and Warren 5)

Placement and Punctuation of Parenthetical Documentation

Parenthetical references should generally be placed at the end of a sentence. Quotation marks, if any, precede the reference; end punctuation, as
well as commas, colons, and semicolons, follow it:

Shaughnessy points out that "the beginning writer does not

know how writers behave" (79).

Was it Shaughnessy who pointed out that "the beginning

writer does not know how writers behave" (79)?

"The beginning writer does not know how writers behave,"

according to Shaughnessy (79).

If confusion might result about the distinction between your own conclusions and an idea from a source, place the parenthetical reference within
a sentence, generally at the end of a clause or phrase:

"The beginning writer does not know how writers behave"

(Shaughnessy 79): all of the research confirms this

conclusion.

(The second half of the sentence represents the writer's conclusion from reading in works other
than Shaughnessy's.)

Entry in list of works   Shaughnessy, Mina P. Errors and Expectations: A Guide for
cited   the Teacher of Basic Writing. New York: Oxford UP,
1977.

For an ellipsis at the end of a sentence, the parenthetical reference follows three points indicating the omission and precedes the period:

```
Berkin and Norton report that "childless households have

once again started to increase . . ." (29).
```

A parenthetical reference at the end of a set-off quotation follows the period. Two spaces separate the period from the reference, which is not followed by a period.

```
Berkin and Norton attribute the decline in the size of the

American household to several factors.
```

```
          An increase in childless households and households
          with one or two children reflects not only lower
          levels of childbearing, but also more older
          couples whose children have grown up and left
          home. (29)
```

Entry in list of works cited

```
Berkin, Carol Ruth, and Mary Beth Norton.  Women of America:
     A History.  Boston: Houghton, 1979.
```

(The original passage appears on page 72 of this book.)

The List of Works Cited

With MLA-style parenthetical documentation, a works cited section at the end of your paper is the key to the references cited in your text. When you have a work that does not fit exactly into any of the categories, follow the principles for constructing bibliography entries outlined above. Follow the guidelines for alphabetizing entries and other instructions given below and on pages 138–40.

A works cited list should not be divided into categories. Your reader needs to be able to locate bibliographical information by looking up the reference in one alphabetized list.

The first word of each entry in a works cited list is of particular importance, since that word, whether the last name of an author or the first word of a title, identifies the entry in the text. In deciding whether to place a translator's or editor's name first rather than the author's name, for example, you need to know the purpose for which you will cite the work in your paper. If your text will refer primarily to the decisions made by a translator, the translator's name should appear first in the entry. If, on the other hand, you plan to discuss only the original work, the author's name should appear first and the name of the translator should follow the title (see page 206).

When you use an edited volume or compilation and refer to more than one of the articles in it, you must list each article by author in the works cited section. The works cited entries should be constructed as follows:

Edited volume

```
Tate, Gary, ed.  Teaching Composition: Ten Bibliographical
     Essays.  Fort Worth: Texas Christian UP, 1976.
```

Article in edited volume

Winterowd, W. Ross. "Linguistics and Composition." Tate 197–222.

(In a bibliography, you could list only the one edited work, since your notes would mention specific articles from the edited volume.)

When you cite more than one work by the same editor(s) or compiler(s), use a shortened form of the title to identify the compilation in the works cited list.

Edited volume

Cooper, Charles R., and Lee Odell, eds. Evaluating Writing: Describing, Measuring, Judging. Urbana: NCTE, 1977.

Edited volume, same editors

---. Research on Composing: Points of Departure. Urbana: NCTE, 1978.

Article in first edited volume

Lloyd-Jones, Richard. "Primary Trait Scoring." Cooper and Odell, Evaluating 77–99.

Article in second edited volume

Petty, Walter T. "The Writing of Young Children." Cooper and Odell, Research 73–84.

Publishers' names

MLA style shortens the names of publishers to one word whenever possible, as in *Holt*. *University* and *Press* are abbreviated, as in *U of Chicago P.* MLA also puts the name of the imprint, or division, of a publisher before the name of the publisher, citing a book published in the Colophon series as Colophon-Harper. See Appendix A for a listing of numerous publishers and imprints in MLA format.

Works Cited

Berkin, Carol Ruth, and Mary Beth Norton. Women of America: A History. Boston: Houghton, 1979.

Brooks, Cleanth, and Robert Penn Warren. Modern Rhetoric. 4th ed. New York: Harcourt, 1979.

Columbia University. Faculty Handbook. New York: 1987.

Cooper, Charles R., and Lee Odell, eds. Evaluating Writing: Describing, Measuring, Judging. Urbana: NCTE, 1977.

---. Research on Composing: Points of Departure. Urbana: NCTE, 1978.

Lauer, Janice M., et al. Four Worlds of Writing. New York: Harper, 1981.

Lloyd-Jones, Richard. "Primary Trait Scoring." Cooper and Odell, Evaluating 77–99.

Moffett, James. Teaching the Universe of Discourse. Boston: Houghton, 1968.

Murray, Donald. A Writer Teaches Writing. 2nd ed. Boston: Houghton, 1985.

Newman, Ernest. Great Operas: The Definitive Treatment of Their History, Stories, and Music. 2 vols. New York: Vintage, 1958.

"New Parliament Installed in Grenada." New York Times 30 Dec. 1984, sec. 1: 5+.

Petty, Walter T. "The Writing of Young Children." Cooper and Odell, Research 73-84.

Shaughnessy, Mina P. "Diving In: An Introduction to Basic Writing." The Writing Teacher's Sourcebook. Ed. Tate, Gary, and Edward P.J. Corbett. New York: Oxford UP, 1981. 62-68.

Tate, Gary, ed. Teaching Composition: Ten Bibliographical Essays. Fort Worth: Texas Christian UP, 1976.

White, E. B. Charlotte's Web. New York: Harper, 1952.

White, Helen C. The Mysticism of William Blake. New York: Russell, 1964.

Winterowd, W. Ross. "Linguistics and Composition." Tate 197-222.

Works Cited Forms

▪ Books

The bibliographical listing for a book includes the name(s) of the author(s) or of the editor(s), compiler(s), or translator(s), as appropriate for the particular book (the name that begins an entry is listed surname first); the title of the book with any subtitle; and the facts of publication, namely the city of publication (and, if needed, the state), the publisher, and the date of publication. (If it is necessary to mention the state in order to identify the city, U.S. Postal Service abbreviations of state names are used.)

MLA Style

Book by a single author	Henderson, Hazel. <u>Paradigms in Progress: Life beyond Economics</u>. Indianapolis: Knowledge Systems, 1992.
An edited volume or compilation	Baum, Robert ed. <u>Reform and Reaction in Post-Mao China: The Road through Tiananmen</u>. New York: Routledge, 1992.
Book by two or more authors	Simonds, Wendy, and Barbara Katz Rothman. <u>Centuries of Solace: Grief in Popular Literature</u>. Philadelphia: Temple UP, 1992.
	McPherson, William, Stephen Lehmann, Craig Likness, and Marcia Pankake. <u>English and American Literature: Sources and Strategies for Collection Development</u>. Chicago: ALA, 1987.
Book by more than four authors	Lauer, Janice M., et al. <u>Four Worlds of Writing</u>. New York: Harper, 1981.
Book by a corporate author	Bicycling Magazine. <u>Reconditioning the Bicycle</u>. New York: Rodale, 1989.
Anonymous book	<u>Times Atlas of the World</u>. 8th ed. London: Times, 1990.

If you know the name of the author, provide it within brackets.

[Scarborough, Dorothy]. <u>The Wind</u>. New York: Harper, 1925.

Work in an anthology, particular work singled out	Burghardt, Gordon M. "On the Origins of Play." <u>Play in Animals and Humans</u>. Ed. Peter K. Smith. Oxford: Basil Blackwell, 1984. 5-42.
Work in an anthology, reprinted work	Ten, C. L. "Mill on Self-Regarding Actions." <u>Philosophy</u> 43 (1968): 29-37. Rpt. in John Stuart Mill, <u>On Liberty</u>. Ed. David Spitz. Norton Critical Edition. New York: Norton, 1972. 238-46.
Work in an anthology, assigned new title	Langer, Suzanne. <u>Feeling and Form</u>. New York: Scribner's, 1953. Rpt. as "The Great Dramatic Forms: The Comic Rhythm." In <u>Comedy: Plays, Theory, and Criticism</u>. Ed. Marvin Feldheim. New York: Harcourt, 1962. 241-53.
Introduction, preface, foreword, afterword	Howard, Maureen. Foreword. <u>Mrs. Dalloway</u>. By Virgina Woolf. New York: Harvest-Harcourt, 1981. vii- xiv.
Multivolume work	Bowsky, William M., ed. <u>Studies in Medieval and Renaissance History</u>. 4 vols. Lincoln: U of Nebraska P, 1963-67.

MLA Style

When you use one volume of a multivolume work, include the title of the particular volume along with that of the complete volumes.

Freehling, William W. The Road to Disunion. Vol. 1 of
    Secessionists at Bay, 1776-1854. 2 vols. New York:
    Oxford UP, 1991-92.

Edition of a literary work

Conrad, Joseph. Lord Jim. Ed. Thomas C. Moser. Norton
    Critical Edition. New York: Norton, 1968.

Translation

Appelfeld, Aharon. Katerina. Trans. Jeffrey Green. New
    York: Random House, 1992.

If you wish to emphasize the name of the translator, place that name in the author position of the entry.

Green, Jeffrey, trans. Katerina. By Aharon Appelfeld. New
    York: Random House, 1992.

Republished book

Markham, Beryl. West with the Night. 1942. Berkeley:
    North Point, 1983.

Article in reference book

"Vicksburg Campaign." Encyclopaedia Britannica. 1973 ed.

"Advertisement." Webster's Third International Dictionary.
(Because the number of the edition appears in the title, the date is not needed.)

"World Climatology." Times Atlas of the World. 1990 ed.

Holman, Harriet R. "Page, Thomas Nelson." Collier's
    Encyclopedia. 1987 ed.

In the case of less well known reference works, provide full publication information.

Brasingly, C. Reginald. "Birth Order." Encyclopedia of
    Psychology. Ed. Raymond J. Corsini. New York: Wiley,
    1984.

Pamphlet

The entry for a pamphlet follows the rules for that of a book in every respect.

Government publications

When the author of a government publication is identified, list it like a book.

Gates, Jane Potter. Educational and Training Opportunities
    in Sustainable Agriculture. U.S. Department of
    Agriculture. Beltsville, MD: National Agricultural
    Library, 1991.

Otherwise list the document by the government agency that produced or sponsored it, using the following abbreviations:

Cong. for Congress
Dept. for Department
sess. for session
Cong. Rec. for *Congressional Record*
S. Rept. for Senate Report
H. Rept. for House Report
S. Res. for Senate Resolution
H. Res. for House Resolution
GPO for Government Printing Office

When used as an author entry, United States is spelled out; otherwise it is abbreviated as U.S.

United States. Cong. Senate. Committee on Environment and
      Public Works. Construction and Repair Programs to
      Alleviate Unemployment. Hearing. 97th Cong., 2nd
      sess., 1 Dec. 1982. Washington: GPO, 1983.

United States. President. Proclamation. Martin Luther
      King Day. 15 Jan. 1988.

Cong. Rec. 17 Nov. 1980: 3852.

Book in a series

Eiser, J. Richard, ed. Attitudinal Judgment. Springer
      Series in Social Psychology 11. New York and Berlin:
      Springer-Verlag, 1990.

Publisher's imprint

Bell, Derrick. Faces at the Bottom of the Well: The
      Permanence of Racism. New York: Basic-HarperCollins,
      1992.

(See Appendix A for a listing of publishers and their imprints in MLA format.)

Multiple publishers

Shelly, Percy Bysshe. Selected Poems. Ed. Timothy Webb.
      London: Dent; Totowa: Rowman, 1977.

Published proceedings of conference

Ferrua, Patricia, ed. Proceedings of the First
      International Symposium on Letterism. Paris: Avant-
      Garde, 1979.

Books in a language other than English

Entries for books in other languages may be treated precisely the same as books in English. If you wish to clarify any portion of the entry with an English translation, place it in brackets immediately following the original language.

Buendía, Felicidad. Libros de caballerías españoles
      [Spanish Novels of Chivalry]. Madrid: Aguilar, 1960.

Book with a title within its title   When the interior title would normally be underlined, leave it without underlining.

The Four-Gated City: The Summer before the Dark

The Plays of Samuel Beckett: Waiting for Godot and Endgame

When the interior title would normally be in quotation marks, underline the entire title.

Coleridge's "Kubla Khan"

Book without stated publication information or pagination   Use the following abbreviations for missing information at the appropriate place in the entry: n.d. for *no date*, n.p. for *no place*, n.p. *for no publisher*, n. pag. for *no pagination.*

Eliot, George. Felix Holt. Edinburgh: William Blackwood,
    n.d.

Eliot, George. Felix Holt. N.p.: William Blackwood, n.d.

Eliot, George. Felix Holt. Edinburgh: n.p., n.d.

Eliot, George. Felix Holt. Edinburgh: William Blackwood,
    n.d. N. pag.

Unpublished dissertation   Virgili, Carmen: "Literature of the Spanish Civil War."
    Diss. New York U, 1990.

Published dissertation   Moskop, William W. The Prudent Politician: An Extension of
    Aristotle's Ethical Theory. Diss. George Washington
    U, 1984. Ann Arbor: UMI, 1985. 85-13289.

▪ Articles in Periodicals

Citations for articles include (1) the name(s) of the author(s) or editor(s); (2) the full title of the article within quotation marks; and (3) the facts of publication, which usually include the name of the periodical (underlined), the series name and number if any, the volume number (for a scholarly journal), the date of publication followed by a colon, and the page numbers on which the article appears. When an article does not appear on consecutive pages, MLA uses only the first page number followed by the symbol +, as in 67+ for an article appearing on pages 67–79 and 84–89.

Article from newspaper   Rasky, Susan F. "Senate Calls for Revisions in New Tax for
    Health Care." New York Times 8 June 1989: A20.

Article from magazine

Kinoshita, June. "The Mapping of the Mind." New York Times Magazine 18 Oct. 1992: 44+.

Article in scholarly journal with continuous pagination

Gingrich, Owen. "Astronomy in the Age of Columbus." Scientific American 267 (Nov. 1992): 100-05.

Article in scholarly journal paginating each issue separately

Gardner, Thomas. "An Interview with Jorie Graham." Denver Quarterly 26.4 (Spring 1992): 79-104.

Journal using only issue numbers

Nwezeh, C. E. "The Comparative Approach to Modern African Literature." Yearbook of General and Comparative Literature 28 (1979): 22.

Article from journal with more than one series

Dwork, Bernard M. "On the Zeta Function of a Hypersurface." Annals of Mathematics 2nd ser. 83 (1966): 518-19.

Editorial or other regular column

"Potomac Yard Decision." Editorial. Washington Post 16 Oct. 1992: A24.

Anonymous article

"Distant Deposits Hint at Huge Eruption." Science News 142 (17 October 1992): 260.

Letter to editor

Lightfoot, Frederick S. Letter. New York Times 21 Oct. 1992: A22.

Review

Moore, Walter. "Great Physicist, Great Guy." Rev. of Genius: The Life and Science of Richard Feynman, by James Gleick. New York Times Book Review 11 Oct. 1992: 3.

Kienitz, Gail M. Rev. of Tennyson and the Doom of Romanticism, by Herbert F. Tucker. Religion and Literature 24 (Spring 1992): 87-90.

Article whose title contains another title

Change double quotation marks to single quotation marks when they appear within another quoted title.

"A Reading of Coleridge's 'Kubla Khan'"

An underlined title appearing within a title in quotation marks remains underlined.

"A Principle of Unity in Between the Acts"

Dissertation Abstracts in *Dissertation Abstracts International (DAI)*

Blair, Catherine Pastore. "Mark Twain, Anatomist." DAI 41 (1981): 4387A-88A. U of Topeka.

Serialized article McPhee, John. "Annals of the Former World." New Yorker 7
Sept. 1992: 36+; 14 Sept. 1992: 44+; 21 Sept. 1992:
39+.

▪ Other Sources

Computer software Microsoft Windows. Computer software. Version 3.1.
Redmond, Wash.: Microsoft, 1990. MacIntosh DOS 3.1,
640 KB, disk.

Material from a computer service Laroche, Jacques M. "Typology of Instructional Theories."
International Review of Applied Linguistics in Language
Teaching 22 (Feb. 1984): 41–52. DIALOG, PsycINFO file
11, 72-03548.

Material from an information service, not previously published Groark, James J. Utilization of Library Resources by
Students in Non-residential Degree Programs. ERIC,
1974. ED 121 236.

If the material has been published elsewhere, treat it like a book or
article and, after the date, add the name of the information service and
the number.

Television and radio programs Jonathan: The Boy Nobody Wanted. With JoBeth Williams and
Chris Burke. WNBC, New York. 19 Oct. 1992.

"The Best of Friends." Masterpiece Theatre. WNET, Newark,
NJ. 18 Oct. 1992.

Recordings Monteverdi, Claudio. L'Orfeo. Dir. Nikolaus Harnoncourt.
With Lajos Kozma. Concentus Musicus Wien. Telefunken,
SKH 21/1-3, n.d.

Karajan, Herbert von, cond. Brahms's Symphony no. 1 in C
minor, op. 68. Vienna Philharmonic Orchestra. London
Records, STS 15194, 1960.

The Beatles. "The Long and Winding Road." Let It Be.
Apple Records, n.d.

Thomas, Dylan. "Fern Hill." Dylan Thomas Reading. Vol. 1.
Caedmon, TC 1102, n.d.

Paolucci, Anne. Audiocassette. Dante and Machiavelli.
Deland, FL: Everett/Edwards, n.d.

Films, filmstrips, videotapes

Robinson, Phil Alden, dir. Field of Dreams. With Kevin Costner, Amy Madigan, and James Earl Jones. Universal, 1989.

Shepherd, Jean, Leigh Brown, and Bob Clark. Videocassette. A Christmas Story. Culver City: MGM/UA, 1984.

Performances
Concert

Mehta, Zubin, dir. New York Philharmonic. Avery Fisher Hall, Lincoln Center, New York. 25 Nov. 1980.

Ballet

Kylian, Jiri. Return to the Strange Land. With Cynthia Anderson and Michael Bjerknes. Joffrey Ballet. City Center, New York. 19 Nov. 1980.

Play

Parker, Stewart. Pentecost. Dir. Kevin Kinley. Round House Theatre, Washington, DC. 25 Oct. 1992.

Musical compositions

Mozart, Wolfgang Amadeus. Piano Concerto in B-flat major, K. 595.

Schubert, Franz. Symphony no. 8 (Unfinished).

Works of art

Gainsborough, Thomas. The Morning Walk. National Gallery, London.

Vallayer-Coster, Anne. The White Soup Bowl. Private Collection, Paris. Plate 52 in Women Artists: 1550–1950. By Ann Sutherland Harris and Linda Nochlin. New York: Knopf, 1977.

Letters

Crane, Stephen. Letter to Lily Brandon Munro. March 1894? Bradley, Sculley et al., eds. The Red Badge of Courage. 2nd ed. Norton Critical Edition. New York: Norton, 1976. 129.

Smith, John. Letters to author. 7 Feb. to 22 Mar. 1992.

Interviews

Lipkowitz, Ina, and Andrea Loselle. "An Interview with Julia Kristeva." Critical Texts 3.3 (1986): 3–13.

Kristeva, Julia. Interview with author. 20 Oct. 1992.

Maps and charts

World Climatology. Map. Times Atlas of the World. 1990 ed.

MLA Style

Cartoons   Schoenbaum, Bernard.   Cartoon.   <u>New Yorker</u> 2 Nov. 1992: 82.

Lectures,   Jochens, Jenny.   "Gender Equality in Law?: The Case of
speeches   Medieval Iceland."   Center for Medieval and Early
         Renaissance Studies, 26th Annual Conference.
         Binghamton, NY, 15 Oct. 1992.

Manuscripts and   Scarborough, Dorothy.   <u>The Wind</u>, ms.   Dorothy Scarborough
typescripts   Papers.   The Texas Collection, Baylor U, Waco.

         The Oral Memoirs of J. R. Smith, ts.   Oral History Division.
             Butler Coll., NY.

9 American Psychological Association Style

For providing documentation, the American Psychological Association (APA) requires citation within the text rather than endnotes or footnotes. The author's last name, the year of publication for the work, and any other information necessary for locating the material cited may be incorporated into the text itself or placed within parentheses, as the particular sentence allows (see explanations below of specific cases). Complete information about each source cited in the text is provided in an alphabetical reference list at the end of the research paper. For an example of such a list, see the reference list on pages 216 and 217, which provides bibliographical information for the works used in the illustrations of APA reference citations.

Parenthetical Reference Citations in Text

Whether you quote directly or indirectly, you must provide the source of your information. If you have questions about whether you should include parenthetical documentation in any given situation, refer to Chapter 3. When you do need documentation, it should be entered in a way that avoids duplication while still making the identity of the source entirely clear.

Author cited in text   If you mention the author's name in your text, cite only the date of publication in parentheses, immediately after the author's name.

Gould (1989) attributes Darwin's success to his gift for

making the appropriate metaphor.

Author not cited in text   When you do not mention the author's name in your own text, that name, followed by a comma and the date of publication, appears in parentheses at the end of your sentence. Use the last name only in both first and subsequent citations.

As metaphors for the workings of nature, Darwin used the

tangled bank, the tree of life, and the face of nature

(Gould, 1989).

Author and date cited in text   If you use both the name of the author and the date in the text, parenthetical reference is not needed.

In a 1989 article, Gould explores some of Darwin's most

effective metaphors.

Direct quotation with name of author   When your sentence contains a quotation and includes the name of the author, place the publication date and page number in parentheses. Abbreviate the word *page* or *pages* (*p.* or *pp.*). The publication date should follow the name of the author; the page number should follow the end of the quotation.

Gould (1989) explains that Darwin used the metaphor

of the tree of life "to express the other form of

interconnectedness--genealogical rather than ecological--and

to illustrate both success and failure in the history of

life" (p. 14).

Direct quotation without name of author   When you quote but do not identify the author in the sentence, the name of the author, date of publication, and page number appear in parentheses at the end of the sentence.

Darwin used the metaphor of the tree of life "to express the

other form of interconnectedness--genealogical rather than

ecological" (Gould, 1989, p. 14).

Two authors   When you refer to a work by two authors, cite both names each time the reference appears. Within the parentheses use an ampersand (&), but within the text spell out the word *and*.

Sexual-selection theory has been used to explore patterns of

insect mating (Alcock & Thornhill, 1983). . . . Alcock and

Thornhill (1983) also demonstrate . . .

Three, four, or five authors   For a work by more than two authors but fewer than six authors, cite all names in the first reference. In subsequent references, cite only the name of the first author and use et al.

DeLong, Wickham, and Pace (1989) devised a new staining

method of cell identification. . . . The new staining

method (DeLong et al., 1989) allows for identification . . .

Six or more authors   For a work by six or more authors, give only the last name of the first author followed by et al. in both first and subsequent references.

Pan et al. (1992) have studied synthetic diamonds . . . Pan

et al. (1992) suggest industrial applications . . .

Authors with the same last name   When you cite works by two or more authors with the same last name, use initials to identify the authors in the text even if their dates of publication differ.

R. Dawkins (1986) and M. S. Dawkins (1980) have contributed

to an understanding of consciousness in animals.

Work identified by title   When a work is noted in the reference list by title alone, a shortened version of the title is used in the text to identify the work. The title of a book is underlined; the title of an article appears within quotation marks.

The National Endowment for the Humanities supports

"theoretical and critical studies of the arts" but not

work in the creative or performing arts (<u>Guidelines</u>, 1988,

p. 1).

Changes in the Medical College Admissions Test to begin in

1991 should encourage more students to pursue general

studies in the humanities, natural sciences, and social

sciences ("New Exam," 1989).

Corporate author   When you cite a work by a corporate author, use the name of the organization as the author.

APA Style

Retired officers retain access to all of the university's

educational and recreational facilities (Columbia

University, 1987, p. 54).

You may use well-known abbreviations of the name of a corporate author in subsequent parenthetical references. For example, you might use NSF for National Science Foundation, NIH for National Institutes of Health, and NEH for National Endowment for the Humanities.

Reference to more than one work

Parenthetical references may mention more than one work. Multiple citations should be arranged as follows:

List two or more works by the same author in order of date of publication: (Gould, 1987, 1989).

Differentiate works by the same author and with the same publication date by adding an identifying letter to each date: (Bloom, 1987a, 1987b). The letters also appear in the reference list, where the works are alphabetized by title.

List works by different authors in alphabetical order by last name, and use semicolons to separate the references: (Dawkins, R. 1986; Gould 1989).

References

Alcock, J., & Thornhill, R. (1983). The evolution of

    insect mating systems. Cambridge: Harvard University

    Press.

Bloom, H. (Ed.). (1987a). Eugene O'Neill. New York:

    Chelsea.

Bloom, H. (Ed.). (1987b). John Dryden. New York: Chelsea.

Columbia University. (1987). Faculty handbook. New York:

    Author.

Darwin, C. (1964). On the origin of the species: A

    facsimile of the first edition (Introd. Ernst Mayer).

    Cambridge: Harvard University Press. (Original work

    published 1859)

Dawkins, M. S. (1980). Animal suffering: The science of

    animal welfare. London: Chapman & Hall.

Dawkins, R. (1986). The blind watchmaker. New York: Norton.

Gould, S. J. (1987). Time's arrow, time's cycle: Myth and

metaphor in the discovery of geological time. Cambridge:

Harvard University Press.

Gould, S. J. (1989). The wheel of fortune and the wedge of

progress. Natural History, 89(3), 14, 16, 18, 20-21.

Guidelines and application form for directors, 1990 summer

seminars for school teachers. (1988). Washington, DC:

National Endowment for the Humanities.

New exam for doctor of future. (1989, March 15). The New

York Times, p. B-10.

Pan, L. S., Kania, D. R., Han, H. C., Ager III, J. W.,

Landstrass, M., Dai, Y., & Landen, O. L. (1992,

February 14). Electrical transport properties of

undoped CVD diamond films. Science, 255, 830-833.

Reference Forms

A reference list at the end of the paper, the equivalent of a bibliography, includes all works cited in the text. In APA style, this list of sources is entitled "References." The first line of the entry begins flush left; the second and successive lines are indented three spaces from the left. Entries appear in alphabetical order according to the last name of the author; two or more works by the same author appear in chronological order by date of publication, beginning with the earliest; two or more works by the same author and with the same publication date appear in alphabetical order by title. When you have two or more books or articles by the same author, repeat the name of the author in each entry. (See pages 138–40.)

■ Periodicals

Basic form   The basic entry for an article in a periodical begins with the last names, followed by the initials of all authors. The year of publication follows in parentheses; for magazine and newspaper articles, give the month and day (if any). Next come the title of the article, not enclosed in quotation marks; the title of the periodical, underlined; the volume number, underlined; and inclusive page numbers. A period follows the author, the date, the title of the article, and the end of the entry. The name of the periodical, the volume number, and page numbers are separated by commas. Only the first word of the article title, the first word of the article subtitle, and proper names within both are capitalized. All words except articles and prepositions are capitalized in the title of the periodical, and the title is underlined. All digits are repeated in page citations. The abbreviation *p.* or *pp.* is used in references to magazines and newspapers but not to journals. The closing page number is not shortened.

Malkiel, B. G. (1989). Is the stock market efficient?

   Science, 3, 1313-1318.

Article by more than one author

For an article by more than one author, invert and list the names of all the authors. Use commas to separate surnames and initials. Place an ampersand (&) before the name of the last author.

Dornbusch, S. M., Carlsmith, J. M., Bushwall, S. J., Ritter,

   P. L., Leiderman, H., & Hastorf, A. H. (1985). Single

   parents, extended households, and the control of

   adolescents. Child Development, 56, 326-341.

Journal paginated by issue

If each issue of a journal begins with page 1, give the issue number in parentheses after the volume number.

Brunsdale, M. M. (1991). Stages on her road: Sigrid

   Undset's spiritual journey. Religion and Literature,

   23(3), 83-96.

Magazine article

The entry for an article in a magazine without volume numbers includes the month and day (if any), as well as the year, and the abbreviation *p.* or *pp.*

Grover, R. (1988, September 19). A megawatt power play in

   California. Business Week, pp. 34-35.

Newspaper articles

An entry for a newspaper (or magazine) article without a byline or signature begins with the headline or title in the author position without underlining or quotation marks.

New exam for doctor of future. (1989, March 15). The New

   York Times, p. B-10.

When a newspaper article appears on discontinuous pages, give all page numbers and separate the numbers with commas.

APA Style

Broad, W. J. (1989, March 14). Flight of shuttle begins

flawlessly. The New York Times, pp. A-1, C-7.

If appropriate, indicate the nature of an article in brackets following the article title.

Williams, R. L. (1992, May 13). National university is an

outmoded idea [Letter to the editor]. The Chronicle of

Higher Education, p. B-4.

Special issue of a journal

In an entry for a special issue of a journal, identify the editors (if any) of the issue and the title of the issue. If the issue does not specify its editors, the title of the issue occupies the author position.

Political and social issues in composition [Special issue].

(1992). College Composition and Communication, 43(2).

Monograph

In an entry for a monograph, identify the nature of the material within brackets and give the volume number of the issue. Place additional identifying numerals, such as issue and serial (or whole) numbers in parentheses after the volume number without an intervening space.

Shumaker, W. (1954). English autobiography: Its emergence,

materials, and form [Monograph]. University of

California English Studies, B.

Kreutzer, M. A., Leonard, C., & Flavell, J. H. (1975). An

interview study of children's knowledge about memory.

Monographs of the Society for Research in Child

Development, 40(Whole No. 1).

Abstract or synopsis

If you wish to cite only the abstract of a published article, provide a complete entry for the published article and cite the source of the abstract, if different, in parentheses.

Dorin, J. R., Inglis, J. D., & Porteous, D. J. (1989).

Selection for precise chromosomal targeting of a dominant

marker by homologous recombination. Science, 243,

1357-1360. (From Science Abstracts, 1989, 75, Abstract

No. 1153)

APA Style

Article in press
When an article has been accepted for publication, the phrase *in press* takes the date position, and the name of the journal follows. (But no volume or page numbers are given.)

```
Smith, S.  (in press).  An experiment in bilingual

     education.  Journal of Bilingual Education.
```

▪ Books

Basic form
The entry for a book begins with the last name of the author, followed by a comma and the author's initials (not the entire first name) followed by periods. The date of publication follows in parentheses, followed by a period. Only the first word of the book title, the first word of the subtitle, and proper names within both are capitalized. The entire title is underlined and followed by a period. Facts of publication include the city of publication. If the city might be confused with another location, use U.S. Postal Service abbreviations to identify the state (see Appendix D). The name of the location is followed by a colon and the name of the publisher. The entry ends with a period. The names of university presses are spelled out.

```
Nagel, P. C.  (1992).  The Lees of Virginia: Seven

     generations of an American family.  New York: Oxford

     University Press.
```

Two or more authors
For a book by more than one author, invert and list the names of all the authors. Use commas to separate surnames and initials. Place an ampersand (&) before the name of the last author.

```
Forsyth, A., & Thornhill, R. (1983).  The evolution of

     insect mating.  Cambridge: Harvard University Press.

Campbell, W. G., Ballou, S. V., & Slade, C. (1990).  Form

     and style: Theses, reports, term papers (8th ed.).

     Boston: Houghton Mifflin.
```

Edition other than the first
Identify an edition other than the first within parentheses following the title without any intervening punctuation.

```
Dreyfus, H.  (1989).  What computers can't do (2nd ed.).

     New York: Harper & Row.
```

Reprinted work
The entry for a reprinted work indicates the original date of publication within parentheses.

Darwin, C. (1964). <u>On the origin of the species: A</u>

  <u>facsimile of the first edition</u> (Introd. Ernst Mayer).

  Cambridge: Harvard University Press. (Original work

  published 1859)

The parenthetical reference in the text includes both dates: (Darwin, 1859/1964).

Edited volume Indicate that a book is an edited volume by placing the abbreviation for editor (*Ed.*) or editors (*Eds.*) within parentheses in the author position.

Stanton, D. C. (Ed.). (1987). <u>The female autograph:</u>

  <u>Theory and practice of autobiography from the tenth to</u>

  <u>the twentieth century</u>. Chicago: University of Chicago

  Press.

Article In an edited collection In a reference to a chapter or article in an edited book, place the name of the author of the chapter in the author position. The second part of the entry identifies the book in which the article appears. The name of the editor(s) is not inverted. The page numbers for the individual chapter or article appear in parentheses after the title of the book.

Burghardt, G. M. (1984). On the origins of play. In Peter

  K. Smith (Ed.), <u>Play in animals and humans</u> (pp. 5-42).

  Oxford: Basil Blackwell.

Even when the author of the article and the editor of the book are the same, list the name in both the author and editor positions.

Olney, J. (1980). Autobiography and the cultural moment: A

  thematic, historical, and bibliographical introduction.

  In J. Olney (Ed.), <u>Autobiography: Essays theoretical and</u>

  <u>critical</u> (pp. 3-27). Princeton: Princeton University

  Press.

Reprinted article When an article in a collection was published previously, give the original citation in parentheses. The parenthetical citation in the text includes both publication dates.

Howarth, H. L. (1980). Some principles of autobiography.

  In J. Olney (Ed.), <u>Autobiography: Essays theoretical and</u>

critical (pp. 84-114). Princeton: Princeton University

Press. (Reprinted from New Literary History, 1974, 5,

363-381)

Within the text, cite this work as (Howarth, 1974/1980).

Anonymous book Enter and alphabetize a book without an author or editor by title alone.

Guidelines and application form for directors, 1990 summer

seminars for school teachers. (1988). Washington, DC:

National Endowment for the Humanities.

Multivolume work For a multivolume work published over several years, place in parentheses the year of publication of first volume and that of the last volume, separated by a hyphen.

Ripley, C. P. (Ed.). (1985-1992). The black abolitionist

papers (Vols. 1-5). Chapel Hill: University of North

Carolina Press.

When referring to the entire multivolume work within the text, cite it as (Ripley, 1985-1992).

To refer to a single volume in a multivolume series, include only the relevant date and volume number after the title without any intervening punctuation.

Ripley, C. P. (Ed.). (1987). The black abolitionist

papers (Vol. 2). Chapel Hill: University of North

Carolina Press.

When each volume has an individual title, provide both the volume and the multivolume titles.

Freehling, W. W. (1992). The road to disunion: Vol. 1.

Secessionists at bay, 1776-1854. New York: Oxford

University Press.

Translation Indicate the name of a translator within parentheses after the title. If you have used only the English translation, you do not need to include the original title within brackets, but you may choose to do so.

Derrida, J. (1976). Of grammatology (G. Spivak, Trans.).

Baltimore: Johns Hopkins University Press. (Original

work published 1967)

Translated article

The parenthetical reference in the text should indicate the original date of publication as well as the date of the translation: (Derrida, 1967/1976).

In an entry for a translated article, you may choose to give the original title within brackets.

```
Gusdorf, G.  (1980).  Conditions and limits of

    autobiography [Conditions et limites de

    l'autobiographie].  In J. Olney (Ed.), Autobiography:

    Essays theoretical and critical (pp. 28-48).  Princeton:

    Princeton University Press.  (Reprinted from Reichenkron,

    G., & Haase, E. [Eds.]. [1956].  Formen der

    selbstdarstellung [Forms of self-representation].

    Berlin: Duncker and Humblot)
```

Book in a foreign language

Within the text, cite this work as (Gusdorf, 1956/1980).

When you cite from a book in a foreign language, supply an English translation of the original title within brackets. Use your own translation if the work has not been translated or the English title by which the work is known.

```
Kristeva, J.  (1983).  L'Histoires d'amour [Tales of love].

    Paris: Denoël.
```

Work in a series

The entry for an individually titled work in a series provides both the volume and the series titles.

```
Eiser, J. R.  (Ed.) (1990).  Attitudinal judgment.

    Springer Series in Social Psychology, no. 11.  New York

    and Berlin: Springer-Verlag, 1990.
```

▪ Technical and Research Reports

Basic entry

Entries for technical and research reports should follow the basic format for a book entry. The series or number of the report should be identified in parentheses immediately after the title.

```
Gates, J. P.  (1991).  Educational and training

    opportunities in sustainable agriculture (U.S. Department

    of Agriculture).  Beltsville, MD: National Agricultural

    Library.
```

Report from an information service

For a report that comes from an information service, such as the National Technical Information Service (NTIS) or Educational Resources Information Center (ERIC), identify the service and document number in parentheses at the end of the entry.

Groak, J. J. (1974). Utilization of library resources by

students in non-residential degree programs. Washington,

DC: U.S. Government Printing Office. (ERIC Document

Reproduction Service No. ED 121 236)

Report from a university

When a university (as opposed to a university press) is the publisher, provide the name of the university, followed by the name of the specific unit or department.

Carter, G. E., Parker, J. R., & Bentley, S. (Eds.).

(1984). Minority literature and the urban experience.

LaCrosse: University of Wisconsin, Institute for Minority

Studies.

Author as publisher

When the author of a report is also the publisher, as in the case of many newsletters, name the publisher as author.

Teachers Insurance and Annuity Association, College

Retirement Equities Fund. (1992). The participant.

New York: Author.

▪ Proceedings of Meetings

Published proceedings

When contributions to a meeting appear in book form, the entry follows the format for a book.

Ferrua, P. (Ed.). (1979). Proceedings of the first

international symposium on letterism. Paris: Avant-Garde.

Unpublished proceedings

For an unpublished paper presented at a conference or symposium, indicate the place and date of the meeting.

Peltonen, K. (1989, June 16). Colors in "Ulysses". Paper

presented at the James Joyce Conference, Curtis Institute

of Music, Philadelphia.

APA Style

▪ Doctoral Dissertations

Microfilm of dissertation
When you use the microfilm of a dissertation as the source, give the microfilm number, as well as the volume and page numbers in *Dissertation Abstracts International.*

Baker, C. A. (1985). Multiple alliance commitments: The

role of the United States in the Falklands war.

Dissertation Abstracts International, 45, 4445B.

(University Microfilms No. 85-77, 123)

Typescript of dissertation
When you use the typescript copy of a dissertation, give the university and year, as well as the volume and page numbers in *Dissertation Abstracts International.* If the dates are different, provide the date of the dissertation after the name of the university.

Moskop, W. W. (1985). The prudent politician: An extension

of Aristotle's ethical theory (Doctoral dissertation,

George Washington University, 1984). Dissertation

Abstracts International, 45, 4445B.

▪ Unpublished Materials

Completed material
When unpublished material is in completed form, underline the title and indicate the unpublished status at the end of the entry.

Johnson, S. J. (1992). The teaching of twelfth-

grade advanced placement mathematics. Unpublished

manuscript.

When an unpublished manuscript has been submitted for publication, indicate that fact at the end of the entry.

Little, C. A. (1992). Forms of childhood autism.

Manuscript submitted for publication.

Draft material
When unpublished material remains in draft or unorganized tabular form, put the name of the topic in brackets in the title position; do not underline the topic. Indicate the status of the material at the end of the entry.

Jensen, H. C. (1992). [Settlement patterns for Norwegian

immigrants, 1890-1920]. Unpublished raw data.

APA Style

Unpublished dissertation or thesis

Treat a dissertation or thesis that does not appear in *Dissertation Abstracts International* as an unpublished work. Underline the title.

Virgili, C. (1985). <u>Literature of the Spanish civil war</u>.

    Unpublished M.A. thesis, New York University.

Publication with limited circulation

When a work, although published, is not available in any library, give the address at which a copy might be located or obtained.

Inouye, L. (1993, April). GECA—The organic agriculture

    training school, El Salvador. <u>Oxfam America project</u>

    <u>report</u>, pp. 1-4. (Available from Oxfam America, 26 West

    Street, Boston, MA 02111-1206)

▪ Reviews and Interviews

Book review

Indicate the subject of a book review within brackets following the title.

Broyard, A. (1989, January 22). Fiction: A user's manual

    [Review of <u>The company we keep: An ethics of fiction</u>].

    <u>The New York Times Book Review</u>, pp. 3, 27.

If the review does not have a title, use the material within brackets as the title, retaining the brackets.

Courage, R. A. [Review of <u>Literacy in the United States:</u>

    <u>Readers and reading since 1880</u>]. (1992). <u>College</u>

    <u>Composition and Communication</u>, <u>43</u>(2).

Movie or film review

Indicate the subject of a movie or film review within brackets following the title. If the review does not have a title, use the material within brackets as the title, retaining the brackets.

Canby, V. (1992, May 22). Cruise and Kidman in old-

    fashioned epic [Review of <u>Far and away</u>]. <u>The New York</u>

    <u>Times</u>, p. C-10.

Published interview

Follow the basic format appropriate for the book or periodical in which the interview is published. The name of the interviewer occupies the place of the author, and the person interviewed is identified by both first and last names within brackets.

APA Style

Jahanbegloo, R.   (1992, May 28).   Philosophy and life

[Interview with Isaiah Berlin].   <u>The New York Review of</u>

<u>Books</u>, pp. 46-54.

Unpublished interviews and personal communications, such as letters and telephone calls, are cited parenthetically within the text but not listed as references.

▪ Nonprint Media

In entries for nonprint media, place the name of the principal organizer or creator in the author position, and in parentheses identify the function of the organizer or creator. The nature of the medium should be indicated in brackets immediately after the title. Enter the place and date of publication as for a book.

Film   Eastwood, C.   (Director).   (1992).   <u>Unforgiven</u> [Film].

Hollywood: Warner.

Cassette   Lake, F. L.   (Author and speaker).   (1989).   <u>Bias and</u>

<u>organizational decision-making</u> [Audiocassette].

Gainesville: Edwards.

Dalton, D.   (Author and speaker).   (1992).   <u>Aristotle's</u>

<u>Politics: The golden mean and just rule</u> [Videocassette

No. BM-G001].   Dubuque, IA: The Teaching Company.

(Here *Politics* is capitalized because it is the title of a work by Aristotle.)

Numbered material   When you have a number for a cassette or other material, include it with the description within parentheses.

Hunter, K.   (Speaker).   (1989).   <u>Family counseling</u> [Cassette

Recording No. 1175].   Washington, DC: American

Psychological Association.

Electronic database, CD-ROM   University Publications of America (Producer).   (1992).

<u>Scholarly book reviews</u> [CD-ROM].   Bethesda.

Computer software   In an entry for computer software, include the name of the author or producer, the year of development or publication, the title underlined, the facts of publication, and any additional information necessary for locating and running the program.

Knowledge Revolution (Producer). (1992). <u>Interactive</u>

    <u>physics II</u> [Computer Software]. San Francisco. (Apple

    Macintosh)

Lingo Fun (Producer). (1987). <u>German context, levels 1 and</u>

    <u>2</u> [Computer software]. Westerville, OH: International

    Software. (Network version)

APA Style

Appendix A

MLA-Style Shortened Forms of Publishers' Names and Imprints

In MLA style, publishers' names are shortened. When the name of the publisher is that of a person (J. B. Lippincott), cite the last name only (Lippincott). When the name of the publisher includes more than one surname (Houghton Mifflin), cite only the first (Houghton). Abbreviate *University* as *U*, and *Press* as *P*. The following is a selected list of shortened names.

SHORT FORM	COMPLETE NAME
Abrams	Harry N. Abrams, Inc.
ALA	American Library Association
Allen	George Allen and Unwin Publishers, Inc.
Allyn	Allyn and Bacon, Inc.
Appleton	Appleton-Century-Crofts
Ballantine	Ballantine Books, Inc.
Bantam	Bantam Books, Inc.
Barnes	Barnes and Noble Books
Basic	Basic Books
Beacon	Beacon Press, Inc.
Benn	Ernest Benn, Ltd.
Bobbs	The Bobbs-Merrill Co., Inc.
Bowker	R. R. Bowker Co.
Cambridge UP	Cambridge University Press
Clarendon	Clarendon Press
Columbia UP	Columbia University Press
Cornell UP	Cornell University Press
Dell	Dell Publishing Co., Inc.
Dodd	Dodd, Mead, and Co.
Doubleday	Doubleday and Co., Inc.
Dover	Dover Publications, Inc.
Dutton	E. P. Dutton, Inc.
Farrar	Farrar, Straus and Giroux, Inc.
Free	The Free Press
Funk	Funk and Wagnalls, Inc.
Gale	Gale Research Co.
GPO	Government Printing Office
Harcourt	Harcourt Brace Jovanovich, Inc.
Harper	Harper and Row Publishers, Inc.

SHORT FORM	COMPLETE NAME
Harvard Law Rev. Assn.	Harvard Law Review Association
Harvard UP	Harvard University Press
Heath	D. C. Heath and Co.
Holt	Holt, Rinehart and Winston, Inc.
Houghton	Houghton Mifflin Co.
Humanities	Humanities Press, Inc.
Indiana UP	Indiana University Press
Johns Hopkins UP	The Johns Hopkins University Press
Knopf	Alfred A. Knopf, Inc.
Lippincott	J. B. Lippincott Co.
Little	Little, Brown and Co.
Macmillan	Macmillan Publishing Co., Inc.
McGraw	McGraw-Hill, Inc.
MIT P	The MIT Press
MLA	The Modern Language Association of America
NAL	The New American Library, Inc.
NEA	The National Education Association
Norton	W. W. Norton and Co., Inc.
Oxford UP	Oxford University Press
Penguin	Penguin Books, Inc.
Pocket	Pocket Books
Popular	The Popular Press
Prentice	Prentice-Hall, Inc.
Princeton UP	Princeton University Press
Putnam's	G. P. Putnam's Sons
Rand	Rand McNally and Co.
Random	Random House, Inc.
St. Martin's	St. Martin's Press, Inc.
Scott	Scott, Foresman and Co.
Scribner's	Charles Scribner's Sons
Simon	Simon and Schuster, Inc.
UMI	University Microfilms International
U of Chicago P	University of Chicago Press
U of Toronto P	University of Toronto Press
UP of Florida	The University Presses of Florida
Viking	The Viking Press, Inc.
Yale UP	Yale University Press

MLA also shortens the names of publishers' imprints (names given to groups of books within a company's publications) to one word, unless more are needed for accurate identification. To distinguish Laurel Editions from Laurel Leaf, both imprints of Dell, the second word should be included. In MLA style, the name of the imprint, followed by a hyphen without spacing on either side, precedes the name of the publisher.

Below is a partial list of well-known imprints.

CHICAGO MANUAL STYLE	MLA STYLE
(Words modifying the name of the imprint, such as *Books* and *Editions*, may be omitted unless they are required for accurate identification.)	
Dell, Laurel Editions	Laurel Editions-Dell
Dell, Laurel Leaf Classics	Laurel Leaf-Dell

Doubleday, Anchor Books	Anchor-Doubleday
Doubleday, Dial Press	Dial-Doubleday
Doubleday, Image Books	Image-Doubleday
Doubleday, Quantum Press	Quantum-Doubleday
Harcourt Brace Jovanovich, Harbinger Books	Harbinger-Harcourt
Harcourt Brace Jovanovich, Harvest Books	Harvest-Harcourt
Harper and Row, Colophon Books	Colophon-Harper
Harper and Row, Perennial Library	Perennial-Harper
Harper and Row, Torchbooks	Torchbooks-Harper
Holt, Rinehart and Winston, Owl Books	Owl-Holt
Houghton Mifflin, Clarion Books	Clarion-Houghton
Houghton Mifflin, Riverside Editions	Riverside-Houghton
Alfred A. Knopf, Dragonfly Books	Dragonfly-Knopf
William Morris, Reynal	Reynal-Morris
New American Library, Mentor Books	Mentor-NAL
New American Library, Plume Books	Plume-NAL
New American Library, Signet Books	Signet-NAL
Pocket Books, Poseidon Press	Poseidon-Pocket
Simon and Schuster, Touchstone Books	Touchstone-Simon

Appendix B

Legal Citation

Most legal writing, particularly briefs and other documents filed with courts, employs only notes. Citations are made either parenthetically in the text or in footnotes. There is only one format for legal references, whether they are placed within the text or at the bottom of the page. If you wish to include legal documents in a bibliography, the entries should take the same form as the notes.

The Harvard Law Review Association booklet *A Uniform System of Citation* (revised periodically) is the standard guide in matters of format and interpretation of entries. For meanings of abbreviations not contained there, consult *Black's Law Dictionary*.

In the United States, primary sources are judicial, statutory, and quasi-statutory material.

■ Judicial Material

The most common category of judicial material includes the reported decisions of court cases and the documents related to these decisions, such as briefs submitted by the parties or the transcript of a trial. The order of the elements in the citation of a reported decision is as follows: (1) names of the parties (only the first party on each side); (2) volume number; (3) name of the report or service in which the decision appears; (4) page on which the decision begins, or paragraph number of the decision, followed by the page on which the cited material appears; (5) in parentheses, the court of decision (if not apparent from the name of the report) followed by the year of decision; and (6) the subsequent history of the case.

U.S. Supreme Court

[41] Traux v. Corrigan, 257 U.S. 312, 327 (1921).

The decision in the *Traux* case, cited in note 41, is contained in volume 257 of the official reports of decisions of the United States Supreme Court (*United States Reports*). It begins on page 312; the cited material appears at page 327. The decision was handed down in 1921; the court of decision is apparent from the name of the report.

State court, parallel citations

[42] 3 N.Y. 2d 155, 143 N.E.2d 906, 164 N.Y.S.2d 714 (1957).

Note 42 gives the citation to *Sabo* v. *Delman*. The name of the case appears in the text, where it is italicized; only the citation is given in the note. The fact that the abbreviation of the official report—*N. Y.* for *New York Reports*—is also the abbreviation of the name of the state indicates that the decision was handed down by the state's highest court (in this case, New York's Court of Appeals). The designation *2d* indicates that the decision is found in the second series of *New York Reports*. A parallel citation is also given to two unofficial reports, the *North Eastern Reporter, Second Series*, which gathers cases from several states into a single volume, and the *New York Supplement, Second Series*, which reports New York cases from several different levels.

Many decisions are reported only in unofficial reporters, particularly loose-leaf services, which attempt to compile the decisions relevant to a particular subject matter:

Decisions in unofficial reporters

43 Omega-Alpha, Inc. v. Touche Ross & Co., [1976-1977 Transfer Binder] Fed. Sec. L. Rep. (CCH) 95,663, at 90,268 (S.D.N.Y. 1976).

The decision cited in note 43 is reported at Paragraph 95,663 of the *Federal Securities Law Reporter*, compiled by the Commerce Clearing House, Inc. Although the decision first appeared in the "Current" binder of that service (updated weekly), it has now been transferred to the permanent binder of decisions handed down in 1976 and 1977. The particular material cited within the case is found at page 90,268 of the volume.

When the citation is to an unreported decision, the docket number of the case, the court in which it is pending, and the actual date of the decision are given:

Unreported decision

44 Lannen v. Simpson, No. 79-1527-J (162nd Jud. Dist. Ct. Tex., Feb. 3, 1980).

Materials submitted to a court or generated during court proceedings are cited by reference to a reported decision, if one exists, or to the case name, docket number, and court, if one does not.

Brief, U.S. District Court

45 Brief for Plaintiff at 10, Jones v. Smith, 139 F. Supp. 730 (W.D. La. 1956).

The reference in note 45 is to material appearing at page 10 of Jones's brief submitted to the United States District Court for the Western District of Louisiana in connection with a case with a decision reported in volume 139 of the *Federal Supplement*.

▪ Statutory Material

The second kind of primary source material includes constitutions, statutes, bills and resolutions, and international agreements. Some of the elements found in judicial material are obviously not a part of statutory citations. The order of those elements that are relevant is the same, at least by analogy. The following examples indicate how this kind of citation can be read by someone who is familiar with legal abbreviations.

U.S. Constitution

⁴⁶ U.S. Const. amend. XXI, § 2.

⁴⁷ U.S. Const. art. III, §§ 1-2.

Notes 46 and 47 refer to the United States Constitution, section 2 of the twenty-first amendment and sections 1 and 2 of article III, respectively.

State constitution, with date

⁴⁸ N.Y. Const. art. II, § 6 (1894, amended).

In note 48, citation of section 6, article II of the New York Constitution includes a date because the portion referred to has since been substantially amended or is no longer in force.

Statute, official and common names

⁴⁹ Labor Management Relations (Taft-Hartley) Act § 301 (a), 29 U.S.C. § 185 (a) (1986).

In note 49, the citation is to a federal enactment by both its official and common names, section 301, subsection (a); the law is codified in title 29 of the *United States Code,* section 185, subsection (a), 1986 edition. The citation should also be to the latest edition of the code.

Bill not enacted into law

⁵⁰ S. 1975, 89th Cong. 1st sess., 111 Cong. Rec. 10502 (1965).

Note 50 refers to Senate Bill 1975, introduced in the first session of the Eighty-ninth Congress and cited in volume 111 of the *Congressional Record,* beginning on page 10502; the bill had not been enacted into law at the time of citation, 1965.

Senate resolution

⁵¹ S. Res. 218, 83d Cong., 2d sess., 100 Cong. Rec. 2972 (1954).

Note 51 refers to Senate Resolution number 218, adopted at the second session of the Eighty-third Congress, 1954, and recorded in volume 100 of the *Congressional Record,* beginning on page 2972.

International agreement

⁵² Agreement on Rural Health Services, Sept. 30, 1976, United States-Egypt, 28 U.S.T. 8877, T.I.A.S. No. 8775.

The agreement cited in note 52 was signed on 30 September 1976 and can be found in volume 28 of *U.S. Treaties and Other International Agreements,* the official source of such treaties, beginning on page 8877. Parallel citation is made to the Department of State publication *Treaties and Other International Acts Series,* number 8775; the latter is an unofficial source.

▪ Quasi-statutory Material

Rules, regulations, and the like that are promulgated by nonlegislative organs of government are classified as quasi-statutory material. By analogy, citations to them are read in the same way as are citations to judicial and statutory sources.

**Presidential
Executive Order**

[53] Exec. Order No. 10540, 19 Fed. Reg. 3983 (1954).

Note 53 refers to Presidential Executive Order number 10540, which is to be found in volume 19 of the *Federal Register* (an official report), 1954, beginning on page 3983.

**Internal Revenue
ruling**

[54] Rev. Rul. 131, 1953-2 Cum. Bull. 112.

Note 54 refers to Revenue Ruling 131, which appears in part 2 of the 1953 volume of the *Cumulative Bulletin*, beginning on page 112. This is an Internal Revenue ruling of the Treasury Department.

Federal regulation

[55] SEC Reg. A, 17 C.F.R. §§ 230.251-230.264 (1980).

In note 55, the citation of Securities and Exchange Commission Regulation A to the Code of Federal Regulations shows that the regulation is currently in force. It is found in title 17, sections 230.251 through 230.264 in the 1980 edition.

Appendix C

Author-Number System of References

The author-number system, like the MLA and APA styles, uses parenthetical references within the text. The parenthetical references, however, do not contain an author's name. References here appear in *Chicago* format; MLA and APA would not permit the use of this system.

In the author-number system, a numbered bibliography of references, with entries arranged in alphabetical order or in order of citation in the text, appears at the end of the paper. The number of each entry in the bibliography is placed within parentheses in the text to indicate the identity of a source. Page numbers, separated from the source number by a colon, follow when needed. Each entry is listed only once in the bibliography, but the number for an entry may be used repeatedly in the text.

Differences of opinion exist about returning to the gold standard. Collins (1) does not believe that the move would help the economy, while backers of the idea, such as Kemp (2), see the gold standard as the key to a stable economy. As Collins puts it, gold is "as beautiful as ever but no cure for what ails us" (1:19). Most commentators agree that gold is a secure investment (1:19, 2:32).

References

1. Collins, Lora S. "An Assay of Gold." Across the Board, 5 Jan. 1982: 19-20.

2. Kemp, Jack. "The Renewal of Western Monetary Standards." Wall Street Journal, 7 Apr. 1982: 32.

Appendix D

Abbreviations of State Names

Usually, the name of the city is all that is needed to identify the place of publication in a note or a bibliographical reference. If one city might be confused with another (such as Lexington, Kentucky, and Lexington, Massachusetts) or if the location of a city is not well known, include the name of the state or territory, using abbreviations. Use these abbreviations only in bibliographical references or in tables; do not use them in the text.

STATE NAME	TRADITIONAL ABBREVIATION (CHICAGO MANUAL)	U.S. POSTAL SERVICE ABBREVIATION (MLA AND APA)
Alabama	Ala.	AL
Alaska	Alaska	AK
American Samoa	Amer. Samoa	AS
Arizona	Ariz.	AZ
Arkansas	Ark.	AR
California	Calif.	CA
Canal Zone	C.Z.	CZ
Colorado	Colo.	CO
Connecticut	Conn.	CT
Delaware	Del.	DE
District of Columbia	D.C.	DC
Florida	Fla.	FL
Georgia	Ga.	GA
Guam	Guam	GU
Hawaii	Hawaii	HI
Idaho	Idaho	ID
Illinois	Ill.	IL
Indiana	Ind.	IN
Iowa	Iowa	IA
Kansas	Kans.	KS
Kentucky	Ky.	KY
Louisiana	La.	LA
Maine	Maine	ME
Maryland	Md.	MD
Massachusetts	Mass.	MA
Michigan	Mich.	MI
Minnesota	Minn.	MN
Mississippi	Miss.	MS

STATE NAME	TRADITIONAL ABBREVIATION (CHICAGO MANUAL)	U.S. POSTAL SERVICE ABBREVIATION (MLA AND APA)
Missouri	Mo.	MO
Montana	Mont.	MT
Nebraska	Nebr.	NE
Nevada	Nev.	NV
New Hampshire	N.H.	NH
New Jersey	N.J.	NJ
New Mexico	N.Mex.	NM
New York	N.Y.	NY
North Carolina	N.C.	NC
North Dakota	N.Dak.	ND
Ohio	Ohio	OH
Oklahoma	Okla.	OK
Oregon	Oreg.	OR
Pennsylvania	Pa.	PA
Puerto Rico	P.R.	PR
Rhode Island	R.I.	RI
South Carolina	S.C.	SC
South Dakota	S.Dak.	SD
Tennessee	Tenn.	TN
Texas	Tex.	TX
Utah	Utah	UT
Vermont	Vt.	VT
Virginia	Va.	VA
Virgin Islands	V.I.	VI
Washington	Wash.	WA
West Virginia	W.Va.	WV
Wisconsin	Wis.	WI
Wyoming	Wyo.	WY

Glossary

This glossary lists terms and abbreviations that occur in notes, parenthetical literary references, and bibliographical entries. Many of these terms, particularly those in Latin, are no longer recommended for current use, but because they are part of the tradition of scholarly research and writing, they appear frequently in literature.

When you are deciding whether to use one of these terms or abbreviations, your first guide should be the requirements of the style you are following. Your second consideration should be brevity and clarity. If an abbreviation will save space and contribute to understanding, you should use it; if it will merely obfuscate or confuse, write out the word or expression.

Foreign words and phrases not yet Anglicized should be italicized (underlined in typing). Conclusions concerning which foreign words have become Anglicized vary among disciplines, institutions, and journals, but the trend seems to be toward Anglicizing abbreviations and terms. Italicized words in parentheses are the Latin originals.

You will find words and expressions not listed here in a dictionary.

ABBREVIATION OR TERM	MEANING
abr.	abridged
anon.	anonymous
art.	article
b.	born, brother
bk., bks.	book(s)
c., cc.	chapters (in legal citations only)
ca. or c. (*circa*)	about (with dates)
CD-ROM	compact disk read-only-memory
cf. (*confer*)	compare
ch. or chap., chaps.	chapter(s)
col., cols.	column(s)
colloq.	colloquial, colloquialism
comp.	compiled (by), compiler
cont.	continued
copr. or ©	copyright
d.	died, daughter
diss.	dissertation
div., divs.	division(s)
ed.	edited (by)

ABBREVIATION OR TERM	MEANING
ed., eds.	editor(s) or edition(s)
e.g. (*exempli gratia*)	for example
esp.	especially
et al.	and other(s)
et passim	and here and there
ex., exs., or exx.	example(s)
f., ff.	and the following page(s), line(s), etc.
fig., figs.	figure(s)
fl. (*floruit*)	flourished
fn.	footnote (cf. n.)
fol., fols.	folio(s)
f.v. (*folio verso*)	on the back of the page
ibid. (*ibidem*)	in the same place
id., *idem*	the same (person)
i.e. (*id est*)	that is
illus.	illustrated (by), illustration(s), illustrator(s)
inf., *infra*	below
introd.	introduction (by)
l., ll.	line(s)
loc. cit. (*loco citato*)	in the place cited
misc.	miscellaneous
MS, MSS, ms, mss	manuscript(s)
n., nn.	note(s), endnote(s), footnote(s)
NB, N.B. (*nota bene*)	take notice, mark well
n.d.	no date (of publication)
no., nos.	number(s)
n.p.	no place (of publication), no publisher
n.s. (also NS, N.S., ns)	New Series, New Style
obs.	obsolete
op. cit. (*opere citato*)	in the work cited
o.s. (also O.S., OS, os)	Old Series, Old Style
p., pp.	page(s)
par., pars.	paragraph(s)
passim	throughout
PC-DOS	personal computer disk operating system
pl., pls.	plate(s)
pseud.	pseudonym
pt., pts.	part(s)
pub.	published by, publisher
q.v. (*quod vide*)	which see
rev.	revised (by), revision; review; reviewed (by)
rpt., repr.	reprint, reprinted
sc.	scene
sec., secs.	section(s)
ser.	series
sic, sic	thus
sup. (*supra*)	above, earlier in the text
suppl.	supplement (APA)
s.v. (*sub verbo or voce*)	under the word or heading

ABBREVIATION OR TERM	MEANING
syn.	synonym, synonymous
tech. rep.	technical report (APA)
trans. or tr.	translated (by), translation, translator
ut sup. (*ut supra*)	as above
v. (*vide*)	see
v.	versus (in legal citations only)
v., vv. or vs., vss.	verse(s)
viz or viz. (*videlicet*)	namely
vol., vols.	volume(s)
vs. (*versus*)	against

Index

Numbers for sample pages are in italics.